Table of Contents

Barracking from the Sidelines 2019

(My personal political commentary on politicians and political events in 2019)

By Greg Tuck

Preface

Australian Politics

Dominated by a federal government, in a three-tier system of government, Australian politics is based on a constitution written in the 1890's that is extremely difficult to change via referendums. It is a Westminster system of government that has two separate chambers that are dominated by two major parties whose ideologies differ and both the sides are very combative to the extent that agreement on issues except politician wage increase, are hard won battles. If one side thinks of an idea, the other side shoots it down in flames, whether the idea is good or not. The public have become disillusioned and feel impotent to change things and see most politicians as merely sucking on the public teat and lining their own pockets. A good few of the political rank's behaviour does nothing to dispel that idea.

Politics changed a lot in Australia from late 2013 onwards, although many will attest to the fact that it hasn't changed at all. There are still lies, deception, obfuscation and manipulation and these have had to become more sophisticated as social media has come to the fore. I have been adding my own comments to mainstream media and my own political blog in those years and on reflection I am amazed at the types of characters that are regularly unearthed and come to the forefront in our political climate.

Some characters have developed over that time. Some were just fleeting shadows on the political spectrum. Others rose from obscurity and some may have also have faded back into it. Characters and events overlap. Views change and political manoeuvres take place. Ideology dictates much of what goes on. Hopefully my blog entries and reflections will help paint a picture of these characters and events that dominated the political scene in this period. This is not a chronological history of the time, merely one person's thoughts that he wanted to scream at the major players in Australian politics at the time.

However, the disappointing thing about all these comments and research is what I still really don't understand is, how does the Canberra bubble still remain intact with so many pricks in it? Are there special properties of moral vacuums?

January

- A far-right political rally held in Melbourne is attended by Independent Senator Fraser Anning, who admits to using tax-payer funded travel to attend the event in a state he doesn't represent.
- A mass fish die-off occurs on the Lower Darling River at Menindee Lakes. Up to 1 million fish, including endangered species, die in the largest fish die-off in Australian history. Drought and poor water management operations by government are seen as the cause.
- The U.S. Justice Department charges Chinese tech firm Huawei with multiple counts of fraud, raising U.S./China tensions

It seems that Sarah Henderson and Linda Reynolds are doing their own type of affirmative action. They are affirming that the status quo is okay. To me that sounds like conformative action.

At the end of every year, humans pause and celebrate the fact that for yet another year they have not blown themselves out of existence. They make promises such as changing attitudes on racism and say that they will be better, be smarter and learn from past mistakes. Before the last firework fades, they realise just how resolute their species is and begin to pray that they may make it through another year.

There is also a great deal of apathy within the walls of the parliamentary chambers. How many of the representatives actually represent their electorate? How many really see politics as anything more than a game? How many of them take responsibility for the decisions they make or don't make? They are not only apathetic they are pathetic as well.

So, who defines Australian values? Pauline Hanson would love to. It was tried on Cronulla beach not that long ago. Values are different to laws. Australians have a diverse set of values, no bill of rights and a wonderful mix of ethnicity and culture. Sometimes I wonder however whether the values of the today's Australians whose ancestors were here before January 1788 might have been better served by their ancestors telling Arthur Phillip to F off and directing him to Manus and Nauru.

It is amazing that we white Australians declare ourselves non-racist but continue to denigrate others. We are quite happy to invade other countries, sell our guns, ammunition and booze to anyone without any regard to the consequences. When things go awry, it can't possibly be our fault. It must be because "those sorts of people" can't handle what they get. However, the thing we can't handle, is the truth.

This common sense idea to back the opposition amendments to help small business is another test of the unwritten rule that says, "if the opposition like it, it must be wrong". There's a lack of maturity within the party dominated political system. A growing number of independents have shown that. Now it seems that the shackles may be coming off the saner members of major parties. Crossing the floor isn't a sin. It is a sign that you have actually thought about something and not been told what to think.

I looked up the word 'honest' in the dictionary and nowhere did the word 'politician' come up, not as a synonym or in an example. I thought that they must be mutually exclusive words until I noticed lower down 'politician' appeared in antonyms.

Perhaps if the politicians were held to account much better over their perks, then GetUp! may not even be needed. If politicians were treated like other employees who were found to be diddling the company, they wouldn't merely have to pay back what had been misspent they would be fired and possibly charged with theft. But then again politicians make their own rules, don't they?

In a recent non-existent poll, people were asked to rate occupations and surprisingly politicians rose in status. It seems that they are still below used car salespeople but now are marginally above bankers and clergymen.

The way the Liberal party is going they may soon get their 50/50 aspirations for women senators and MP's. They already have a plan. Lose enough seats at the next election and it's a done deal.

The saying is "if you pay peanuts, you get monkeys." We are paying more than peanuts and all we get are nuts!

The first rule about travel expenses is that there are no rules.

And so many senators in particular rack up travel expenses as if they don't mean anything. "Unrepresentative swill," one former Prime Minister described them as and you can understand why. The quota system is wrong and the fact that parties can replace an outgoing senator with anybody and no election being held is laughable. That means there is no equality between the houses. In the Reps a by-election must be called. In the Senate an internal raffle is held.

What is this "pass the pub test?" Very seldom have I seen politicians pass the pub. They are often seen having a frothy to appear fair dinkum and one of the people. They then go home rinse the taste out of their mouth and have a Grange chaser.

I've got a plan to make a fortune! Set up an Uber jet company in Canberra and undercut the Defence Force flying chauffeur service.

The quieter Australians need to ask some questions. With a Federal election just around the corner, it is important that all voters look at the promises of all candidates carefully and then envisage how their candidate will vote on the floor of Parliament on issues of concern. That is where the actual vote counts. It doesn't matter what is argued in party rooms because the parties almost always vote in a block and elected representatives may be forced to vote against the wishes of their electorate to maintain party solidarity. This puts some representatives in a bind as they were pre-selected by their party, but elected by their electorate. More often than not, they choose party first.

So many pieces of legislation are always voted on party lines and recently we have had years of forestalling Same Sex Marriage, a workable energy policy and a Financial Industry Royal Commission because of a small dominating group within a party.

Party ideologies form the basis on which people generally choose a person on a ballot. It is the easiest way for electors to understand what a candidate actually supports. However, we place trust that our representative will actually honour the commitments made.

The challenge will be for whomever we elect, to stand up on the floor of parliament, not just in the party room, and actually represent his/her electorate. If that makes a representative unpopular within their own party, so be it.

Before we fill in our ballot it would be beneficial if all candidates could make detailed, personal (and not just party) commitments about major issues including: asylum seekers, energy, climate change, national debt, immigration, employment, health, education and social services. That way we can make a more informed choice and in three years' time hold them to account more effectively.

Why is everything about the economy with the Coalition. Yes, we need a strong economy to function but it seems that is all they care about. Social issues, equality, the environment can all go to hell but if the economy is doing well, all is right with the world.

There is a belief in the public that politicians should be available 24/7 but hardly work at all. Some politicians try to let people know that they do work 24/7 which is a myth in itself. Many of the best politicians are the quiet ones who go about their tasks and duties without wanting to be noticed. they have a job to do and just do it. Party work should be seen as out of hours and voluntary but so many of our politicians think that lobbying on behalf of their party is the main part of their job. Their job is to represent their electorate and make judgments on behalf of these same people. Nothing more, nothing less. The public should expect nothing more and nothing less. When the day is done, you go home to your family. Our political setup is so 19th century. Politicians do not have to be in Canberra to communicate. They should use the technology that is available to them. Many do but sadly it is to communicate with their families because these politicians are trapped in other parts of the continent doing party work. Accountability to their families isn't there. Public accountability is only there every three years. There are no KPI's for politicians but I'd suggest there should be at least one or two. Firstly: achieve a work life balance. Secondly: ensure that at least 90% of your time is allocated to your main role and not your party role.

If government becomes even more about the economy then heaven help us. Social and environmental issues should be main focuses of the government. A balanced economy with a small surplus and no debt may be a great target but if that is only due to the fact that repressive policies divide our nation, what have we gained? Already there has been a great division between rich and poor. We have rising household debt caused by a huge bubble in real estate. People are struggling to put food on the table and pay for basic utilities. But that is seen by one side of politics as just collateral damage to getting the economy just right. Health and education and care for the disabled and aged are willingly sacrificed to get a better budget bottom line.

I am impressed with the strength of the lobby groups within Australia and the capacity for governments to cave under the slightest whiff of pressure that their voting base may be affected by good policy. The coal and mining lobby, the banks and now the Catholic schools must be patting themselves on their collective backs over their efforts during the last six years. Maybe we need a lobby group for the ordinary citizen...... oh, wait a minute... we have one already.... it is comprised of our elected representatives.

You would think that with the economy booming that so would infrastructure and construction but that it seems doesn't seem to be part of the Liberal/National way of doing things. Happy to take our money but not spend it except on themselves and pork barrels.

The government will be looking for a perfect example of how an average citizen will be affected by Labor's proposed changes to negative gearing. I reckon they will choose someone from Tampa Crt.

Is the weakness in the housing market actually a major concern? It will drive investors out of the market and let owner occupiers in. First home owners may be able to buy in to the great Australian dream. Many rental properties are in reality tied to the property's value. some people will be caught but why should they be compensated because they took a risk? Are shareholders compensated? Are gamblers? Investing in property is a gamble. Current investors should be grateful and consider themselves as very fortunate their negatively geared properties are being grandfathered. Some people put their trust in their belief that house property values would always rise. Electors put their trust in a government that said that they were the adults in the room and that they were the best at economic management. Disappointment is part of life.

The federal government is about to release details of lots of tax cuts ($9.2 billion) in an attempt to buy votes.

To misquote the Beatles
"Can buy us votes, yeah
Can buy us votes

*Books don't need balancing my friend even though the debt's
too high*
We'll promise anything my friend to win on election night
*Cos we don't care too much 'bout money, money just buys your
votes*
It's all about an election win so we'll give anything to you
The economy's in a tail spin but what's left we'll give to you
*Cos we don't care too much 'bout money, as money's to buy your
votes*
Can buy us votes, everybody sells their soul
Can buy us votes, keep the status quo"

Graphs are a bit bamboozling but the one that sticks out is the increase in tobacco pricing which must be due to tax hikes. Given the huge reduction in the use of tobacco and the underlying savings in health costs, surely governments should start looking at increasing taxes on alcohol. Alcohol is often associated with family violence, car accidents and loss of production. The drop in crime statistics and health costs alone should see the government look at making this area a high taxing one. Alcohol and tobacco should be treated equally but they aren't because the liquor industry has such a powerful lobby group and politicians a healthy appetite for the stuff. Cheers Scomo! Have another frothy.

We are in for yet another election cycle of power politics but it is the politics of power that we should fear the most. Already established industries such as coal who have benefited from subsidies for years will no doubt confuse the issue with cries of job losses, but they refuse to admit to the job losses they are creating through automation. They will rail against other industries getting start up subsidies, overlooking at the way they structure their business so that profits disappear overseas. It is about time the power was taken out politics and independent scientists and economics produced a workable way forward to

combat climate change, move to renewables and maintain a working power industry for the benefit of all Australians, not just big coal companies and parties who accept donations. People power at the ballot box may be the answer.

Tony Abbott and co. will be able to spin such data as "fake news". However global warming/climate change etc needs to be front and centre when it comes to election issues. It is a major differentiating point between parties and hopefully will be used to rally people.

The Coalition are in denial about climate change, it's effect on our economy and the reason why uncommon severe droughts and heatwaves are devastating inland economies, native animals and the environment. Maybe it is because in de Nile there is more water than in de Murray-Darling.

Look over here. See that sparkly thing. Isn't it pretty? A few years ago, it was Abbott and knighthoods. Now it's Morrison and board shorts. Massive heatwaves. Drought chewing up the rural economy. Water being syphoned from rivers leading to massive fish losses. Board shorts is the best he can come up with???? Meanwhile our Special Envoy for Drought Assistance and Recovery is nowhere to be seen.

Climate change sceptics will see this record of the 15 hottest places on Earth on Tuesday being in Australia as not a sign of global warming because it is just localised.

"No such thing as global warming," the naysaying flat earth people say. No, they are right. Right now, it is just Australia warming or baking as it is more like. As Robin Williams character in Good Morning Vietnam said, "What's the weather like out there? It's hot! Damn hot! Real hot! Hot as it is, is my shorts I can cook things in it, a little crotch-pot cookin'. Well can you tell me what it feels like? Fool! Why it's hot I told you again. Were you born on the sun? It's damn hot!"

Part of the issue regarding power is the fact that each vested interest has a vested interest! Their industry is by far better than any other. No-one is really looking at a mix. This has been going on for decades. They have modelled their discussions on the adversarial approach that we have embedded in government. Working together and each getting some part of the whole pie is seen to be by them as tantamount to admitting defeat and anti-competitive. To the general public, it is seen to be just plain stupid. We have a vested interest too. We are the consumers and we are also concerned about climate change. But we have only a small voice......... for now.

The Nationals may be positioning themselves to being the majority party in the Coalition after the next election. That would make Michael McCormack Leader of the Opposition. Yikes!!!

I think we are far more mature than the politicians give us credit for. I don't want to see bunting and balloons and buses. if a politician stepped out of one with an entourage including marching band, I would hope they were playing "Hit the road Jack and don't you come back no more no more...." Save the money and tell us about your policies and what you will do before some enterprising TV producer steps up and makes a reality TV show about elections.

"Canberra, we have a problem!" No-one wants to work there especially those who can't stop the inexorable slide into opposition. The coalition are staring down the barrel of a six year or more stay in oblivion. Many from either of the parties are looking at whether they can best fulfill their potential sitting in the opposition seats. The way many are choosing to opt out before the next election makes you wonder how full those seats will be and which of the two parties will have the majority in the Coalition. "Oh Scotty boy, the pipes the pipes are calling...." The piper is from Hamelin and many of Morrison's colleagues are falling over themselves to follow the piper.

You can imagine how Shakespeare would have seen this electioneering by Shorten and Morrison

"A bus! A bus! My kingdom for a bus!"

"Some are born great, some achieve greatness, but these two have a long way to go and will probably never make it."

"Men at some time are masters of their fates. These guys fates are sealed."

"Lord, what fools these wannabe immortals be!"

"All the world's a stage,

And all the men and women merely players:

They have their exits and their entrances;

These two need to exit as soon as possible."

"No surplus is so rich as honesty."

"Hell is empty and all the devils are here in Queensland"

"Please don't shout. Listen to many, speak to few"

"the voters will have their say. Now is the election to show their discontent."

"No zingers please. Better to be a witty fool than a foolish wit."

"Uneasy lies the head that wears the crown. Watch out for Dutton and Albo."

On the Coalition many are resigned to their fate, some have just resigned.

"Man the lifeboats!" That was the more than apt call that emanated from some and echoed across the Coalition. There is no cry of "Women and children first!" because there are very few women and the childish antics of those who have driven the ship onto the rocks disqualifies them from the lifeboats anyway. Some of the davits swing empty as a few have already cut and run, trying to distance themselves from the upcoming turbulence as the ship capsizes. The mutiny didn't achieve what it hoped and the stand in captain is wondering whether he actually has to go down with the ship. Meanwhile the band plays on. The tune is 'Six Months in a Leaky Boat'

Has anyone really looked at the seriousness of the next election? There will be a vast number of unemployed people seeking assistance from the government purse...... all those Coalition MP's and senators, their staff, their hangers-on, the people who were receiving grants with little or no accountability and paperwork. The election could send the debt completely out of control.

I think it a wasted opportunity by parties to not declare at each election a true spill of the seat. Incumbents should not get a free pass to pre-selection. They need to earn the right and compete against other viable members of their own party. No-one should be parachuted in either. Local members should have the final say. They after all are the ones wanting someone to represent them.

If, as some predict, Labor could end up winning Kooyong, is the new entrant vying with Josh to be the biggest loser?

It's like that line in Jaws when you see how many independents have a chance of winning, "We're gonna need a bigger cross bench."

There are a large number of new young voters who have enrolled because of the Same Sex Marriage vote. Many wouldn't have. Labor's policies target these people well in a positive way. These people struggle to get into the housing market because of negative gearing and capital gains issues assisting investors. Money is being tied up in non-productive assets, money that could be flowing through the economy and helping young people get a foothold through ongoing training. The middle-class welfare largess of years gone by needs to be identified for what it was, a vote buying exercise. There are so many loopholes in tax law that are exploited by the wealthy and companies that it is a wonder that revenue for the government actually can grow. A massive overhaul needs to happen and hopefully by laying out what will be targeted before the election, a proper mandate will be given. We were sucked in by the Coalition in 2013 and won't be again by either party. It will be up to the best party at selling their message this time knowing that creating fear and telling lies will not work as effectively again.

The fish kill has been put down by many members of the Coalition as being caused solely by the drought.... you know the My Country poem...."Land of droughts and flooding rains". The severity of the heat wave, drought and other climatic conditions has been agreed by over 95% of the world's scientists to be the fault of man-made activities causing global warming. So, it is not just another drought. The Coalition has no real effective policy in place which will let Australia do its little bit to control global warming. It also turns a blind eye to the draining of our rivers for crops that are no longer sustainable. So, the cause isn't drought. It is the mindless stupidity of the people in power welded on to big business and the mining industry. The believe there is no such thing as global warming and that coal is king.

If I go into a shop and illegally take something, I am hauled before the courts and appropriately punished. If I illegally syphon off water which leads to the death of fish and possibly other ecosystems, I get more water in the form of a light tap of a wet lettuce. Something is vastly wrong with our judicial system. White collar crime doesn't seem to matter. I wonder what an outcry there would be if the owners of the rice and cotton farms were black young Africans.

The current Ministerial setup hampers any sort of cohesive policy being developed, let alone enacted. You have:

Minister for Agriculture and Water Resources: David Littleproud

Minister for the Environment: Melissa Price

Minister for Resources and Northern Australia: Matthew Canavan.

All have overlapping portfolios when it comes to the Murray Darling. They have changed the original design and implemented a camel rather than a horse when it comes to water management across Australia. The best part about it is as far as they are concerned, each one can say that the water problems being faced are not their responsibility.

Tony Abbott showed himself to be not a very bright spark. He lost power!

If Tony really knew his onions, he would be careful how he presents himself as a candidate. Saying that people would be better off voting for a Labor candidate rather than an independent won't endear him to those Liberals who still support the Liberal party but despise him. Maybe he has bitten off more than he can chew.

Normally I worry about people trapped in landslides and avalanches, but in Dickson I hope that this self-inflicted one that is due in May has one particular casualty. Please Dicksonians keep your St Bernards at home and just enjoy the silence that normally comes after the landslide ends.

You have to wonder how much pressure will come from Border Force on the voters of Dickson. Dutton has built his own powerful fiefdom and now will seek a tithe from the people in Dickson in the form of votes. If he is prepared to use absolutely anything to stop refugees coming into Australia, what lengths is he prepared to use to exact.

Very soon Peter Dutton may be told by the people of Dickson to consider another vocation. Ireland is well known for potatoes and now with Brexit happening, they will be wanting someone to deal with those ungrateful would-be asylum seekers from Britain. Manus Island to us, Isle of Man to them. For Dutton this could be a match made in heaven post May. (both Theresa and the month)

How many au pairs will become registered to vote in Dickson before May?

Dutton's maxim has always been similar to John Howard's "We will decide who comes to this country and the circumstances in which they come." He likes to change the We to I though. Imagine his horror when the electors of Dickson say, "We will decide who goes to Canberra and the circumstances in which he/she does."

Not only will pork barrels be needed to save Dutton's bacon but also required will be lots of smoke, mirrors and any spare whiteboards that Michaelia Cash is not using.

It will be an interesting choice for the people of Kooyong to make. The "I'm not Josh. I'm for the environment" candidate will have to broaden his horizons a little or he will become just a Clayton's option, "the Lib you have when you are not having a Lib." If he wants a seat, he will have to stand for something more than one issue.

Is Joe Hockey a lifter or a leaner? In receipt of a government pension courtesy of superannuation. Has an extremely well-paid job as ambassador to the US which includes travel, chauffeur and housing. Is that double dipping? That's capitalism 101. Get all you can, while you can and bugger the rest.

Barnaby Joyce is no plumber. Give him a break. How can he possibly fix the leaking taps that 'accidentally' lead into cotton and rice farms in the Murray Darling? He also has a dislike for all those fishing programs on TV.

Are we getting value for money from our PM? Is he spending more time campaigning than doing what he is being paid for? We may scoff at the huge salaries that sports people get but they are actually doing what they are supposed to do.... okay maybe not Bernard and Nick. Perhaps the Liberal party should pay some of the PM's wages but they could easily ask are they getting value for

money. I think most politicians are having a lend of us. Neither a leaner or a lender be.

If you are too busy screaming and shouting, Scott Morrison, how can you say you are listening?

How prescriptive will Morrison's new dress code for Australia Day ceremonies be? Will a hijab or niqab be banned? Will nuns have to dress differently? Is it a case of "clothes maketh the man"? A white Anglo-Saxon, old white man is dictating what must be worn to be sworn in as an Australian citizen. Is that how we now judge a person's character and value to society?

I keep reading that Morrison is PM and am hoping that is fake news.

We will decide who comes to Australia. We will decide what they can wear. What next? Which religion they must follow? Which footy team? Why Morrison is trying to dictate terms of what being Australian looks like as well as means, is beyond me. But that is what dictators do. They want to control and thus they begin to erode the freedoms that have been bravely fought for. So what does an Australian look like? If you drew a caricature based on the averages from the 2016 census, it would look nothing like Scott Morrison believes. He is looking at it through his old white Anglo-Saxon male eyes. What may have been true in his childhood, or as he looks around his party room, is vastly different now.

Clive Palmer is spending money on his political campaign as if it was going out of style. And where is the money coming from? A few displaced nickel workers would like to know. It will be a titanic struggle which will sink and he will become another old fossil like a dinosaur.

February

- Four people are killed and over a thousand people remain evacuated from homes in Townsville, Queensland from flooding after, a metre of rainfall in one week.
- The Coalition government becomes the first Australian federal government to lose a vote on its own legislation in 78 years, after a defeat on the floor of the House of Representatives
- Major bushfires in Northern NSW
- U.S. President Donald Trump confirms that the U.S. will leave the Intermediate-Range Nuclear Forces Treaty of 1987

The figure released that unemployment remained steady at 5.1% doesn't give the whole picture. Of the employed, how many were underemployed, how many were part-time, how many had ongoing employment, how many had more than 10 hours per week, how many had more than 20 hours per week, how many were self-employed, how many were without superannuation etc. Until the full details are consistently published and compared over time, then the 5.1% is just a number that doesn't tell us much.

"Court rules out Hunter Valley coalmine on climate change grounds". I see it but Adani believe it.

Melissa Price hasn't gone missing, she has just borrowed one of ScoMo's flood jackets and no-one can see her. Makes a change from wearing a high-vis vest which makes her a target for all those 'do-gooder greenies' with their climate change and global warming nonsense.......... Okay, I can't go on. Drafting a press release for someone purporting to do something positive for the

environment is such hard work, especially if all that she does is sit on her hands.

Lost and Found.

Found in Canberra - a Coalition climate policy. Believed to be very rare and much sought after. However, use (abuse) by date is nearly up. Found with it is some funding which was thought never to be seen again. However, money allocated to pensions, Centrelink and implementing Royal Commission findings seems to have a shortfall. If the policy bears a resemblance to yours please call and ask for the man in the camouflage jacket who is trying to now blend in with others

Lost - An environment minister. She has been missing since her appointment. If found please return to parliament. No reward is available but many Australians are concerned for her whereabouts. We are not sure where abouts she stands on coal, climate change or emissions. Last seen babbling about Paris targets. We are not sure whether that was to do with cut "price" French clothing stores or anyone who looks like that Hilton girl. If you call her and say Environment Minister she will glance around, look bewildered and respond with, "Who? Me?"

The Coalition will run the same old campaign that they have always run; that Labor is bad for the economy and bad for border security. They haven't learned anything. They will target the people who will be affected by franking credits, negative gearing and capital gains tax. These however are no longer in the majority. There is poor wage growth, the opportunities for young people to buy their own homes have diminished and community services and support are in decline. The "reds under the beds" message will fall on to more deaf ears than ever. People are more aware of how things are these days. Social media shows us that. The Libs may be preparing for a fightback but their weaponry is old and dated, the troops are likewise and their communication

is behind the times. The plebiscite they ran on Same Sex Marriage will come back to bite them. So many young people enrolled just to have their say, and they will also have their say on the Coalition's performance over the past six years and the old-fashioned hectoring that will be the majority of their pitch to voters.

The definition of what is notionally a Coalition seat and what is a marginal seat was turned on its head at the Wentworth by-election and in the Victorian state election. So, given the analogy that climate change has so graciously given us in Northern Queensland, the Coalition better not worry about the seats that they thought were marginal at the last election, they need to start sandbagging their formerly safe seats. The storm of protest and the tide of public opinion may leave them high and dry in only a few places.

When asked about the election, Morrison's only comment was that it would be a Mayday! We are not sure whether that is a cry for help or not.

Given that so many men are voted in at pre-selection for the Libs because of "merit" does that mean women who make it are equally meritorious? This can't be the case because many of the men have little or no merit based on their performance and the women who are there put most of the men to shame. The merit argument therefore does not hold up in argument. Perhaps there is a hidden part of the Australian Constitution in section 44 that prohibits too many talented Liberal women from being in parliament at the one time.

"To fund this policy, we have had to let go a few people.... Julie Bishop, Kelly O'Dwyer, Michael Keenan, Nigel Scullion, Malcolm Turnbull, Julia Banks, Andrew Broad, Ann Sudmalis and possibly Craig Laundy, David Coleman and Ken Wyatt. These are all cost savings but Craig Kelly, Barnaby Joyce, Kevin Andrews and Tony Abbott weren't seen as much of a loss, so

nothing would be gained by moving them on. There is a chance in May that we will be further downsizing."

So, all these wonderful announcements being made and parliament not sitting. Coincidence obviously. Money can be found when needed. How big is the slush fund or rather how big is the pork barrel? Amazing how things suddenly are promised before an election and then suddenly are unheard of again post-election. Politicians think that we have the memory of a goldfish. Perhaps they are right we might just forget to vote for the Coalition this time around. Scott Morrison????? Never heard of him.

Julia Banks is now railing against the attitude of the Libs to any sort of sensible environmental policy and is now copping a lot of invective for her troubles. She forgot that part of the baptismal rites when entering the broad church of the Liberal Party reads: "We respect your right to disagree, but please do so behind closed doors, or we will pour all the scorn we can muster on you." Julia Banks you have been well and truly excommunicated.

I think that politicians should be bought back, like the water buy-back for the Murray Darling. Let them have a wealthfare payout, so that we can get some others in who will actually do the job they were elected to do and that is to provide a fairer social system, economy and taxation system for all. We could tax the billionaires higher to fund the buy-back. This is not class envy; it is a reality that the first million is harder to make than the second and it gets infinitely easier after that. There needs to be a cut off where taxation support peters out. Do I feel sorry for the imposition of such a scheme? Yes, just as much as I feel sorry for the poor millionaires who are having difficulty spending their money........ the poor (actually not so poor) sods!

Like in Aldous Huxley's Brave New World will we be categorised into various groups via the information passed on by

our doctors? Our social class, education level, career path etc will be predicted and later predetermined. The politicians will see us as Epsilons to their Alphas. Eugenics is how far away????

I wonder if the government was asked to hand back all the health records, it might proffer the excuse "the dog ate my database."

The first case that comes up of an insurance company or a health insurance company refusing to give coverage or a payout because of data that has been mined from hacked "My Health Record" data should be quite interesting. From my understanding, it is the security of the database that is the least healthy thing of all.

How many actual positive ideas have come from this government? They are always on the defensive and it takes a huge effort to get them to do anything. Most of the ideas come from the crossbench, the general public or the opposition. The government is really conservative. They have been conserving their innovation since 2013. Time is running out or is it that the ideas have run out or were never there. They will have the same Abbott opposition spiel after May. It comes in the three-word slogan, "No, No, No."

If the Liberal Party was a bird, it would be going around in circles with such a large number of right wings.

I have seen the acronym LNP used everywhere so I looked it up and found it to stand for Losing National Prominence.

Welfare isn't wealth fair. It is a safety net for those people who are the most disadvantaged in our community. Not everyone needs it but there may be times in one's life when people may. It is the way a society functions. To criticise and hurt those who are in difficulties due to circumstances almost invariable not of their own doing shows a lack of humanity. MP's and senators are quite content to take their salary and perks from the government purse but, particularly those in the Coalition believe that any small scrap of welfare has to be hard gained. By making things

too difficult for those in need to apply for welfare just adds an extra burden in a very difficult time. The government has tried to homogenise people into simple stereotypes but each case is different and should be treated individually. People needing support should not be shamed. They should be able to make easy contact with Centrelink and get a quick response. Heaven forbid that any parliamentarian should have to wait over six weeks to get their government paycheque. All hell will break loose. If the Coalition actually saw how people lived then they might have a different perspective. Full time jobs are becoming scarce, ongoing employment is hard to obtain, wage rises are a thing of the past, Newstart is inadequate and all the while basic essentials such as food water, gas and electricity are going up. This is predominantly happening in Labor held seats so the Coalition doesn't seem to notice or care about the difficulties people in those electorates face. Hopefully many of these politicians will find themselves in a Centrelink queue after May and they may see first-hand............ wishful thinking, as I bet they have jobs already teed up.

For the last five and a half years Labor has been practising to be in government. At the same time the Coalition have been practising to be in opposition and they are getting bloody good at it.

So, these leaners will have to lift their game and actually spend some more time sitting in parliament. They should actually earn their money. Two weeks sitting is not enough in five months. Even Pauline should be saying, "Please explain". There's a banking royal commission report to discuss and other legislation as well so perhaps Morrison shouldn't spit the dummy like Trump and close the government down.

Someone should check the health records of the actual health department computer system...... oh that's right; no-one could possibly access any health records of anybody or anything....

Forget buying the submarines, our biggest risk is through the internet. Perhaps Malcolm was right to give us a poor quality NBN. That way it might mitigate against high speed hacking.

What we need is a renewable government. The power that this one has, is damaging our environment and, with the hidden subsidies to the coal industry, is actually damaging our economy. The old fossils in power on the far right are fuelling a dying system, but they don't care as long as they get the support of the powerful mining lobby.

The following issues will count as baggage for the Coalition as they head into the next election and no amount of spin will change that.

a) inaction on climate change

b) low wage growth

c) asylum seeker detention

d) banking royal commission

e) blatant over advertising of Coalition 'successes' at taxpayer expense

f) Murray Darling management

g) performance at a state level

h) incompetence of ministers

i) the Turnbull dumping

j) the Great Barrier Reef funding decision

k) cost of living increases particularly energy

There are too many others to list but if they are hoping that another Tampa is on the horizon, they better hope for a whole fleet of them.

No fence for Australia. Apparently Border Force, at Dutton's behest, are making plans for a moat.

The scare campaign is ramping up. Expect more news and fake news on African Gangs, Rapists and Paedophiles being brought to Australia from Manus and Nauru, Muslim extremists,

hacking by Chinese and Russians .... Australia will be made out to be under immediate and serious attack. However, the truth of the matter will be that the only attack we will be under, will be by middle aged white men who wish to retain their seats in Parliament. We will be bombarded with advertising, speeches and gross over exaggeration. But we will get through, we're tough. The footy season is almost upon us. There's another long weekend coming up. Easter hols aren't too far away and then mercifully the election will be over and we will find that the spectre of invasion has disappeared along with the smoke and mirrors used to create it.

Tim Wilson, already under his own pressure from his insane political stunts over franking issues is out their tweeting today. He would be better off keeping a low profile. These tweets merely emphasise what a twat he is.

The leaders of the Coalition must have been cock-a-hoop when the franking issue gave them a chance to have a point of difference with Labor. Then along comes Tim Wilson and his half-cocked action of combining an investigative committee with a sales pitch for a Coalition return. Great coordination and combination of the one voice approach by a dysfunctional team. There will be more ill-disciplined acts as individuals try to promote themselves into the public light so that they will be seen. Many may even try to distance themselves from Coalition policies. Long time until May. Plenty of time for people to cock their weapons, shoot themselves in their feet, while those said same feet are in their mouths, in a complete cock up.

We are in for a bit of biffo today. Morrison, Pyne, Frydenberg and Dutton all launched into the fray over the weekend while Labor just danced around the ring, ducking and weaving, evading hard right jabs. Points went to the Coalition in the first round but they are looking like they already are struggling to lay an effective blow.

Meanwhile Tim Wilson is back in the dressing (down) room after a self-inflicted blow. Labor seems to be pacing itself for a long fight. It is used to southpaws who always lead with the right but doesn't know what to make of its opponent who doesn't have a strong left side to back it up with. Expect the rules to be forgotten and the gloves to come off shortly............ and maybe the watching public may pay a little more attention.

Predictions: QT will be a full-on attack by the government on franking credits, border security and refugees. Labor will try unsuccessfully to mention the Royal Commission into Banks (that's the financial institutions, not Julia's defection to the cross-bench). There will be an attempt to suspend standing orders to move that the sitting days be increased. That will go down as Katter will want to keep his water and be in the good books with his constituents, even though Kennedy has had more water than it needs the past few weeks.

I have a feeling that the amended bill will pass in the house and then go back to the Senate. That little-known senator from the back of beyond, Phil E. Buster will again take to the floor and this two-week sitting will be done and dusted before we know it.

Some possible texts that may have been at the church ceremony for parliamentarians this morning:

When a foreigner resides among you in your land, do not mistreat them. The foreigner residing among you must be treated as your native-born. Love them as yourself, for you were foreigners in Egypt. (Leviticus 19:33-34)

For I was hungry and you gave me something to eat, I was thirsty and you gave me something to drink, I was a stranger and you invited me in, I needed clothes and you clothed me, I was sick and you looked after me, I was in prison and you came to visit me.' (Matthew 25:25-36)

For the entire law is fulfilled in keeping this one command: "Love your neighbour as yourself." (Galatians 5:14)

Ann Sudmalis must have picked up some frequent flyer points with her back and forth flight last year. But will she declare them? Come to think about it did Bronnie Bishop declare hers for the helicopter flight?

Will there be a condolence motion for the death of common sense?

Now think back a few months. Turnbull was PM, Julie Bishop was Foreign Affairs Minister, the Coalition were at 49% in the polls, Julia Banks was still a Liberal and the Government had a one seat majority. Now which idiots decided that a contest for the leadership was a good thing?

You just gotta love democracy when it works. All the stalling tactics, the furphy of it being a money bill, the filibustering, the argy bargy of threats from the government, the fake news, the untruths stood for nothing when it came to a vote on the floor and people stood up to be counted. The only shame is that some members of the government who have a conscience should have crossed the floor.

Morrison is hoping that he has done Labor a mortal wound by bringing border security back on the agenda. We will have to see which side of politics gets hurt the most. Morrison is claiming that he has stopped the boats but yesterday he couldn't stop the votes.

So, the media is to be awash with re-runs. We had the original series in 2001. It was reincarnated in 2004 and again in 2013. Now we hear it is coming back in 2019. It has always been promoted as reality TV, but like all reality TV, very little of it is real. It is heavily edited. The performers are wannabe celebrities and the acting is atrocious. Aren't the producers of this rubbish aware that the public aren't interested. There is nowhere on the repetitious surveys where the public is asked, "Do you care?" The

program is there for a long season and the final ratings are in May. The producers, Morrison, Dutton & Co. will then find out in all probability that their revamped "Border Security Scare" program probably should not have been remade after the first incarnation. It's like Starwars I, II, III and every Rocky after the first one. I hear Changing Rooms is making a comeback too. I think that Morrison, Dutton & Co are a sure thing for that too....... from government party room to opposition party room.

All the pious hypocrites of politicians at church services prior to Parliament opening and them then doing and saying all the things contrary to their religion, summed up this week in politics and it amazes me. You would think that a bolt of lightning wouldn't go astray. I am quite happy for religion to be a personal inward held belief. If that's what people want. I won't shove my views down their throat as long as they don't shove them down mine. But as far as religious faith being an active determinant of governance, well, whatever religion and whatever culture and whatever form of government, I would say bugger off. History tells us that it always ends up badly. But there are ignorant people who think that with faith, history won't repeat itself.

People with religion can tell me after I am dead that there is a God and there is a heaven. I will have marshmallows on toasting forks in my coffin and celebrate their accurate predictions. The problem with a lot of zealots, both religious and political ones (or both), is that they believe they have all the answers. They may have, but they have therefore not asked enough, or the right questions. Soon as you stop asking questions then I think your brain atrophies. If politicians argued and listened to both sides of political debates, they may see the different stances raise more and more questions and their grey matter gets some stimulus. Now I would like them to leave me alone to pray to any and every god to try to get them to end both religion and politics.

It seems strange that for so long the Nationals have been weak as water. Now, in this time of drought and flood, no-one is sure anymore.

The boat is sinking and it should be women and children first. Okay, most of the politicians are childish and yes, there is a definite shortage of women in the Coalition, but it seems like it's every man for himself. The Nationals are making a rush for the lifeboat as the orchestra plays on. Sadly, the tune is Six Months in a Leaky Boat. Dutton is on the helm wishing he could stop this boat and Morrison and is contemplating another possible rearrangement of deck chairs to keep everyone from seeing what is going on. Orders are being bellowed but that is Morrison's normal mode of speech. It's an on-water matter so the public won't be fully informed. The garbled message comes across as "Boats will come. Deaths at Sea" The first is hope and the second is inevitable as the SS Coalition founders.

Why is it wrong to say in parliament that someone is lying? I thought that was merely stating the obvious. The government over the refugee issue has been telling blatant lies, telling half-truths, omitting important parts, taking things out of context, misinforming, having little or no evidence to back up statements they call facts. Yet they can't be called liars? If they mislead the house, they make a meek apology at a time they can't be questioned and that is then hidden in Hansard. It is a tactic similar to what newspapers do who hide their apologies somewhere in on page 17. We have become so used to the lies and false promises that we no longer hold our politicians to account and have learnt to either just accept what they say with cynicism or tune out altogether. The words "honest politician" have become an oxymoron. They treat us like morons and suck all the oxygen out of the truth.

What gutless wonders the government are. If the legislation is good enough, put it up in parliament rather than use some back-door contrivance. If legislation goes through that you did not put forward, accept it and move on, not cowardly undermine it and sook about it. Morrison through this minority government phase is being tested........... and found wanting.

It sounds like the Federal government wants to do what the State government did in Victoria just prior to the election of the Andrews government. They want to put in place contracts not underpinned by legislation but signed off so that projects can go ahead despite them not being in power. Andrews had to payout a billion dollars to change things because of such shady political deeds. Hopefully the legal advice holds and the Morrison government is held to account by parliament. They are a minority government (by their own hand) and need to negotiate their actions through parliament. Julia Gillard did it so well, particularly by acknowledging that her decisions were not final and handed down by God.

David Coleman's "Those processes are a matter for the department. They are run by the department and not by ministers. My understanding is that is the case for all of these sorts of contracts and they are subject to the usual rules, including audit rules of the commonwealth and so on and the department has stated quite clearly that it's followed all of those correct rules." makes you wonder whether ministerial accountability exists anymore.

I hope that Parliament doesn't have to be evacuated this afternoon. All this talk on Medivac and boats could see smoke detectors go off. Not from the smoke and mirrors. but so many pants catching fire to the Speakers right.

On the house being plunged into darkness:

Doesn't bode well for the budget if the government can't pay the power bill!

Perhaps it was the reliance on renewables as in South Australia's case?

Politicians kept in the dark? I thought that was the public?

The Energy Minister is where?.................... Can't see. It is too dark.

Isn't it the right thing to do for MP's to be in the house and Senators to be in the Senate when maiden speeches and valedictory speeches are made? That is just manners. perhaps someone on the coalition side was passing around fruit during Swannie's speech and they all had to leave the chamber suffering from the sour grapes on offer.

Australia is supposed to be a democracy. Everyone's views matter and have the right to be heard. Parliamentarians are there to represent the multitude of views and opinions of their electorate.................... yet Parliament is meeting for just a few days before June. Obviously, our views aren't as important as we thought. If Australia had a meritocracy instead (a system where government or the holding of power is by people selected according to merit) then most of our parliamentarians wouldn't be there, despite claims by parties that the candidates are chosen on merit. Maybe we should have a combination of democracy and meritocracy but that might be called a demeritocracy or a mediocracy. Can't win, can you???

Christian Porter probably wants us to have a proper gander at his Solicitor General's advice. Or is it just propaganda?

There are some terms that politicians should consider when making decisions:

Insider Trading (the illegal practice of trading on the stock exchange to one's own advantage through having access to confidential information.) is against the law

Corruption (dishonest or fraudulent conduct by those in power, typically involving bribery) is against the law

Turning a blind eye (to ignore something that you know is wrong) is often against the law

The use of propaganda (information, especially of a biased or misleading nature, used to promote a political cause or point of view.) can be against the law

but ALL should be against the moral code of ethics that politicians should abide by. Ministers have a supposedly higher code of conduct which it seems isn't practised or enforced.

It is also about time that the government dealt with another sort of power and the price we have to pay for it. It is the power of those people who think that they are above the law or at least go beyond ministerial standards and basic ethics. With so many of their snouts in the trough, is it any wonder that the politicians concerned in the rorts as outlined this week can't smell the stink around them? The next thing the public should be concerned about is how big and deep is the trough and how many more noses are pressed in it.

The issue that the public has to deal with when listening to the Coalition on any issue is to work out what parts are true, what parts are spin and what parts are downright lies. Given all the jobs for the boys and the freebies added to the lack of ministerial standards, the public have become sceptical and assume lies are the standard fare. Good luck to the Coalition selling their message at the election!!!!!!

With the Pell guilty finding out this week, it really is a whole week of putting out the trash as nothing will make the news. It has caught out the Coalition's push for an environment change of heart and that will now be buried pages deep in the news and not get much more than a sound bite on the TV news. They had a win though as the blown budget in Border Force that caused a reduction in patrols, has gone through to the keeper. People won't be able to focus on the fact that there's a drought and the rivers are dying at the same time that the Snowy and Tasmanian hydro improvements are being advocated. To run these hydro schemes, more and more water is hoarded upstream and thus

punishing the people and environment downstream at a time when they can ill afford it. Maybe this is another piece of trash that is a good thing for the Coalition to throw out this week.

Outsourcing responsibilities to the private sector has always had issues and potential corruption involved. There are many things that a government should provide and is capable of providing at a better price than private companies can do. The government doesn't have to make a profit that is added on to the overall cost. If we are detaining people in detention centres and gaols that is a social issue and the social obligation of a government. They should not absolve themselves of responsibility. We have offloaded many other responsibilities along the way. Healthcare and insurance, education, aged care, welfare, telecommunication, even banking have all been hived off to the private sector under the foolish notion that they can best be done by people who want to make money out of them. There is no net gain for society as a whole. The government and thus the public lose control and we pay a high price for that economically, morally and politically. The government should be a not for profit institution and run basic social services with that in mind.

The vote on doctors assessing medical health of refugees is not a no confidence vote in Morrison. He has had that already. O'Dwyer, Kennan, Scullion and Banks surely had no confidence in him winning or their decisions to retire may have been harder to make.

I think that the Wilderness Society will have no success similar to the Ghosts of Christmas Past had with Scrooge. Abbott's, Hunt's and to a lesser extent Frydenberg's "Global Warming. Bah! Humbug!" won't change. At best the Wilderness Society can highlight the incapability these people to see the bleeding obvious and do something about it.

The logical questions that need to be asked is that if all 1000 people on Manus and Nauru will end up in Australia because

doctors will swear they must for health reasons, as the Coalition claims, then how bad are the conditions there that would cause such mental health issues, and why hasn't the government acted sooner?

Should Phelp's Medivac Bill get passed, how long does it take for assent to be given and the law to actually be actionable? Morrison said he would ignore it. Probably until May. If the turn back the boats policy has been so effective and will continue, surely Border Force has got it all down pat by now. Any mass number of boats that do set out should be turned back if the Border Force are any good, or if the Minister is any good............. has anyone too just seen the flaw?

"I'm told that the full shadow ministry is due to meet to discuss the medical evacuation bill nowish." This is actually crunch time for Labor. What the shadow cabinet and caucus decide will determine the election result. If the stand shoulder to shoulder with the independents, they win. If they buckle, they lose. Not only the election but credibility.

Under the Phelps' bill, rapists, paedophiles and murderers would be excluded because of the crimes committed, they wouldn't qualify as refugees, so Morrison is just fear mongering when he says the bill will allow such people to enter and remain. They deserve treatment, yes but then they should return to detention. The whole thing revolves around the fact that Dutton's inept department can't process these people quick enough. If they qualify as refugees, why are they still imprisoned offshore.

Labor is actually in a winning situation whether the Phelp's bill gets passed or not. They have offered a compromise to the Coalition, which the Coalition will as a matter of course reject. Should the bill go down, Labor can therefore say that they have tried to work through the issue, but the Coalition were just too pig-headed to graciously accept an amended bill. Should the bill pass, Labor will be seen as the calm collected moderator who

escorted the bill through. All the while, the Greens will be wedged. If they vote against the amendments and the bill goes down, they will be viewed as the ones who sent it down. If it passes, they will get no credit. If the bill goes down, then Labor has great ammunition to throw at the Coalition in the election campaign..........." hard-hearted, dispassionate bastards" will taint the Coalition. Labor will take the middle ground and are one step closer to a win.

Morrison could solve the border crossing problem easier than Trump.... Morrison could dig a moat!

That PNG statement could make it a dark day for the government. A real film noir moment for them. All we get are lies and the government seem to get away with it because that is what we have come to expect. Ministers' noses must be poking holes in the bottom of the trough by now surely.

"Donald Trump's Muslim travel ban is influencing Australia's offshore processing system – with all Iranian and Somali refugees rejected for resettlement in the US." Dutton will explain that one away by saying that the US don't want black African gangs and Muslim extremists roaming the streets and making US citizens afraid to go out at night.

I don't understand why people who are deemed to be refugees aren't able to be released. I don't understand why it takes so long to process people for qualifying as refugees when the US can do it so much quicker. I don't understand why the New Zealand option isn't being accepted for those deemed to be refugees. Then again, I don't understand how an Indigenous Australian who was born in New Zealand can be deported back to New Zealand simply because his parents were visiting there when he was born. There are lots of things I don't understand about our immigration laws but the biggest one, I guess, is why hard and fast rules aren't tinged with compassion and common sense,

unless of course you are a sportsperson or can gain influence with the Minister.

So, we are to get the asylum seekers that John West (Trump) rejects? What isn't explained is that if they are brought to Australia for treatment, those with a criminal history will not be released into society. They will still be in detention and merely get the proper medical treatment they warrant. Lying to the public may be a possible vote winning strategy, but it discredits the brand and the individual. Peter Reith never recovered from the Tampa and John Howard has WMD's and the need for the invasion of Iraq as crosses to bear. Politicians can't understand that winning isn't everything. But they don't know how to lose graciously either.

If Christmas Island had all the doctors, beds and facilities to treat the asylum seekers that will needed to be removed from Manus and Nauru, then that would be fair enough. However according to the Administrative staff on Christmas Island, they don't have. In effect what will happen is that people will be transferred to Christmas Island (a distance of 6,851 km from Nauru) only to have to be assessed after a wait and then transferred to the mainland. The nearest place in Australia from Nauru with proper staff and treatment available is Cairns (a distance of 2,946 km). Logically, why would you send people over twice as far away as need be? But logic is another one of those things like common sense and compassion that are missing from the Coalition policy on asylum seekers.

Oh No! I have climbed into the DeLorean and accidentally pushed the wrong button and it's August 2001 again........... Where can I get some fuel for my Mr. Fusion Home Energy Reactor and move forward in time? There's a Peter Reith look alike telling me that rapists, murderers and paedophiles will be invading us in leaky boats.

It is sad that we have gone down the Trump path, where our politicians can tell outright lies which they seem to be held as absolute truths. I was disappointed that our local member, Russell Broadbent, who has always been a champion of refugees, didn't stand up and say that what was being said was blatantly wrong. The new law, commonly known as Medivac, that was passed by federal parliament against the government's wishes, will NOT release murderers, rapists and paedophiles into our community. Any such people on Manus Island or Nauru who need to have physical or mental health treatment that can only be done in Australia, will still be in detention here. They will not be released. If they have such significant criminal history and records, they will not qualify as refugees and be able to join the general community.

The new law will ONLY apply to those on Manus Island and Nauru at the moment. Many have languished there to our shame for over five years because 'processing' has been obscenely slow. Any others arriving afterwards will NOT be covered by the Medivac law. The law will only act as a lure to people to make the dangerous journey if it is promoted as a relaxation of current procedure. The government seems to be doing the promotion itself, perhaps for political reasons or because they are ungracious losers. That in itself is a problem because the Medivac law was a sensible and compassionate compromise to deal with a real problem affecting real people. Government should not be a game where winning and losing is all that matters.

The turn back the boats policy, which has worked so well according to the government, has NOT changed. No new boats should get through as long as the Border Force is allowed to do its job. The hectoring that has gone on saying we will be 'invaded' doesn't stand up to scrutiny of any proper analysis. The government is scaremongering, praying on our fears and hoping

that we will return them at the next election. They shouldn't need to win based on a concoction of lies. The reopening of Christmas Island detention centre to treat those physically and mentally ill on Manus and Nauru is poor economics and merely an expensive way for the government to save face. It does nothing to help those in real need. According to the administrative staff on Christmas Island, they don't have the medical expertise and beds to cope. People on Nauru will be transferred 6,851 km to Christmas Island whereas they could be transferred 2,946 km to Cairns which has all the appropriate facilities and medical practitioners.

The Medivac law is a sensible compassionate way of aiding people who are in desperate need of our help. For over five years we have effectively turned our backs on them. We have finally turned around and faced our responsibilities. Hopefully our incumbent federal MHR will continue to call the government out on its attitude toward asylum seekers on our behalf.

The government seems to be all at sea over its on waters matters. Is it out of its depth? Has the tide turned against it? Do they see the Medivac legislation as a mere drop in the ocean of what is to come? Do they wish us to drown in a sea of lies and misrepresentations? Is propaganda the only port in a storm that is available to them?

I'm not buying Morrison's change of heart and his $2 billion plan over ten years but somehow, I am still paying for it. Every taxpayer is paying for yet another political stunt under the saving one's bacon scheme. Last week it was Christmas Island re-opening. What will it be next week? Where did this magic pudding of taxpayer dollars come from? Maybe the subs have been cancelled. One can only hope. By the time they are built and are in use they will be so outdated just like the Tony Abbott Direct Action plan that is being refloated. Still, the subs will be handy for future generations to view a dead coral reef and where Kiribati and the Maldives once were.

A pork barrel from a known ham trying to save his own bacon. Nothing rasher than what he is proposing because it will encourage more snouts to get into the trough. The oink has yet to dry on the last about turn, the NEG.

I blame Dorothea MacKellar. Her poem about a sunburnt country with droughts and flooding rains has become the ready-made excuse for us doing nothing to mitigate the effects of human influenced climate change. It has allowed sceptics to proudly boast that this is the way the world has always been. Yet the facts get in the way. Heatwaves have become more extreme, so have floods, cyclones, cold snaps and droughts across the world. There is a gradual rising of sea levels and melting of polar caps, but in the true Aussie spirit of "she'll be right, mate", our government does nothing and can't even get together a cohesive environment and energy policy. They are too busy worrying about the economy and how any change away from fossil fuels towards renewables will affect the hip pockets of voters and even more so, how their donors in the mining industry will react. The argument that if we do something it will have little impact across the whole world, should not be a reason to do nothing. Generations following ours will be wondering 'what were they thinking?'

Is the Coalition hoping things will coalesce at the same time so many people are hoping that things will Coal Less?

If the Coalition steps aside, stops ramping up the use of coal and lets the market dictate, as it said it would, then we will probably meet the targets. Actually, if they just stepped aside completely by calling an election that would guarantee the targets would be met.

"The House moves on to a motion acknowledging the natural disasters across the country." No acknowledgement of climate change and lack of a proper environment policy of course.

The new energy plan, power from smoke and mirrors. The Coalition hope to retain power using this new source.

"These people just can't help themselves. They are all negative. They don't know what they're for, but by God, they know what they're against." And this was said by "flip flop" Dr No in opposition who went on to become the PM where he just flopped.

Tony Abbott: "I have a lot of respect for the medical profession but we all know that doctors always err on the side of compassion." Border Force and Dutton must err on the side of hard heartedness (assuming a heart can be found in the Minister.)

Good to see that Tony Abbott's green army is finally paying dividends in lower energy prices. He said it was a cure-all for everything to do with energy and the environment. What a forward-thinking man perfectly placed in the industrial revolution of the nineteenth century.

How many white boards does the Federal Court have? Cash may have to appear there today or is that disappear there?

"If it looks like a duck, swims like a duck, and quacks like a duck, then it probably is a duck."

If it looks like corruption.......................................

If it looks like a lie..............................

If it looks like a coverup........................

If it looks like a whiteboard................... Hang on it could be Michaelia Cash.

I agree with Julie Bishop that the Coalition will win...... enough seats to form an Opposition; and that she should stay to be Leader of the Opposition.

We now have Sergeant Schultz being played by an Arnold Schwarzenegger sound alike.

The Minister in charge of Finance overlooks his own financial transactions? Not a great recommendation for the job. Maybe it was just a flight of fancy.

One wonders whether, instead of an Arnie Schwarzenegger voice, Mathias Cormann has a distinctive phone voice like Lionel Richie's. When he books his flights, it would sound like this:

Hello, this is me you're booking for
As I smoke my huge cigar
I've got some money just for you
You'll win the tender only, if there's some kick back from you?
So, don't charge my credit card
But I'll put the blame on you
If somehow someone finds out the truth

"A fire alarm appears to be going off in the room where Mathias Cormann is facing his estimates grilling." Someone's pants are on fire!!!!!

Mirrors don't last when Dutton is around. Like the rest of us they are shattered that such a being without a conscience and any compassion could walk the earth.

Josh Frydenberg seems to be demanding that Labor take action on the Banking Royal Commission report. He fails to realise that the government is the only one that can take action. They have the power to do something. Labor does not and will not until May 2019 at the earliest. Frydenberg should not demand such things. He is not in opposition........... yet!

"I'm an elected representative. It is my God-given right to remain unchallenged by anyone else in the Liberal Party". Craig Kelly didn't actually say this nor the Liberal Party executive but I hope someone looks at the way that pre-selection occurs in the Liberal Party. If Craig Kelly is the best that the Liberals have to offer in the seat of Hughes, there must have been no-one at the bottom of the barrel with him.

If the government can issue a gag order in parliament, they should extend it to Michael McCormack when he is out and about. I wonder whether Scott Morrison regrets that hasn't been

done? If so, I bet the voice in his head is saying, "We're all experts in hindsight."

The fuel emissions taskforce seems to have run out of energy, or at least had the supply cut off. You set up a taskforce to bury something that you don't want published. The important thing is to choose the right chairperson to run it. Michael McCormack is the right one to bury any outcome. After all he has had his personality interred years ago and doesn't even remember where the grave is.

We have full page ads in the paper, long ads on TV and in social media and apart from the Clive Palmer ones that cause nausea, they are all about how the government is great and wonderful. We are paying for these government ads just like we are paying for Tim Wilson's committee junket. The public have become quite cynical over such advertising. It is counterproductive towards a good election result for the incumbent government. Who are the people pushing for this quasi election approach? Dumb & Dumber?

Rudd rails against the hard right and encourages the far left to action. The majority of people are in the centre. The centre is where the votes lie. The centre is the group that needs to deplore the hard right and to a certain part, the hard left. Radical policies further divide us. Radical policies won't win an election, only lose one.

March

- Cardinal George Pell is sentenced to six years in prison following his conviction over the sexual abuse of two choirboys
- North Korea–United States summit between United States President Donald Trump and the North Korean Chairman Kim Jong-un is held in Hanoi, Vietnam
- 51 people are killed and 50 others injured in terrorist attacks on two mosques in Christchurch, New Zealand.
- Europe's antitrust regulators fine Google 1.49 billion euros for freezing out rivals in the online advertising business. The ruling brings to nearly $10 billion the fines imposed against Google by the European Union.
- The final territory occupied by ISIS located in Syria, is liberated.
- An estimated 400,000 people march in central London in protest against Brexit
- A four-page summary of Special Counsel Robert Mueller's report into U.S. President Donald Trump's 2016 election campaign is released. It concludes that there was no collusion with Russia but states "While this report does not conclude that the president committed a crime, it also does not exonerate him"

Song of the farmers:
"Up in the mornin'
Out on the job
Work like the devil for my pay
But that politician has nothin' to do
But go around talking all day"

Barnaby Joyce's and Angus Taylor's seats are under threat by disillusioned voters in the bush. That should come as no surprise. The fact that it is now being reported on as something serious, is. There is a born to rule mentality that exists with many coalition members. There is also a reluctance on people in country seats to change their voting patterns. However, they are now not about to be bulldozed and conned into choosing someone who doesn't represent their views. They can see the way climate is changing and how water in particular is being mismanaged. They are not going to take on board the assurances that the Coalition has finally got the message after six years. It is a case of once, twice, three elections and you're out..........

To paraphrase Deep Purple
"Pollies have no rules
They lie all the time
They treat us like fools
Spinning ev'ry line
Dutton's the worst of them
Tearing the truth down
Talking with a forked tongue
What's that hissing sound?
Smoke about borders
Mirrors with lies
Smoke about borders"

The sad thing is that we have become conditioned to accepting the lies. We expect them to lie and never call them on it. We would be shocked if we heard the truth and so our complacency sets in. This is the way it is, the way it always was and the way it will always be. Not only is it a sad indictment on the standard of politician who is supposed to represent us, but also on the voting public ourselves. David Morrison said it best with, "The standard you walk past, is the standard you accept". When the PM and ministers brazenly lie then they should be held to account. Perhaps we should elect used car salespeople and raise the standards a bit.

Rats leaving a sinking ship? An insult to rats. There is no deceit in rats. There's no corruption in rats. There's some dignity in rats because they know no better.

Morrison is looking for a new cabinet. Soon there will only be Kelly, Abetz, Joyce, Andrews and Abbott to choose from to join Dutton. That's all he needs.......... woodworms in his cabinet.

We were on the good ship Scottus
And look where it's got us
Said Chrissie Pyne
As he called time
The right wing is just not us
They chased away poor Julie
And she was loyal truly
A PM who loves to shout
May too be voted out
By the mob that's so unruly
The mutineer called Dutton
Not the smartest button
Opens up his mouth
And lies tumble out
Who voted this nut in?

Australia has a problem with power. Too many people want it and offer nothing in return. At least that is what the last four Prime Ministers have shown. The Coalition believe that clinging to power by any means is justifiable. Once politicians used to be able to convince us that they were offering a public service by being in Canberra. Now nearly all of them seem to be self-serving.

Figures don't lie. Politicians do.

Do all our excessive emissions come from burning too much coal or from the fires Coalition politicians have in their pants?

If politicians want a seat in parliament only for the power it gives them, why aren't their chairs properly wired up? In Canberra that would be Capital punishment but much deserved.

The strength of anything can only be based on its weakest link. Let's look at Morrison's current crop of ministers: Dutton, Hunt, Cash, Fifield, Canavan, Price, McCormack. Take your pick. The cabinet is pretty dodgy and likely to fall apart even before, Scullion, O'Dwyer and Pyne quit.

I have seen stable teams. Most of the time they just clean the stalls. So, Morrison has a group of people known as muckrakers?????

It is all to do with perception. If you look sideways at line graphs of approval ratings, numbers of people choosing to remain in the team, decrease in debt, etc. Things look they are all on the up. It is the same method that Angus Taylor uses when he talks about emission reductions. Gotta be impressed with the agility of the Coalition. For most of us, we certainly aren't that flexible when it comes to the truth.

"The adults are back in charge.............."

"Lifters not leaners.................."

"Not safe to go to restaurants in Melbourne................"

"1000 asylum seekers will force Australians off waiting lists for medical procedures..........."

"South Australian energy crisis was caused by renewables........."

These are just some of the farrago of lies that the Coalition believe that if said often enough will become truths.

Global warming... blame Labor

Spiralling debt... blame Labor

Rising energy costs... blame Labor

Poor wage growth... blame Labor

Jobs for the boys... blame Labor

Possible recession... blame Labor

Potential arrival of boat people... blame Labor

It seems that the only answer that the Coalition has to its own self-induced problems is ... blame Labor. This is the sort of thing one would expect of people in Opposition. It seems that after six years of continual practice, they actually might get the gig.

How dare the law inhibit what a woman can do with her body. It seems so archaic and a remnant of a male patriarchal society. Of course, abortions and counselling should be offered at hospitals. What century are we in? And also of course the religious right will dump a bucket on Labor for even broaching the topic and thought of change. They were never going to vote for Labor anyway so there will be no votes lost there. I hope that Labor has pledged this for altruistic reasons rather than trying to garner more votes. Yes, like many of us, I have become very cynical of promises around election time.

Hopefully one thing that the Labor Party will do after the next election is to get the attorneys-general of the states to push for uniform laws regarding abortion across Australia. That law should state that a woman has the right to do what she wants with her own body and if she deems it necessary/desirable to have an abortion, then that should not be prevented because of money, being shamed, being harassed outside abortion clinics etc. The current situation merely reinforces the patriarchal leaning society we have. It pays scant regard to the social, physical, mental and emotional wellbeing of the person who in the past has only had the choice to carry the child to full term or seek a backyard abortion. Religious and moral zealots should not impose their own views on others. Nor should laws designed by men, impose restrictions. A woman's body is her own.

We have Barnabus Lacka Joyus, spilling for a fight to retake the leadership of the Nationals in a gladiatorial battle with

Michaelus Can'trmemeberhisnameus. This is while Scottoobee Moronicus is trying to prove he has a strong and stable cabinet. We also have a Coalition caused 'almost recession' and flat wages growth while Moronicus is trying to stress his self-proclaimed excellent economic credentials. The public gathered in the stands watching the arena known as the Canberra bubble will be giving a thumbs down to those who are unsteadily standing but staggering around in their death throes. The blood bath began with the knifing of Malcolm Turnbullshitus and has gone nonstop since. Standing well clear is Shortinarse who seems to be enjoying this internecine battle between one disunited group. He appears ready to take on the last man standing.

It could be argued that with the Coalition that the left hand doesn't know what the right hand is doing. However, with this Coalition it is more a case that the right hand doesn't know what the far-right hand is doing.

You would hope that all members of Cabinet would openly discuss issues within Cabinet and put forward lots of alternative ideas and views. However, as Cabinet solidarity is always being stressed, the expectation that once a decision is made, everyone should speak from the same book. There are some reasons why this is isn't happening with the Coalition. The policy book may be too complex. The literacy levels of ministers may be very low. Or, and this is more likely, the pages are blank and Ministers are forced to ad-lib.

Truth in advertising? Hardly likely. Truth in politics? Even more remote a chance. We have come to expect that anything said by politicians or about politicians is a lie...... that make this a potential lie. Therefore, does that mean that there is truth in politics? Let's not stretch credibility well beyond the bounds of belief.

When something is divided everyone usually gets less. I'm doing the maths too, Mr Morrison. We therefore seem to be getting less and less from the Liberals and the same can be said of the Nats. The only way you don't get less when you divide is when there was nothing there to begin with or if you started with less than nothing and it was divided by something that was also less than nothing.

You have to give credit for the optimism of the Coalition. It's akin to a Field of Dreams scenario. Christmas Island reopens, "Open it and boats will come." A government funded coal fired power station, "Build it and investors will come." Coalition pork barrelling, "Do it and votes will come." Scare mongering, "Lie 'cause voters are dumb." Sadly, the Coalition don't realise that Field of Dreams was a fantasy.

It seems a shame when the terms 'brainwashing' and 'manipulation' are thrust at the protest by young people by those supposedly more educated, older and wiser. If these people were actually more educated and wiser, would they have let the planet slide to the point where students feel compelled to protest at the mess they will inherit? The people who use these terms are actually just older, and probably of a generation who decried the way the then government with older, supposedly more educated and wiser people led us into a war in Vietnam. Age makes people forget what it is like to be young, see a need for change and want an opportunity to express a voice.

The Nationals used to represent the people in the bush but now seemed to be more obsessed with people high up in the towering offices of the mining companies. Farmers are slowly realising that they are being underrepresented and the things that are affecting their livelihood the most are the consequences of climate change. More and more land is being usurped for the mining industry. More and more subsidies that they might have received are being given to the mining industry and to businesses trying to deal with the damage caused by the mining industry, both short and long term.

The Nationals would be better off not cosying up to mining magnates, but addressing the needs of their constituents. Perhaps this election may just reinforce that prediction.

When you think about someone being bold, you need to think of John Hewson and his logical (minus the birthday cake) GST. It was poo-hooed and he was pilloried eventually by both sides of the political spectrum who quickly accepted the idea. Governments have become too scared to take a chance. The window for change is so small in the life of a government who always seem to look forward to ways of winning the next election, the moment they gain power. The safe road is not always the best one to take because change, even positive change gets bogged down in politics. If a government is elected, they claim they have a mandate for everything they promised. That is not true of itself. However, they do need to do something rather than just fight to retain office. If there is a change in government this is because the status quo was not seen as good enough. It is a shame that when we vote we can't also put in our priorities for change so that the government had some idea of what we actually want.

You wonder why Angus Taylor didn't somehow link all this to asylum seekers. Linda Reynolds somehow managed to do that on Q & A last night. But then she said this was no time for politicking. I can see how disconcerting it must be for voters. Watching politicians having their noses extend, while their pants are on fire just as their parents are washing their mouths out with soap and water. Not a pretty sight.

The rise of independents should signal to the two major parties a growing dissatisfaction with the way they conduct business. Blame should not be placed on voters and their supposed ignorance, but should be directed at the ignorance of our current crop of politicians who fight among themselves, conduct themselves abominably and treat the governance of

Australia as a game. They need to get their own house in order before they assume the responsibility of the House. If they continue to refuse to listen to voters, they will continue to pay a high price at the ballot box. They alone should be blamed. Yes, Australia could do with stable government, but it needs to be progressive and respond to the needs of the community it serves. Politicians appear to believe that we serve them, yet it is the other way around. The current government is slow to react, applies Band-Aid measures to big problems and continues to stick to outdated notions based on archaic ideologies. Political parties need to firstly recognise that there is a problem, take ownership of the problem and work swiftly to alleviate the problem. They can't even get to the first part of the solution because they just don't, or refuse to, see the problem as being them.

Years ago, the Nationals were the Country Party and the name change was a huge signal to people but more so to those representatives who were elected. You were there to do the best you could for those in the country, to make sure they had a voice and usually those members of the Country Party looked after issues pertaining to the bush and to farms. Now the Nationals might as well be called, "Just Another Party". They have lost credibility with their former base and by trying to do more than what they were initially doing, have spread themselves too thin and tried to please everyone and ended up pleasing very few. They thought they had their 'base' locked away securely and went chasing votes elsewhere. Well their base has revolted because they were getting lip service only to their needs. Just wearing an akubra does not entitle you to their vote any more.

The comparison between the Coalition and the Labor party becomes relevant only if we talk about promises. We know that once elected, some excuse will be made so that election promises aren't kept. The freeze on payments to doctors through Medicare

was a money saving exercise. It ended up forcing doctors not to bulk bill many patients and the gap between what Medicare offered and what the bill was, increased. Preventative health went out of the window as the public was forced to go to the doctor only when they were seriously ill. To buy some more submarines, more jet fighters, to give themselves more perks and wage rises was deemed more important than the health of the public. In the past six years the Coalition was in power and ran down Medicare. It was deliberate. It went against the promises made in 2013 when they were elected. Can we trust Labor to stick to their promises? That is a moot point, but we know that the Coalition can't. It may need a leap of blind faith on our part. Let's hope that Medicare and our health system can cope with the injuries we sustain when we fall flat on our faces.

You have to look seriously about who the PM's advisers are and the decision making that takes place within his party and within the Coalition. Peter Hartcher's expose on what took place over the last six years is enlightening and makes you wonder about the policy making processes. Teena McQueen, vice president of the Libs made it quite clear on Q&A of the level of talent they are relying on. Yes, she is marginally ahead of James Ashby and Steve Dickson but you have to wonder that if she is one of the puppeteers pulling the strings, just how Punch and Judy the whole show is.

The Coalition looks like a last man, last woman standing affair.... a bloodbath in a Colosseum where every gladiator is out for themselves. Some have escaped, wounded but alive. The penchant for face to face mortal combat is tempered only by the backstabbing. Michaelus McCormackitus is hoping that the meek will inherit the earth and he hopes he will be able to "leave the building, thank you very much. The masterful Unscrupulous Morrisonus believed all his prayers had been answered, but will eventually get the thumbs down by the public. There is an alliance within Queensland working together but only gaining minor ground. The moderates are taking a beating from the lions on the right who are trying to outflank them. All the while, waiting in the wings waiting to cart away the dead and dying, is Bilious Shortenus, himself a victor of previous battles. It seems Maximus Damajus will prevail and that's all that will be remembered by those witnessing what took place in the political arena.

If you think Brexit will cause border issues for Britain and Trump's wall between the US and Mexico is an emergency crisis, think how difficult it will be to lock immigrants out of our cities. Border force may need to change their uniform, at least their shirts anyway, perhaps to colours more reminiscent of Germany and Italy in the 1930's

Scott Morrison says 'just do the maths'. Well something doesn't add up for sure. We spent billions of dollars on off-shore detention and private companies made a fortune providing third world facilities. There were not enough trained medical people to do the work required to maintain the physical and mental well-being of asylum seekers. That was a cost too much to bear and the situation deteriorated so much that we will be spending millions paying for the remediation of a problem that was known. We are opening up Christmas Island and sending people there at huge cost rather than bring them to the mainland where proper care can be given at the fraction of the cost. There are not enough hospital beds there and why would you send people twice the distance from Nauru to Cairns in the first place. To properly look after these people, doctors will need to go where they are needed, wherever that is. I've done the maths and the lies that are being told are on an exponential curve. Hopefully though the Coalition are on a downward spiral. Newton proved mathematically that for every action there is an equal and

opposite reaction. Morrison's and Dutton's distortion of the truth will see the Coalition out of government.

Morrison reached into his bag of tricks and pulled out the xenophobic one, trying to convince us that we are about to be invaded by rapists, paedophiles and murderers from Manus and Nauru. We saw through that one. Michael McCormack pulled out of his bag of tricks the one saying there would be no more night footy. That made a bigger impact on the public.

So, at last we find out where the numbers have come from and why the numbers being quoted by Angus Taylor are so out of tune with reality. Worst case scenario without known factors in play. Sounds a bit like the rapist, murderers and paedophiles claim for asylum seekers. Anything to scare us and repeated often enough must of course be true. The one unique quality a politician must have is not compassion, but the ability to lie with a straight face.

Immigration should not be about demonising people of different races, cultures or religions. It should be above that but we have been conditioned to believe that immigration and invasion are one and the same thing. We spend billions on ensuring those who risk coming by boat are kept at bay or on Pacific islands. Yet more people come here by plane and overstay. If visas were properly enforced and restrictions placed on foreign students, skilled workers, then immigration would be better controlled. However, once the airport terminal doors close and people are in the community, Border Force or Immigration let them fly under the radar. Many of these people are exploited and because their visa status may be suspect, they cannot say anything. Any decent organisation would track people who are here on visas and step in once the visa time has passed. That is not as gung-ho and as visually riveting as high-speed warships though. Australia has the rules and regulations to maintain a good immigration level if the government didn't want to practice its dog-whistling.

A recession after such wonderful economic management and having the delivered a massive reduction in the national debt as promised by the Coalition. How can that be possible? Could it be that we have been told porkies and/or that Morrison's mathematical ability matches his Finance Ministers?

The federal government have been caught out on their trickle-down economic approach. It was supposed to provide incentive for investment but instead, much has disappeared offshore. A trickle up approach which allowed more take home wages, higher Newstart and pensions would allow consumers to spend more, rather than live frugally and constrict the economy. With more money actually out and being used, businesses will invest more. If capital wasn't invested so much in overpriced and inflated real-estate because of the property boom, people would spend more and the wheels of business and industry would keep turning. Currently the economic settings by this government are like a snake that has begun eating its own tail. It will only get so far until it either realises and spits it out or chokes to death.

If you continue just to apply a small amount of liquid fertiliser willy nilly just on the parts that show, then trickle down doesn't work. It doesn't get down to the grassroots. A tinge of growth may show briefly but then it will die. Better off to apply the same amount below the surface where the uptake will be greater and more sustained growth will be the outcome. Works in the garden but apparently not according to the Coalition in economics in Australia. They are using their own same ideology on inland rivers. Just a trickle is being sent downstream and they wonder why the rivers are dying. Too much is being siphoned off before it can be of any use.

So how does big business actually work? Large companies speculate and invest. They take a risk but then that risk is passed quickly down the food chain. Board members and the Executive become exempt somehow for losses. Shareholders assume most of the risk. Employees and sub-contractors are caught in the middle when things go sour. They are not the first in line as creditors. Banks usually are. They get their pound of flesh first and anything (and sometimes there is nothing) left over goes to employees and subcontractors. If things however go well, then the Board and Executive get bonuses, shareholders get a dividend and employees don't get sacked, but they don't get a rise in wages even though their efforts may have propelled the company forward. They get a flat and often stagnant wage. Sub-contractors are still screwed down mightily and are paid as little as possible. so, the ideal thing to be is on the Executive, on the Board or a Bank. It's a win/win situation. Shareholders are in a win/lose situation. Employees and sub-contractors are in a no net gain/lose situation. And as the majority of people in big business are employees or sub-contractors, they are in the worst situation; all the risk in reality for little gain. That is Big Business 101. And next semester we look at Big Business 102 which will cover tax avoidance, lobbying, corruption, bonus structures, nepotism and politics.

The question needs to be asked whether the economy is in a smaller slump than the Coalition. The Coalition can't really go into the election now spruiking its economic achievements because they can't really spin the truth of: spiralling debt, flat wage growth, per capita recession and other very unflattering economic data. The promise of a surplus at a budget is really an optimistic guess which always seems to fall flat. Lately they have had to reduce their highly touted Border Force operations because they ran out of money. No wonder the Coalition is scaremongering; they have nothing really positive to say, nor positive policies and actions to change the current state of play. Business confidence is down, consumer confidence is down and confidence in the Coalition to do anything about these things is

way down. Scott Morrison will need all his advertising genius to pull this one out of the bag. He hasn't started well though and if this is a sign of things to come, then "Victory, where the bloody hell are you?" will be all that he can utter on election day.

The party of the rational economists, the party that believes in non-government interference in business, the party that wants the market to set the agenda now seems to be quite socialist in nature by expressing a desire for a government run coal fired power station. Are we in some sort of Bizarro world? Japan has seen the need for change, China has too, despite the smog from its out of date power supply. It seems that it's only the Coalition who refuses to see the light unless it is powered by coal.

Who would have thought that giving tax cuts to the wealthy whilst deliberately flattening wages would have seen money taken out of the economy and reinvested overseas? Surely the adults in charge, the best economic managers and the party that is asking the public to trust them as they know what they are doing, would have foreseen that. But sadly, they overlooked that. The economy is stalling except it seems for those who already had money. And the Coalition wonder why they are losing votes. If they are always talking about themselves, you would think some sort of self-reflection would be taking place. There is an image crisis that they refuse to see.

Soon we will hear complaints from people who were all too keen to join the boom cycle of housing prices. They will expect the government to step in quickly and subsidise their gambling losses. That is what they are. They have invested in things just as a punter does at the TAB or on the stock market. They would have been only too happy to cream the profit, but will feel dudded by a loss. Meanwhile those in the rental market may actually be able to get a foothold and be able to buy a house for something like it is worth. So, what will the government do? They have shown the best example of what could happen by devaluing Parliament House by their presence, actions and corruption over the past decade or more. Will they try to prop up a market that sucks money out of the economy or will they go against their market forces ideology? I guess it depends where the votes are.

The response from one political party about the wage stagnation appears remarkably similar to Marie Antoinette's. But what GST is to be paid on the cake that they want people to eat? Perhaps John Hewson can explain. If productivity and profits are up and the wages don't rise accordingly then the divide between rich and poor is exacerbated. If a government doesn't intervene perhaps heads will roll, figuratively not literally like in France years ago. If people have no discretionary spending money, the economy will slow down, house prices will continue to fall, the dollar will become unstable and the GDP will take a battering. Worst case scenarios are recession leading to depression. Good economic managers listen to the market, listen to the guiding remarks of the Reserve Bank Board and the OECD and look at long term trends. Good figures in one quarter aren't enough to rely upon. They can be artificially contrived especially around election times. Australia has a burgeoning debt simply because the main increase in spending is being driven by public and public/private partnership projects. The debt rise is unsustainable and sooner or later, as the world market stumbles, loans will be called in, just as they were in the late 1920's. The result will be massive unemployment, loss of the government's high credit rating and an economic face-plant that took fifteen years and a world war to recover from. Right now, profits are being syphoned overseas thus proving the trickle-down approach was never going to work. The Coalition will muddy the waters over the true state of our economy and claim to be the best economic managers. The facts don't support that, but since when has there been truth in advertising and in politics?

It is the stagnant wage growth that is causing a lot of disaffection with government policies. With everything going up except wages, low income earners had little discretionary income to help boost the economy. Each day now without a change means that necessities feel the pinch. Wage growth has grown by only 2% over the past three years. If this was to continue, for someone now on the average wage of $86,000 per year that 2% amounts to nearly $33 per week. The average is just that and the median yearly wage is actually $66,000 so a 2% increase for most Australians is around $25. But consider a person earning the minimum wage of $37,000 a year a 2% rise amounts to $14 per week. Prices of household necessities are rising much faster than 2% each year let alone over three. Everyone is feeling the pinch except those at the top getting the benefit of a trickle-down economic ideology. There is a drought just below the surface that is not being addressed. A living wage in an egalitarian and just society makes sense.

The Coalition have often said that Australia should not make energy and environmental changes alone to combat climate change because nothing would change across the world and we would suffer economically. Yet now we find that the Coalition has set us apart from the world by going it alone and using climate funding to spend on the upgrades to coal fired power plants. How they don't lisp when they speak amazes me. Perhaps their forked tongue has been doctored.

If coal is actually the cheapest form of power, as has been spruiked by the likes of Abbot and other right-wing politicians, why are companies making an economic decision to get out of coal fired power stations? The market, according to the Coalition, is supposed to determine things and yet that doesn't apply to coal. It hardly seems rational and logical. The public is being denied facts when it comes to actual costs and subsidies for all types of power production. We need to be able to make a rational decision when it comes to voting at elections, not one based on spin. do we just choose who lies the least?

The science is in. It is there with 99% accuracy for all to read and yet slightly less than half of the population still dispute it. Our coal coveting and carrying PM should not be heading the country. All these PM changing deniers need to take a look at the cold hard facts. For a government still to be pushing coal mining for any reason, be it for export or for our own consumption is tantamount to putting economics over the future of the planet. Coal has been subsidised for years by the government. State governments have been hoodwinked over the mineral rights for coal, the royalties for its use and have been deluded about the number of people it will employ. They have forgotten that deals they make are with national assets. State governments have sold off power production plants they built to private enterprise for a tiny amount. They also have sold off the control of these. Any company can just say that they do not wish to run them and then mothball them. Many are contemplating that as they have become less and less economically viable. How our PM can advocate on behalf of the coal industry beggars belief. If he continues to push ahead with this fixated ideology and hope that coal will provide more jobs, he will only find out that it will in fact cost jobs. One of which will be his own.

With global warming causing rising sea levels, soon congestion won't be a problem as some cities will be underwater. (Perhaps that is what the subs are for). Border force will be patrolling former streets in rubber rafts. Immigration numbers won't matter. Everything will be classified as an "on water" matter. In all seriousness however, has the government factored in the number of climate change refugees that will be coming our way from low lying Pacific and Indian Ocean

Islands. Our shame in contributing to global warming should see us morally obliged to take in these people, but sadly when it comes to morals and immigration there is a cultural divide in our politicians.

And what will the children think? In a hundred years' time when they are doing history. Will they look at Australia as a prime example of a nation that buried its head in the sand and did little despite overwhelming scientific evidence; a nation that toyed with the fringes rather than addressing the problem; a nation that was more obsessed with political infighting than setting up a mechanism to try to combat global warming; a nation that ridiculed its own children who protested that something should be done? History is notoriously written by winners. There appears to be no winners when it comes to climate change, so what history will be written? What will the children think?

This to the tune of Gold by John Stewart
Counting the days to the election in May
And the Libs all seem to be leaving
How did it get this far? They'll ponder at the bar
It started with Dutton's deceiving
*A few "F*** me's" and "Bless my souls*
We're bloody good at kicking own goals"
Well people are bailing fast, seen their future at last,
Seeking jobs in the final hours
Postings to far off lands, making huge demands
They didn't come down in the last shower
*A few "F*** me's" and "Bless my souls*
We're bloody good at kicking own goals"
ScoMo's career's unsure, though the writing's on the wall
Seems he's not too good at reading.
He says strong and stable, but didn't say able
No wonder they're going to be beaten

*A few "F*** me's" and "Bless my souls*
We're bloody good at kicking own goals"
*A few "F*** me's" and "Bless my souls*
We're bloody good at kicking own goals"

Has someone come up with an advent calendar for the countdown to the next election? There's a money-making idea! Advertise it saying that behind each picture of a cabinet minister is a workable policy. This is not false advertising if there's nothing behind each one, just disappointment. You get to market new versions weekly as people opt not to continue after the election. They will become collector's items. My rubbish is collected Wednesdays. Of course, instead of Melissa Price's face there will be question mark. Michaelia Cash won't be seen either, just a whiteboard. Mathias Cormann's face will be obscured by cigar smoke and guilt about his travel and ability to count spill votes. Of course, there will be a game released afterwards called Where are They Now? I am running a sweep on which ones will be on Dancing with the Stars and/or I'm a Celebrity Get Me Out of Here. Although something similar to the latter I believe is already in production, I'm a Coalition Member Get Me Out of Here. The location of which is inside a bubble in Canberra which is far more lethal and dangerous than South African jungles I hear.

The Greens have just relaunched with Julian Burnside to take on Josh Frydenberg in Kooyong. It will be interesting to see what impact he has as he has a big personal following and he brings with him a lot of integrity that many politicians lack including some of his own party.

I don't understand why Scott Morrison isn't having Georgina Downer saying things about recession on behalf of the government. Surely, she is in cabinet already as Minister for Hogging the Spotlight.

Looks like the Beijing style atmosphere is coming to the Hunter Valley, or maybe the electors could vote Labor and choose health of the community over a few extra jobs. Could be a hoax as I met someone who was offering me a deal on the scrap steel from the Harbour Bridge when it was being pulled down next year.

If the Libs really badly perform at the next election, it could make McCormack leader of the opposition and alternative PM............... that alone could see them out of power for a few more elections. While doing the dishes, I look in the sink and see that as being much brighter than McCormack. Isn't a leader someone who knows where they are going, knows how to get there and more importantly knows why? McCormack fails all three and you have to feel some sympathy for the Nats who had to put up someone transparently bland to counteract the farcical Barnaby Joyce. The trouble is that he is so transparently bland we can see that there is no substance there at all.

Watch for the sandbagging of old white male seats rather than the money going to the marginal women candidate seats. In Victoria that means the likes of Kevin Andrews, Josh Frydenberg and Greg Hunt will get the lion's share of Liberal election funds. The Libs think that money buys votes. Hopefully this time they will find that they have misjudged the public who think that policies are the things that matter more.

It is sad the notion of a two-party preferred outcome to a poll; when at one time or another either or both major parties are on the nose. All the polls indicate is which side has won the prize as the least worst option. We have somehow conferred a presidential-like visage on our Prime Minister. It will not be a Bill Shorten Labor government, nor a Scott Morrison Coalition government that is elected in May, it will be an Australian government. Australians elect governments and we are all collectively responsible for what we get. The God like status of

the PM needs to be taken down a peg or two. The PM is only one person among many elected.

The Stock Exchange will soon be halting trading on companies that sell barrels and/or pork.

The thing that politicians think we do when voting, is pretend we are going down the confectionery aisle in the supermarket and choosing from the array that is on offer. Which packaging and subliminal advertising will seduce us into selecting them? In fact, we are actually going through the offal section and the pickings are lean. Tripe abounds, sadly no brains, no heart and no guts. Excess fat is there in copious amounts but is no substitute for brains. The tongues are harsh and tasteless. While there are rusted on addicts to this fare, most of the population would find it unfit for human consumption.

This is election season. That is a period in the calendar when numbers are plucked out of the air, distorted and declared to be real, yet strangely have no substance. They are tossed out into the public domain in the hope that some media outlet will pick them up and run with them. The modelling that is supposed to go with the figures is also a product of someone's imagination and the give or take 3% is conveniently ignored. To enhance the numbers even further for their own benefit, worse case scenarios are made to be the norm, extra zeroes are added or deleted as required. There is no end to the data that is available. In fact, what is needed is created. Often statements drive the data rather than the other way around. The statisticians are forced to create a model that will match the result rather than the other way around. The general public doesn't know who to believe and focus on more important things such as sport. Their major concern is how to be able to vote in May and get to their sporting venue. Already they are doing their own modelling to achieve that. There is real and genuine data available for that but not for making the best choice for a government in an election.

Sometimes I think that the voting public should take the elected representatives to the Fair Work Commission. The notion of a fair day's work for a fair day's pay seems way out of kilter for some of them. How many days is parliament sitting prior to the election?

Political parties are held hostage simply because they accept donations from individuals, companies and organisations including unions. These don't pay something to get nothing in return, even if it is only access. The money can also be in the form of a ransom so that groups do not have the reverse of their ideas put forward. In that sense it is a hush money payment. True and honest discussion has been kidnapped and political parties don't seem to mind. They need money to fight an election and winning is everything. They will do and say anything to be in power, including sacrificing ideals and ethics. The sad part of this is that we, the public, have become used to it, expect it and are surprised and often question the real motives of politicians who rail against the accepted standard of paid for political opinions.

There are different battlegrounds forming across the eastern seaboard states and electors have begun to realise that the Coalition have moved to the right after 2013 to try to recoup ground that was potentially being lost and now has been lost to One Nation and other minor right-wing parties. In doing so they vacated the centre which was the reason for their win in 2013. Labor said thank you very much and diligently went about bringing a more centrist approach. This broad sweep they now have has isolated the Greens and Labor has been able to brand their product as the sensible centre. Politically Labor have been kicking goals after the 2013 loss and the Coalition have been kicking own goals. One wonders just how politically smart the coalition is as a whole. It seems that individuals will do and say anything to retain their own seat and as such team Coalition

is fragmented, playing for themselves and trying win the game solely down the right-wing side. Quickest, most productive and often easiest route is down the centre. After the Grand Final in May, the coach and many players are likely to get sacked and the team will be in a rebuild phase for years to come.

If the public voted below the line then the crazies wouldn't get much of a look in. On the Senate ballot paper, you need to only mark 12 names below the line or six above the line. For the sake of the six extra seconds it takes to get to twelve, surely people can do the right thing and rid us of the preference manipulators.

The campaign launch was months ago. I'm thinking August last year when a New Improved PM hit the market and the taxpayer funded ads came rolling out, the sound bites became harder to swallow and baseball caps were given away in abundance. Since then the campaign has rolled on with a monotonous, shouting white noise that we just can't shut out. if we have learned one thing; there is no truth in advertising. This 'all natural' 'bloke endorsed' 'fa(c)t free, 'sustainable', 'environmentally friendly' PM is not all he appears to be. The longer the campaign, the quicker we learned that. Morrison has hit us like a bout of constipation. Even Frydenberg trying to budge it, won't help.

Needn't worry about the NRA buying votes, the Coalition use our own money to buy ours. Talk about trying to influence an election outcome.

The Coalition has discovered the environment. They have discovered global warming and climate change. They have discovered the need for renewable energy. Hallelujah! Praise the Lord! But Melissa Price, the Environment Minister, has been in the wilderness for more than forty days and forty nights. Perhaps she still has her head buried in the sand and can't see the right path or was her portfolio just a mirage anyway?

Coalition politicians are like seagulls at the beach after a chip. The chip being some credibility when it comes to a proper environmental stance. The keep squawking, "Mine mine, mine!" hoping to get our attention, but we can see their real intention because what they are really saying is "Coal mine, Coal mine, Coal mine."

I think that Labor trying to get the banks to somehow not fiddle their books while developing a social conscience will be an entertaining battle. The banks really have come through unscathed from the Royal Commission. Hardly anyone has been sacked and fines have been minimal. What should have been gaolable offences including fraud and theft have not progressed. Domestic violence needs to be allocated more money. Banks need to be punished far more heavily. The Coalition have been weak on both aspects. I am hoping that Labor will do so much more.

The figures that are being compared over a number of years aren't realistic. Apples ain't apples. What was taken as employment years ago referred to full time employment and the 40-hour working week. Now anybody working a few hours is considered to be employed. What is the definition of part-time employed? Does it mean part-time by the wage earners choice or the employers' choice? With the now 38 hour working week, how many 'employed' people are actually underemployed? Graphs and statistical tables look great but without the same baseline, comparing things over time is fraught with the possibility of making generalisations based on false assumptions.

How long ago was it that Dutton was doing his Brando impersonation: "You don't understand. I coulda had class. I coulda been a contender. I coulda been somebody, instead of a bum, which is what I am, let's face it"? This is the sort of person that Morrison has in his cabinet and he has a senior portfolio!

At least Labor is coming up with initiatives to deal with real problems such as domestic violence while the Coalition are ensuring that cronyism is not only allowed to remain rife but is actively encouraged.

You'd think that Dutton would be lying low rather than being a low-down liar.

The Murray Darling should be enough to keep Joyce from getting the Nats leadership if there was any sense in that party.... but it is the Nats. He was water minister at the time when a blind eye was turned to the unlawful siphoning off of water. He has also since been made special envoy for the drought. Barnaby has that anti-Midas touch. But Queensland and Northern New South Wales love him. Maybe there is something in the.......... in the.... (can't say water because that is in short supply and wasted on him) ...... in the dust up there.

Michael McCormack is the public face of the Nationals. Yet the public, particularly in the country electorates are asking, "Michael who?......"

Michael McCormack to the tune of Put Your Hand in the Hand of the Man" by Anne Murray

Don't put your trust in the hands of the man who gave away the water

Don't put your trust in the hands of the man who will damage the Reef

Think Nats supporters at the ballot box

About voting differently

Don't put your trust in the man who wants coal mined in Galilee

The polls will come back to the Coalition with the decisive and inspired input of Michael McCormack about the reliance on solar power. His incisive "There will be no more night footy" could be the turning point in the election campaign.

We know Michael McCormack loves doing Elvis impersonations but his Bee Gees ones are pretty pathetic, like this one to Night Fever

"No lights on the ground
Cause no power can be found
As coal baseload ain't allowed
Because of the Greenies
There's no wind in the air
And it's so dark out there
That solar is nowhere
In the evenings
Night footy, night footy yeah
Won't be able to do it
Night footy, night footy yeah
You're all losers"

Morrison has shown his true nature. He has decided that the only way he can win the election is to buy people's votes. To do that we are having a Clive Palmer blitz style ad campaign using tax payers dollars on our screens and airwaves, telling all the wonderful things the government is about to start doing. He can use government revenue for that, simply because an election hasn't been called yet. The one thing that he can't show is what the government has achieved in the last six years which is what the public should judge an incumbent government on. We've had the budget from hell, constant backflipping on policy, money spent to bolster marginal seats, the race/religion card played, but nothing of structural significance that will take Australia into a more stable future. The Coalition is fragmenting almost as much as the Liberals have fragmented. Morrison was not the right person to unite either of these. He is a salesman, and the public can sense that it is snake oil that he is marketing. He tries to come across as both blokey, forceful and knowing where he is going. The first of which the public see as a sham, the second is all piss and wind and the third, the public will tell him....... into opposition.

Scott has inadvertently (??) used the term "strong and stable", the same as the Tories in Britain used. I don't think that is fair. It is a breach of copyright. Theresa May but

Scott Shouldn't.

Scott Morrison is thinking ahead. The only way he can win an election is to start a war with someone. With all the mods jumping ship and a new Defence Minister in the role, he is positioning for a play against someone. But who? Our submarines are years away and the ones we have are too noisy and can't be used without OHS approval. The new fancy jets are also years away and any spares needed will double our debt. Our army and navy are being seconded to Peter Dutton's strategic command of Border Force. So basically, who does Morrison think we can beat with a paper plane, a rubber duck and nerf arrows? It doesn't matter really because unless he can stop the war in his own party, he won't be able to adopt Baldrick's 'cunning plan' in time.

Morrison has said, "But at the end of the day it's all about results and I'm known for getting results." My proctologist wanted me to have a look at my colonoscopy results. I think they were like Scott Morrison's.... full of sh!t

Physiotherapist and chiropractor to the PM's office please. Hurry. The man who replaced the man with no backbone and who was so good at backflips, himself is having issues. Apparently, he has been stooping so low that he has become rigid in one position and now can only see the gutter. With all those asylum seekers clogging the health system, I understand that it may take time to get there, but it is an on-water matter so the public mustn't be told. Actually, the PM is out of his depth in the flood of his party's commentary at gutter level and that is saying something.

Morrison is all too happy to take responsibility and credit for upturns in the economy but it is always Labor's fault when things go downhill, even if they haven't been in power for six years. If it is on your watch, Scott, the buck stops with you. If you refuse to accept responsibility, watch how quickly the votes top for you.

The score is 54 to 46 and it is time on in the final quarter. Coach Morrison has had to make many substitutions and his star players have been benched or are playing injured and exhausted. Can he rally the troops? He is hoping that the opposing team will fumble the ball but that hasn't happened much all game. Only divine providence will see a turnover and a dramatic turnaround. Appealing to umpires is not helping. Many of his team's fans are already leaving. Perhaps he should try the old Collingwood trick of starting a fight but that is more likely to just spur the opposition onwards. Changing the leadership mid-season hasn't helped and the players are still fighting among themselves instead of working as a team. Many players are retiring at the end of the season and if he thought this season was bad, next season will be far worse. It seems hopeless............... but stranger things have happened in the past.......... (they haven't really) but that is all coach Morrison has to cling to.

Surely the word prime in Prime Minister means that he is the leader and has to accept responsibility for all the things his ministers, such as Peter Dutton, says. He is also leader of the Liberals and whether it is a backbencher or not he should accept responsibility for members of his party. Otherwise why call him a leader? What is he there for/ He doesn't have to be an apologist, but have people toe the line he wants. His reluctance to do so shows that he seems under threat or has a prevailing weakness. "What he walks past is the standard he accepts".

I came away from Waleed Aly's interview with Scott Morrison thinking Morrison, "Where the hell are you?" and the answer echoed around the room. ..... all over the place.

It is not just the Nats who may face the wrath of people in the bush. Around Australia, the Coalition has really fallen out of favour. Scott Morrison as a leader is putting out spot fires in his own party, fails to connect with the public as he comes across as non-genuine and is ultra-defensive over criticism on anything. Australia deserves better than Scott Morrison. We have a free trade agreement with New Zealand. Let's trade him for Jacinta Ardern.

Kicking and screaming all the way, Scott Morrison has finally caved in to public opinion. He has finally realised that PHON(y) is taboo. He still wants to win and that is the only reason he has changed his mind. Hit over the head with the butt of a rifle, he came to the conclusion that even considering not putting One Nation last was going to cost him votes. It is all about winning and nothing about values. But then that is the way he has always been. The jokey blokey man is just a charade and his blindingly obvious sudden enlightenment is all about political tactics.

ScoMo has finally done the right thing, not the right-wing thing. Imagine if he had have told Waleed Aly that days ago. His levels of acceptance with the public wouldn't have plummeted almost to negative numbers.

Morrison is good on captain's calls when he thinks there is a political advantage for himself. However, when there isn't, he says it is all out of his hands and that it needs to go to cabinet or it is an administrative decision. Machiavelli would have been proud.

This Captain's call shows what a General disappointment he is as a leader. Private enterprise will be loving all this. No wonder all the defence force commanders shied away from Christopher Pyne at the press conference.

Scott Morrison hasn't done the ballsy thing after sitting on the barbed wire fence. He has allowed one nation to emasculate him. The public gelding has been painful.

So, I vastly overspent for nine of the last twelve months but I managed to slightly underspend my allowance for the last three months. According to Angus Taylor I am now free from debt. Please come and talk to my bank manager Angus and help me out because my bank manager is thinking of calling in the debt collector. Tell him I am making a profit!

Malcolm may be warning the Brits about Huawei's 5G but I wish Malcolm had warned us about a far inferior NBN. Fibre to the node and then copper after that. Whose dumb idea was that???

When you look at the quality of our politicians, there are few that would rise to the standard that Jacinda Ardern displayed yesterday and has since she has become elected as PM of New Zealand. Her compassion and her leadership were on full display yesterday as she led her country through a crisis. I can't imagine the likes of Bill Shorten or Scott Morrison coming close to that mark. Perhaps, we, the public of Australia, should try to parachute her into a seat and be able to have her lead us. She would unite our country and take us forward in the energy debate, past the immigration xenophobia and get our politicians to start thinking about others rather than themselves. Just a thought. But if we are going to do it, it needs to happen before Dutton gets wind of it or he will deport her. We could smuggle her in as an au pair I suppose.

April

- Retirements of many politicians including Julie Bishop, Christopher Pyne and former treasurer Wayne Swan
- WikiLeaks co-founder Julian Assange is arrested after seven years in Ecuador's embassy in London.
- The full 448-page Mueller Report is released in redacted form
- Comedian Volodymyr Zelensky is elected President of Ukraine.
- North Korean leader Kim Jong-un visits Russia to hold a series of summits with Russian leaders, including President Vladimir Putin

Still waiting on when Murdoch will announce who the next Prime Minister will be............ I mean when his newspapers will say which side they are supporting. Morrison has placed all his trust in Frydenberg........... could be a big mistake.

Greens senator, Mehreen Faruqi said it all with her speech about Christchurch and Muslims. Australian culture post 1788 has had a habit and history of dehumanising anyone who is different from white Anglo-Saxons. We began with the indigenous and then have targeted specific groups, stereotyping them and calling all of them unAustralian at times. If we want to move forward, we need to actually stop stereotyping the typical Aussie.... blond haired, white bronzed male who is good at cutting down tall poppies, doesn't take himself too seriously, is part bogan and loves a beer. These people are rare and not the norm. It's about time that as a country, Australia grew up and recognised that.

With all the valedictory speeches, will any work get done in the all too few sitting days this year?

All politicians need to recognise that all budgets aren't written in stone. They are best guesstimates. They should focus solely on the year ahead. Economic variables impact daily and who knows what will happen four or ten years down the track. If there is a downturn in the economy, we should not be exposed by high debt and excess spending. You shouldn't buy your way into government with false promises or aspirations bought on the never never. There is an overemphasis on the budget and even more so on the surplus/deficit. There should be a strong emphasis placed on making sure that promises are met, not might be met. An optimistic treasurer should be merely a misinformed pessimistic one.

So, what will those leaving parliament think of the battle for tax cut supremacy that will continue after they have left? Will they shake their heads and say that tax cuts mean less services are being provided? That tax cuts mean that the debt is not being wound back? A surplus works the same way. Not enough money was being spent on important things that the community actually needs. The money could easily have been better used to lift Newstart and roll out the NDIs or even have some actual people at Centrelink for example. Promised surpluses and tax cuts should not be used to buy votes because how many times have the public been spurned by their own government? Instead of tax cuts, allow us to sue people in the government for breach of promise. That might make them think again before offering up lies and deception to us on a platter.

We expect a lot of our umpires in a football, netball, basketball game or any other game for that matter. We know that they are doing a good job if we don't even notice their influence on play. They are expected to show no favouritism, nor dominate the game with their own voices and agendas. That is the way our politicians should be. They are elected by us to simply look at and enact legislation in the best interests of us all. They should hardly

be visible at all. Yet somehow, they have taken over the game and dominated the whole scene making the game itself quite farcical. Perhaps the whole set of rules should be changed and the players (public) should be able to red card the umpires (politicians) and not just every three years, or six years in the case of the Senate. Politicians have forgotten what their role is, what their purpose is and who they are working for. It is a job, just as important as any other. It shouldn't give them rights and privileges and status beyond that of anyone else. The question of "Who is our PM?" shouldn't need to be asked. It shouldn't matter. Just as long as that person is doing the job properly, well and good. It is time for some harvesting of tall poppies and that is one thing Australians do better than most other countries.

When there is some sort of disease ravaging a body, all sorts of tests are done. The body politic could do with such a process. A gastroscopy could see just how much the public could stomach. A colonoscopy requires a purging of all the shitty things first and may show us if some intestinal fortitude remains. A brain scan may see if any part is actually working or a lobotomy has been done in the past. A simple ultrasound may show whether there is actually a heart there and if it is beating. An audiologist will find out whether the body is actually capable of hearing the voices of others. A laryngoscopy will show whether the voice has been overused and when added to an MRI may show whether the brain and the voice are connected or whether the brain and the rectum are actually connected. In animals when there are so many things wrong with them, we have the decency to have the animal put down. Yet with the body politic we are prevented from doing that. A post-mortem on this the 45th Parliament of Australia may show that it died a lingering death of self-inflicted but preventable causes.

It's all about money, be it the cost of advertising of the government's agenda at taxpayer expense, the budget itself

organised to woo voters through the hip-pocket and pork barrelling of marginal electorates, or allowing the LNP to sandbag seats in Queensland through skilful negotiation with the coal and hard right lobby. Money will decide the election, not innovative social programs. The NDIS is underfunded at present because the NDIA has been deliberately understaffed and thus the money could not be spent. Saved money has been funnelled into consolidated revenue improving the budget bottom line and giving a surplus. This issue will be whether the public will be fooled again by the shifting around of sums of money from one budget year to the next or from one marginally underfunded program to one that the public could see as seriously underfunded. It is the old pea under the walnut shell trick. The odds are never in favour of the public and sometimes you wonder whether indeed there is a pea in play at all.

Why isn't there a real time list of who ministers meet with published? If lobbyists are meeting with a minister too frequently then the public has a right to know. Each minister needs to be accountable. Surely there is a digital diary available that would make their actions more transparent.

A government should only exist for the good of the public as a whole. The budget should reflect that. Yet we see partisan politics being played out and the best and often the loudest lobbyist is the one who really calls the tune. Budgets are at best forecasts and as variable as the weather forecasts which can only be accurate a short time ahead. The 'forward estimates' is a sham. Budgeting based on what might happen in the next four years never works out. The public has learnt not to believe in the promises and to recognise the politicians who spruik them are foolish. Our budget surplus predicted but not actually in place as Josh Frydenberg and Scott Morrison would have us believe is based heavily on better than predicted mineral sales, higher immigration and underfunding the NDIA causing the NDIS to underspend. It is clever accountancy. In the year preceding the proposed new budget we were in deficit and our debt was not paid down but increased. that is the reality of the situation. So many treasurers have had to eat humble pie after declaring a budget surplus only for "things to change dramatically" No one expected the Spanish Inquisition either! The government is not really in control of the economy and spends tax payers money on whims like Christmas Island reopening and then suddenly closing. The world market has more influence on our economy than anything else and all we have become as a nation is a quarry. That should be what concerns generations in the future. When we have literally sold off our backyard, we will become almost a third world country because we have no industrial base and our innovation and R & D has been shipped overseas.

I may not understand the difference between state and federal government responsibilities and powers but how can the federal parties promise transport infrastructure such as more parking at railway stations as Josh Frydenberg did recently? The land is state government land. The trains are run by the state government but he said that he will make it happen. The same was said about fast rail to Geelong. He has promised it will happen but is also relying on state government funding as well. Who has the final say? Whose jurisdiction is it?

Seems like any policy that the Coalition once supported can be picked up by Labor and be instantly criticised by the Coalition. Think electric cars and the NEG. I am sure if Labor decided that trickle-down economics was the way to go, the Coalition would be against it. However, if Labor has a policy that is working in government, the Coalition will jump on board to match it and beat it when in opposition. Labor's aspirational target will mean that more electric vehicle charging stations will be part of future budgets. But somehow the Coalition will decry that possibly by saying we need many more coal fired power stations to supply them.

Perhaps we should put our politicians into the starting barriers. Which one would be Winx, Black Caviar, Kingston Town, Carbine, Phar Lap, Makybe Diva, Tulloch, Wakeful, Benrborough, Ajax, Manikato? (please note there may be dual citizenship issues with some of these). Which one will be Chautauqua and refuse to leave the starting barrier?

There are so many two-faced politicians around. You don't know which one is Quirrell and which one is Voldemort. Why should we think Bill Shorten is not in the same camp? In front of a microphone, he will play the game. Privately he probably has an opinion and is probably a helluva nice bloke. But who can tell when so much is stage managed these days? Morrison may be a soft talker at home for all we know.

The advertising industry is a good learning place for politicians like Scott Morrison. Fabrication 101, Lies and Deception 101, Snake Oil Derivatives are all first-year subjects for Degrees in Dishonesty and Misrepresentation.

There's wishful thinking and there's reality. Truth has nothing to do with politics. We are shocked when someone actually uses it.

Has anyone really had a look at the fraud being perpetrated by the Coalition almost daily over infrastructure spending? Very little will actually be achieved in the next three years. Spending on projects has been pushed out to nearly ten years for major items. It is like a visit to Utopia where a shovel is turning one sod for a photo op and then nothing happens. All the extravagant promises for congestion busting are promised on the never never. When the Coalition do a promo of an infrastructure promise they should be asked not for just a start date but a completion date. If they can give the latter with some certainty then they might be believed.

I wish I lived in a marginal seat
Politicians I'd like to meet
But the election circus doesn't come to town
And so, I don't meet those clowns
I'd give them all a piece of my mind
About why our electorate's left behind
Marginals get all the treats
Not us stuck here in safe seats
(With apologies to William Shakespeare)
"Bubble bubble, lots of trouble
Libs squirm in Canberra's bubble
After words from James McGrath
He sadly made people laugh
Way worse than Teena McQueen
Made Mal Roberts look serene
Took up Scotty's shouting act
Refused to accept any facts
For the Coalition he is trouble
Both in and out of Canberra's bubble."

Can anyone explain to me what benefit is gained by politicians placing themselves in ludicrous situations like kissing babies, loading a ute dressed in a suit, climbing aboard a military vehicle in camouflage gear etc. That is not their job. Yet they make a big song and dance about it and open themselves up to ridicule. They are employed to do a job which is to make decisions on legislation in the best interests of Australians. Instead they become hollow celebrities or wannabe rock stars but end up being unfunny clowns. Please politicians, simply apply for the job. If you deserve it, you will get it. Then respect the position and get on with doing the job to the best of your ability. That way

you will earn the respect of us all. How you do what you currently do, in the way you do it, yet still claim you have self-respect, is beyond me

If I was a selfish person on $180,000 a year, I would be rubbing my hands with glee for the massive windfall compliments of the Coalition tax plan. But I'm neither a selfish person nor on that income. I think it unfair that some will get an extra $11,640 a year, ten times what I will be getting. I'd rather see the money spent on providing a rise in Newstart, improving healthcare, raising pensions, improving public housing to cater for the many homeless and the standard of living for those more in need. As I said, I am not a selfish person. I wonder how many Coalition politicians will donate their $11000+ to charities who are providing support that governments should be doing.

If I was found to be mishandling funds, making mistake after mistake and trying to cover them up, I would be sacked. It doesn't happen with our politicians. They keep their job with immunity for three years at a minimum. Then they have the temerity to apply for the same job. However, it is the public who show the greatest lack of sense by re-electing them and overlooking their mistakes.

It seems that we now have royal commissions to try to remedy what our elected governments have done badly, turned a blind eye to or had no bloody clue about. Perhaps we should have a board of royal commissioners to run the country properly instead of the people who think the governing a country is just a game, a game that they aren't very good at.

Maybe I am wrong but I thought that the Minister was accountable under the Westminster system. Your department stuffs up, you wear the blame. That's what you earn the big bucks for. That's what the job entails. You are answerable for the decisions made below you. Any opting out of this should see

you sacked. A Minister who allows his department to make gargantuan errors is not focused on his/her job and demonstrates a level of incompetency that doesn't qualify he/she for the job.

Let me see. Is communism and socialism where you tax people and reallocate those taxes according to need? If so, the Coalition certainly aren't communists as they reallocate taxes according to those who aren't in need. Is communism/socialism where you allocate money to projects that will benefit the broader community? If so then the Coalition are anti-communist as they allocate money according to winnable seats and to their mates. Somehow cronyism and nepotism seem to be far worse than the social democracy that Labor espouses. Labor is putting forward policies where all people are legally entitled to certain social rights and services such as: education, health care, workers' compensation, public transportation, child care and care for the elderly. They want freedom from discrimination based on differences of: ability/ disability, age, ethnicity, sex, gender, language, race, religion, sexual orientation, and social class.

Takes a certain form of arrogance to be elected to parliament. Clive Palmer doesn't give a stuff what people think as he is rich as buggery. George Christensen believes those in his electorate don't care whether he has been in the Philippines more than in his electorate. Pauline Hanson can lie straight faced. In fact, lying seems to be part and parcel of most politician's make-up. If it, denigration, negativity and self-righteousness were only part of the Section 44 of the constitution that would ban people with those traits from being elected, imagine what a democratic government we would have.

If Morrison and McCormack had the same sense of fair play as Marcelo Bielsa did as a coach in the Aston Villa and Leeds match where he ordered his team to let an uncontested goal be given, they would have more credibility. Instead they have wooed One Nation and Clive Palmer, offering who knows what in return for a preference deal. They have cosied up to them showing how shallow they are on morals and ethics. What else does that say about them?

How many years in detention will be offered to a person who arrives here 'illegally' by boat, works on a strawberry farm is a vegan and accidentally clicks on a terrorist link while eating at a Chinese restaurant? We could ask Christian Porter about his new laws or go straight to Peter Dutton who might say "That person will be detained on Nauru indefinitely anyway unless they are an au pair, could make an Australian sporting team or come to see me privately with a brown paper bag full of cash"

The public hopefully won't be fooled into believing this is a normal budget. It is the announcing of an election agenda. Normal budgets are merely forecasts of how governments wish to spend money over the next twelve months. They are crystal ball gazing at best. An election budget is a grab bag of wish-lists designed to win selected seats across the country. The budget post-election is always markedly different. Think back to the 2014 budget as a perfect example. What the Coalition promised before the election in 2013 was nothing like what was delivered in 2014. It is almost criminal that parties blatantly ignore economic realities when announcing budgets around election times whether in opposition or in government. The ACCC should investigate false advertising in what amounts to being a company prospectus.

What a perfect time for politicians to play up. Most of the respected journalists are locked away for six hours trying to make head or tail of the budget papers. All those politicians let loose on society without scrutiny. Surely therefore the new security fences at Parliament House should be used to keep the politicians in there so that people of Canberra won't be too scared to go out to restaurants on Budget afternoon/evening.

To the tune of Gonna Build a Mountain as sung by ScoMo and Frydenberg

"Gonna save our bacon
Up on Capitol Hill
Hope to hell this budget
Really kills off Bill
Gonna sandbag some seats
Others are left to die
Gonna use huge tax cuts
We have no idea what we are doing
We only know we're gonna try
Gonna plan some pipe dreams
That's our only hope
Then renege on promises
Once we've got their votes
Gonna stop wage growth
But hide it with lies
Gonna tell great porkies
We have no idea what we are doing
We only know we're gonna try"

So, if there is an underestimation in the budget of what things will cost to fund and an overestimation of revenue coming in because forecasts have been over the top in optimism, what happens then? Will it be like Abbott did in 2013 when he blandly stated "no cuts to education, no cuts to health, no change to pensions, no change to the GST and no cuts to the ABC or SBS"? And then went to do all those things. 'Trust me I'm a politician' is the biggest con ever and I should know as I am still waiting for that big bridge in Sydney to be delivered.

Could Josh Frydenberg please explain the difference between surplus and debt? Australia has spiralling debt and yet the focus is on a surplus to be delivered. There should be no surplus, it

should be a down-payment on debt. We are encouraged to pay down our home mortgages as soon as possible, so why does the government splash money around instead of paying off some of the nation's mortgage. After all we are paying interest on what we have borrowed. It makes you worry about what we are leaving future generations.

"The so-called 'settled science' is not quite as settled as people say. And that's my position. Nevertheless, we've only got one planet. We should do what we reasonably can to rest lightly upon it." Sounds like Tony Abbott is talking 'crap' again or deliberately trying to lose his seat.

Are we surprised that "integrity issues" have arisen with the Coalition's climate change policy according to a government appointed panel? Apparently, they aren't sure that some of the emission reductions claimed by Australia are real. Seems that the Coalition are trying to launder some held over credits but are stuck on a spin cycle. It has all come out in the wash.

"We went through an exhausted process, back four years or so ago, in terms of setting those targets, that was a very exhausted process informed by Treasury" I think Simon Birmingham means exhaustive. Or perhaps you can become exhausted with all the backflips, turnarounds, retreats etc, that the tired and exhausted Coalition went through to get to the non-policy they have now.

How's that song go?
"Roll out the barrel.
There's an election to be won.
Roll out the barrel.
But pork's not for everyone."
"Who will buy the next election?
And sandbag marginal seats
'Specially ones that're blue ribbon
Time for a spending spree"

Yes, it is from Oliver but remember at the same time the other song from Oliver will apply, "Got a pick a pocket or two."

The election tone of the Coalition has been set. It is about refugees and Muslim invasion. It is about carbon tax. It is about Labor's record of economic management. Have they just started up the De Lorean again?

Climate change funding, wage growth, a proper ICAC and Penny Wong moving to the House of Reps. That should be enough to win an election. Bill doesn't need to promise any more than that. Although if the latter happens, let's hope he will do the honourable thing and step aside so that we can have a real leader fill the role as PM.

The Senate was a device used by our founders to ensure that all states would come on board with the Federation. It gave states some power to wield because the Senate was based on a state by state basis not electorates which could span state boundaries. It has since become a mockery because of the quota system that applies and the proportional representation concept it adheres to. First past the post system of voting means that you don't have to actually vote for any other candidate than the one you think will be the best to represent you. Why should you even have to select someone as a second pick who may not meet what you need as a representative. It's like going into a lolly shop and pre-ordering a chocolate Easter egg only to find that you've been given a liquorice one by other some dumb bunnies..........and you loathe liquorice. It should be chocolate or nothing thank you very much.

There needs to be a campaign to get people to vote below the line in the Senate to rid us of some of the types of woeful senators that have been elected in the past. The voting form may be large, but voters aren't made fully aware that they only need to number to twelve for their vote to count. It is not rocket science, but if

you don't know, then the form becomes quite daunting and many therefore just opt to vote above the line.

The public, who are the actual employers of politicians, need to reset the Key Selection Criteria for applicants to the job. Honesty should be one. Representing the views of the electorate should be another. All that are in place at the moment are that you belong to a major political party, are capable of convincing a small number of people in the party to pre-select you in a winnable seat and the job is more than likely yours. It is actually easier to get a job in parliament if you are willing to meet these criteria, than it is to get full-time employment through an employment agency. Perhaps we should convince voters to think before putting their vote in the ballot box, what person meets the key selection criteria to be a fit and proper member of parliament. That would be far better than merely numbering a box according to what a political party tells you to do.

As soon as Morrison calls the election, we will be spared the taxpayer funded advertising of this current government's so-called achievements. Let each party pay for their own. Why should we pay, especially when we are still wondering why we paid a fortune for Scott Morrison's petty tantrum of re-opening Christmas Island detention centre and his trip there because he lost the asylum seeker vote? How many staff are guarding no prisoners there? Sounds like a certain hospital in Yes Minister!

If everyone agreed that the preferred PM was the ultimate in deciding who would win the next election, perhaps we have delved into the unreality of the US democratic way of life. Our PM is one person who is leading a team of Ministers and backbenchers who are supposed to be forming a government in the best interests of the nation. There is no preferred PM section on the form. We do not select between Scott Morrison and Bill Shorten when we go to vote. This is a myth that has been conjured up and extrapolated on and almost now set in concrete. Bill Shorten can only become PM if the majority of voters in his electorate choose him to represent them and subsequently the members of the elected Labor Party choose him AND the Labor Party hold the majority in the House. Scott Morrison is in the same boat on the Liberal side. The extra hurdle he has is that the Liberals must be the senior party in the Coalition. Instead of the truth being explained, we have political party advertising reinforced by the media telling us that we have a presidential type election.

They say that choosing the right government is a lottery. I would think that it is more like being in a poker machine venue. The house has the edge. Whatever you do, you know that you will lose. The flashing lights, frenetic activity and sound after a while become less exciting and almost soporific, lulling you into getting you to just throw your hard-earned money away. Clive Palmer has striven for that effect with his advertising. The government are using taxpayers' money to do the same. It is mind numbing, brain dumbing and headache drumming by nose thumbing, slumming politicians plumbing the depths of depravity............ (sorry about the 'umming' rhymes but I originally started off with bloodsucking politicians and couldn't thing of a word that worked well with an 'ucking' rhyme)

There is a lot of conjecture as to why the calling of an election has been delayed. True, the government can advertise at taxpayers' expense for one or two more weeks, but that could have a negative effect. The government could also finally make a decision on Adani and try to appease the LNP in Queensland. (The same notion was used with the East-West Tollway by the Liberal Government in Victoria just before their savage thrashing) A miracle could happen and Labor could make a stupid last-minute bungle and the Government capitalise on it. However, the government has been the one thus far lacking in political rigour and prone to shooting itself in the foot while that same foot is in its mouth. If the Coalition win, this delay will be seen as a masterstroke. If it loses then it merely means that politicians and ministers get paid for extra time. However, the public could quite rightly ask why, if there is no election yet, the parliament isn't sitting.

Time to call an election. The Adani mine has been approved. Morrison has been waiting for this. What sort of person does that make him?

Oh, to have shares in an advertising agency now. The swathe of ads currently hitting the airwaves, papers and screens is phenomenal and when the election is called more will come but their budget will not be as big. Still it would be enough to pay executives, who were any good at all, bonuses. Those who weren't any good would still get the sack................ that last point remind you of someone?

I can't see why Morrison is telling everyone about his swimming. I thought 'on waters' matters were state secrets. One wonders whether someone should get him to do some due diligence on previous Prime Ministers, especially Harold Holt.................... too soon?????

So, Adani is approved, all the political allies have filled the empty positions on government boards, the LNP in Queensland has been appeased with a possible coal fired power station in the pipeline, ambassadors have been appointed, massive taxpayer funded advertising blitz has happened etc., it is time for an election! The Coalition has done all it set out to do. It stopped the boats, killed the so-called carbon tax and ended waste............. oh, maybe not all when you think of the now you see it now you don't Christmas Island opening. It has nearly tripled our debt, had three Prime Ministers in six years and done bugger all else.......... yes, it is time for an election!!!!

There is only one thing that is at better odds than Winx winning her final race and that is that a politician will lie each day of this campaign.

I may not be very good a mathematics, but the Coalition is saying that Labor is going to tax $387 billion dollars more because they are not going to give the handout to high income earners that the Coalition promises??? That would mean that the figure of $230 billion dollars that will not be going to those taxpayers will actually be benefiting all the rest of us and give us better healthcare, aged care, NDIS and education services and could even boost Newstart. To me that sounds like a saving. I notice that the Coalition are not factoring in the revenue that will come in from negative gearing, capital gains tax and dividend imputation credit reforms into the equation either. Must have slipped their mind. Hopefully there will be an independent assessment shortly of what each major party will have as revenue and expenditure and these fabricated figures being used now will be cast aside for some reality. One would think that truth in advertising is needed more in politics than anywhere else.

Oh, to have shares in a high viz vest manufacturer around election time....... a fortune to be made.

Someone should plot the exaggerations of Labor's tax grab as claimed by the Coalition on an exponential graph. $157 billion on Friday last week became $200 billion on Sunday and now it is $387 billion. Based on my rough calculations it will be $800 billion by next Monday and $1.2 trillion by next Thursday the 18th of April. Heaven only knows how high it will be a month after that on polling day.

Let's hope the AEC has laid out its plan sufficient advertising to tell us that you can just number to 12 below the line on the Senate ballot paper rather than vote above the line. That way there is a chance preference whispering will be a thing of the past. Perhaps the Guardian and other media outlets should encourage us as well.

There is bound to a push for informal voting, but surely, we are smart enough as a nation to choose informed voting instead.

But then again how smart have we been in choosing people to represent us in the past?

What the politicians fail to recognise is that people in poverty vote. The socially disadvantaged become tired of not being recognised or catered for. They think that they are just an afterthought but as wages become suppressed, Newstart continues to not be increased and the cost of living goes up, their anger soars exponentially. Hopefully it will burst at the ballot box and the "Let them eat cake" attitude by parties, particularly the Coalition, will not be enough to quell the shitstorm that will follow. One off handouts will not be enough. Giving them proper recognition and restoring their dignity would be a small step forward, though.

This election and the people in it once again demonstrate why comparatively sane, normal and intelligent people won't go into politics. Senator McGrath on Q & A last night displayed the antithesis of what we want our politicians to be and he was right to be booed, heckled and vain attempts were made to get him to focus on the question. His bully boy antics showed that there was probably a lot of heavy handedness in his approach to Melissa Price over the Adani decision. Politics has become more farcical over the years, moving from second rate comic pantomime to a tragedy. People who have a genuine concern for our society and all in it are choosing not to stand for election and even participate in it. It has become the white noise of life, a wall of sound that few wish to step into for fear of vilification, not having their views heard or worse still, becoming like those who have stepped through the portal.

The same old message is coming out from the parties ad nauseum. "We are good. They are bad." This election is like the Game of Drones.

The Age reports: *"The Coalition says teachers, nurses, tradespeople and police officers will be up to $4000-a-year better* *off by the middle of the next decade, as an escalating tax cut battle takes centre stage in its election campaigning."* The issue is that the government can promise what it likes in five years' time and walk away from it anytime. They have done so in the past so trying to tap into the hip pockets to find votes there is hardly a winner. They have already had six years and are only promising things will get better for these people after eleven years of their government. Everything is based on false promises and false hopes.

Captain GetUp is probably one of the dumbest things that someone has thought up. If it was to push the right-wing approach then all it has succeeded in doing is rubbing people the wrong way.

The leaders' debate.......... Let's have it in an MMA octagon ring or perhaps in a sound proof room or maybe even in a padded cell.

There is one benefit about being in a notional safe seat, we don't get to see our politicians. I have never had my door knocked. I just get a pamphlet stuck in my letterbox once every three years and a Christmas card paid for with taxpayers' money. Has my local member ever been down my street? Unlikely.

Is the IPA trying to sabotage the Coalition? Perhaps it has backed Labor to win with the bookies? That is the only reason I can think of why it has suddenly released (according to the Age) a manifesto asking for the selling the ABC, slashing the company tax rate, pulling out of the Paris agreement on climate change, repealing the ban on offensive speech in the Racial Discrimination Act and scrapping the Fair Work Act including its provisions on the minimum wage. One would hope that the IPA got really good odds. Perhaps it is looking at using any winnings to bankroll an election three years hence to make up for what Malcolm Turnbull and Julie Bishop used to raise.

The conservative right wing of the Coalition is weighing in heavily today. They seem determined to undermine any move to the centre, which is where the majority of votes are. Not sure red necked Neanderthals fully understand how the voting system works. You may save the few votes that are trending towards one nation but lose the undecided who will switch to Labor. Is the right wing mathematically challenged?

No surprises here. Adani has made generous contributions to the election campaign funds for Michelle Landry who is the current sitting Liberal MP in Capricornia. She has come out even more strongly in her support of the mine. Coincidental? Perhaps her advertising should carry a cover note saying that the ads are paid for and supported by Adani. We will find out months after the election just how generous they have been.

The AANA established the self-regulatory system for advertising and marketing communications in 1997 with the release of the AANA Code of Ethics. They have codes of conduct for almost everything, but politics seems to get a free pass. Seems strange. Perhaps there should be a separate regulatory body that oversees all advertising including some of the ludicrous things hitting our airwaves during the election campaign. We need to raise the standard of our spin doctors!

The Coalition bulk billed all those government ads prior to calling the election. Do all spin doctors bulk bill their clients? I'd like to see the Medicare code for that one.

Captain Getup shows a dearth of talent in the advertising industry or maybe those luminaries who back the campaign are very short of money. Ads reveal that (in this case) there is no truth in advertising, no humour and wit, no political awareness and an incredible optimism that the intelligent people of Australia would actually buy what they are selling. James Ashby and Steve Dickson must be relishing the fact that someone else is stupider than they are.

The night of the long knives will happen post-election but I think that will involve not public servants but the advisors for the right-wing Liberals who have cost the LNP an election.

Is there anyone else doing any press conferences for the government? It seems it is just Morrison. Wong, Plibersek, Burke and others are out there talking for Labor and thus giving an impression of a formidable team behind Bill Shorten. Morrison stands there front and centre and occasionally looking over his shoulder like Julius Caesar. Beware ides of May when all debts will be settled.

Not sure about the colours that parties have latched onto. The Greens have obviously chosen green, Labor has red and the Libs have blue. Those in Indi supporting an independent wear orange and of course Clive has yellow, but it seems that Fraser Anning's supporters are behaving as if their shirt colours are like the black and brown shirts of the thirties. Which colour will they settle on?

Pre-polling begins next week. What a great way for people to avoid the running of the gauntlet of how to vote cards. And vegans to miss the sausage sizzle. After six years of one party's government, I am sure that many people will have made their mind up already. That is the problem Morrison has. He has to hope that he is the Steven Bradbury in a two person skate off.

Morrison's new theme song (apologies to Leo Sayer)
"Well I'm a one-man band
Nobody knows nor understands
Is there anybody out there want to lend me a hand
With my one-man band"
Meanwhile the right-wing politician, Fraser Anning's supporters don't let other's practice what they themselves preach. It's all about the rights and rites of the right. This is their theme song (Apologies to Supertramp)

"Right (right) you're bloody well right
You got the bloody right to say
Right, you're bloody well right
You know you got a right to say
Ha, ha you're bloody well right
You know you're right to say
Yeah, yeah you're bloody well right
You know you're right to say
Me, I don't care anyway!
Write your problems down in detail
Take them to a higher place
You've had your cry, no, I should say wail
In the meantime, hush your face
Right (quite right) you're bloody well right"

Incumbency used to be the winning edge that previously elected candidates had at an election. However, it may now prove to be a double-edged sword because their voting record comes under heavy scrutiny and they also wear the blame for all the shortcomings that their party has demonstrated. It appears for this election that people are seeking change and incumbents are being seriously challenged, especially if they have formed part of a government that has been in power for quite a while. With so many new enrolees voting for the first time, questions will be asked, such as: What has your government done on climate change? Did your party abolish penalty rates for low paid workers? How did you vote on the Same Sex Marriage Bill? What is your stance on immigration and asylum seekers? How did you vote on the numerous leadership spills in your party? An incumbent can't hide from the truth, can't make promises that contradict past votes on legislation, can't state arguments that were put forward in party rooms because they don't count. All incumbents can do is state the reasons why they voted the way

they did. It is called accountability and this election it appears many incumbents will be called to account perhaps for the first time. They may find themselves out of a job as voters push them down as preferred representative to let a new voice be heard, perhaps an independent or just someone from a different party. This election safe seats may be a thing of the past and incumbents may only have themselves to blame.

There's a lot of eggs in the one basket that Bill Shorten is carrying around. He is doling them out carefully like some latter-day Easter bunny in the hope that they won't become addled. There is a lot riding on this. Scott Morrison is trying to do much the same but he does not have the team around him to ensure that the eggs don't fall from the basket. All he can do is walk carefully keeping focus on one or two things so that he won't become distracted and lose his balance. While Bill is going through an open meadow, Scott is going through a minefield. He can only rely on what he knows from the past and has to walk a fine line. With three weeks to go, it may well come down to how each hold their nerve.

I've been on the AEC site and can't find the spot on the ballot papers where I assign my vote for Preferred Prime Minister. Maybe I am looking in the wrong place or it just isn't there. This gives me rise to question just who is delusional? The one who insists that it matters or the one who doesn't.

"Reds under the bed". How the out of date catch cry has surfaced is anybody's guess. It is just the latest in unthinking comments that the Coalition parties are trying not to let slip. No wonder Morrison has virtually banned any of his ministers from speaking. He thought he had them all in the cone of silence but I'm afraid that never works. How long he can keep hiding away Cash, Price and others is anyone's guess. We won't hear from Tehan again for a while now. Tehan will now be forced to join the silent majority .... of Liberal party candidates.

Has anyone done a poll on pre-poll votes? I am a bit concerned that with so many people opting to do that, schools that run sausage sizzles on election days to make up for the Coalition's shortfall for public schools, may go broke. Antony Green could also be facing unemployment.

Good to see that out of the $54,305,319,500 proposed expenditure by the Coalition including tax cuts to big business, my electorate of Monash is being given a "massive" $3,500,000 or .006%. That's what happens if your electorate isn't marginal or you have an incumbent who doesn't want to rock the boat and ask for more.

The battle for ratings was lost without a whimper. The only major battle that was worth watching took place at Winterfell and not in Western Australia with the Game of Clones/Drones/Clowns. The debate was not of epic proportions. To make a bad pun, it was a Stark reality of the inability of politicians to answer questions and in Morrison's case, to speak with respect and courtesy to his opponent as he tried for the gotcha moment by trying to dominate his rival. The moderators were barely moderate and did little to keep Morrison and Shorten on topic, instead they allowed the 'contest' to become just a long boring ad. On content Shorten talked about policy and Morrison talked about Labor's policies indicating that there was little substance behind his own. It was a bit like the battle at Winterfell in one way. All the strong characters formed an even stronger team to take on a sole leader whose major skill was to try to bring about a victory by raising the dead and defeated as his army. Winter is here and who will be cut down in its wake?

Morrison says that Labor hasn't outlined all the details and so isn't ready to govern. The truth is that Labor has a swathe of policies that have been out there in the public domain for a long time. They have an excellent team of leaders who will be formidable as Ministers. By comparison, so many of the Coalition Ministers have pulled the plug or look like not being re-elected that Morrison, Birmingham and Frydenberg are the only ones to be put forward as leaders. The Coalition hasn't got the depth of talent and the detailed policies. All they can do is try to tear down what Labor has and what they haven't. Watching Morrison over the next two weeks will be like watching the Black Knight on Monty Python and the Holy Grail.

So, let me get this right. We have to buy back water that falls from the sky freely. Some people believe that they have a notional claim on it and want some recompense for not taking free water from a stream that they don't own. Those downstream don't have access to the 'free' water upstream that greedy people have decided they have more right to. Fish have no right to it either despite it being what they need to live and flourish in. Our water minister has given away the water, despite it not being owned by anyone. Now we have environmental damage and drought like conditions because of some property rights that never existed in the first place. Was the Emperor's New Clothes the foundation for this policy debacle?

I suggest that the people seeking an environmental grant in Chris Crewther's seat use the skill and expertise of the Great Barrier Reef Foundation. Who knows you may get more than $20,000 after all the Great Barrier Reef Foundation got $444 million for a non-application

Adani should be renamed Petard. Morrison's government has been hoisted on their own one.

With Adani getting approval, other companies will be lining up. Frack that for a joke.

The Nats members of the LNP are not worried about supporting Adani. They won't lose seats in Victoria because of that................ there are so many other reasons that come to mind: instability, no separation of agenda from Liberals, looking

after mining companies ahead of farmers, water mismanagement, climate change etc.

Consulting the share ownership of the Adani companies may give us some clues as to whether it will go ahead. If there are links between Helloworld, Murdoch's Newscorp, and shell companies where politicians have interests, then it is a done deal. I wonder how many Industry Super Funds have also an interest. Politicians have only three years to feather their nests in some cases (more in the Senate) so put money on their self-interest. It is better odds than Winx has in her last race.

Do the inflated jobs figures for the Adani mine stack up? If it is like many other mines, there is a helluva lot of automation after initial setup. The tourism jobs lost as the Reef dies because of excess shipping traffic may balance out any new jobs. Surely a renewable energy industry could be constructed in Townsville that would create as many long-term jobs.

Given that the Adani mine will require a lot of government support to get up and running and possibly be unprofitable, would you call the owners lifters or leaners?

If Labor needs and gets Greens or crossbench independent support to stop Adani, the Libs and Nats will accuse them of working together...... like a coalition!!!

Michelle Landry has outdone herself again talking about cow dung fuelled cooking in India, in order to promote the Adani mine. I think she could have been seen to be speaking bull shit too.

Scott Morrison says water buybacks are 'at arm's length' They are at arm's length but only when it comes to accountability. They make the rules, they give the heads up to mates, they agree with lobbyists rather than scientists and they refuse to accept responsibility when they are caught being incompetent.

Can we please see the expenditure receipts for the funds that went to the Great Barrier Reef Foundation? I'm sure that a lot of it has been spent by clever bookkeeping but what has actually been achieved in the first ten months of it having access to the funds.

All you journos seem to use acronyms or initials for each other e.g. PK and KM. Do you do the same for the leaders of the two major parties because it is very confusing because it might make it look like Morrison is into sado-masochism and Shorten into bullshit.

I worry about the journalists covering politics. They survive on coffee during the day and drown their sorrows in alcohol of an evening. Perhaps Scott Morrison worries about them too and that's the real reason why there were so few sitting days. Journalists' health issues may blow out Medicare and Health budgets and the PBS may have to expand to cover the sorts of drugs needed to make them function. That might be a more understandable Scott Morrison concern.

Journalists seem to want to bully politicians into saying something that the journalists want to hear. Even Shorten upbraided one journalist yesterday when the Sky News journalist asked a question and then proceeded to answer it himself. Shorten has said a few things about Adani. It will have to stand on its own two feet and will not get any federal government money. He said it can only go ahead if it environmentally and economically stacks up. He cannot say at the moment whether he is against it simply because he does not have the facts yet. They have been kept secret by the Coalition who called an election rather than have the CSIRO be questioned in Senate Estimates. So, journalists who wish to put words in his mouth would be better off getting the facts together from the Coalition, presenting them to Bill Shorten before asking the questions they are asking right now.

Personal attacks shouldn't be allowed but you'd have to think that if Michaela Cash was out of politics or at least as a minister, she may use less hair spray and thus global warming may be abated somewhat. So, saving the planet is another reason to get her out of the limelight.

Scott Morrison refused to call out Peter Dutton for being insensitive and then proceeded to call out Israel Folau for being insensitive. How many faces does Morrison have? Out of which side of his mouth does he speak for each one? That would mean at least two forked tongues. A bit like Professor Quirrell and Voldemort perhaps, although with all the shouting he does a spare one with pristine vocal cords would be an asset.

Just wondering.... If it costs $20,000 for an audience with Peter Dutton, how much should I charge each candidate who wishes to seek an audience with me?

Eddie McGuire chose to stand down from a match and made a formal apology when he ridiculed a coin toss by a disabled person. Dutton has less morals than a Collingwood president!!!! Perhaps he should stand himself down for this election before the electors of Dickson do so permanently.

Christopher Pyne is leaving a legacy of billions of dollars spent on submarines that one day cabinet documents may query why so much money was sunk into a possible bottom of the harbour scheme?

Pyne should have closed with "Goodbye, Farewell and Amen" which was the last MASH episode. A series, like Pyne's career, that ran way longer than it expected to. The Korean conflict ended in that last episode but the Cold War continued. Christopher Pyne leaves behind a Cold War between moderates and hard right elements in his party. You have to ask yourself which members of the Coalition over the past six years match the characters in MASH? Who would play the snivelling Frank Burns?

What a shame Christopher Pyne has left with so much still left to do. Known as 'the fixer' the one thing he needed to fix remains in disrepair; the Liberal Party. It is a mockery of its former self. Shattered dreams lie on the floor like shards of table top marble. Blood has been spilt and no Pyne-o-cleen will remove the stained reputations of many members. Pyne will be remembered as being a faster runner than Tony Abbott in the race to leave the chamber and so it is fitting that he departs first again before Abbott who too may join him on the speaking/lobbying circuit after the votes are counted.

Josh was apparently good at junior tennis? Hardly a master of spin now.

You have got to respect Josh Frydenberg. His acting ability is superb. To be able to deliver lines like he did in the budget speech, in post budget interviews when he doesn't believe them is astounding. No wonder he has changed his Twitter background to an Oscars style format. The only question is whether his award will be as light entertainment, comedy or drama.

So, the special envoy for drought paid a whole heap of money for water that didn't exist and may only exist in times of flood. Is Barnaby Joyce's job to actively promote drought or help alleviate it?

Given everything that has happened to Barnaby about the buyback scheme do you think he's in a little bit of hot water at the moment? And if he is, how much will he sell it back to the government for?

Michael McCormack's national press club address will be all about his cure for insomnia. The video will be released and available on the PBS shortly.

Would a trip to Yarralumla on Wednesday afternoon be a tax-deductible expense for Scott Morrison? I mean it could be also his retirement farewell.

Scott Morrison just said "the PBS to me, spells H.O.P.E" He can't spell and he can't even see the writing on wall. Shoulda gone to Specsavers.

I wonder if someone will ask Morrison when the fast rail will be completed and whether he has even had discussions with the Victorian government yet. Perhaps also whether the Nation Building Authority has checked it out and if Tony Woodford (Rob Sitch) thinks it is a good idea.

Scott Morrison will be in his element today. His shouts will be an important part of his communication strategy at last as he addresses seniors. Perhaps his health policy will include new hearing aids (coal or petrol driven of course as electricity powered things are taboo). I certainly hope those seniors with hearing aids already have turned the volume down.

Everyone seems to wonder what makes Morrison tick. There seem to be so many facets to him. It's almost as if different parts of others have been used, a touch Menzies, a touch Trump, a touch Howard, a touch Dutton, a touch Reagan and Thatcher. The last time such a person was made he was jump started by lightning and had bolts in his neck....... ah, I can see why he wears a Cronulla Sharks scarf and the cap hides the scars.

Morrison wants even more debates. When you are losing, it is common to play the man and not the ball. It seems that Morrison has dropped the ball. Common practice for those in a winning position is to reduce the chances for slip ups by excessive political debates. Morrison would do that if he was sure of winning but right now it seems he is the only fit person on his team with so many subbed out or unable to assist positively. He is alone and looking for a very long field goal in golden point time.

We have seen Scott Morrison auditioning for other jobs during this election campaign: sheep shearer, cheerleader, truck driver, tennis professional, beer taster, pool hustler, vegetable picker etc.

Hope he is successful, but his new employers need to be wary as he doesn't always do what he's supposed to do.... like his job!!!!

If Clive Palmer has failed to pay his workers and is/was the subject of criminal proceedings as a director of a company, is he entitled to stand for a Senate seat? Just asking.

Down at Clive Palmer's camp, they are burning money as if they had plenty to spare after not paying nickel workers. They are gathered around Clive who has decided to release a single as part of his multimedia approach

Gonna get a senate seat
Up on Capitol hill
Gonna get me a senate seat
'Cause Scomo's scared of Bill
Gonna get a senate seat
One that money can buy
Sure as hell I'm gonna do it
And I don't even know why (yeah yeah)
Gonna build me a campaign (yeah yeah)
As a little joke (yeah yeah)
Gonna use that campaign (yeah yeah)
To say I'm a nice bloke (yeah yeah)
Gonna use that campaign (yeah yeah)
And won't tell the truth (yeah yeah)
Gonna spend money that isn't mine
'Cause that's all I know how to do (yeah yeah)"

"Clive Palmer will also announce his preference deal with the Liberals today" I am going to do the same. My preference is that Clive Palmer doesn't get elected nor Fraser Anning. I would also prefer that the numbers in right wing parties decline. Not sure if the preferential voting and how to vote card legislation will let me. First past the post voting in both houses and no quota system for the senate however top my list of preferences.

May

- Scott Morrison's Liberal/National Coalition Government is narrowly re-elected
- Former Prime Minister Tony Abbott loses his seat.
- Anthony Albanese is elected Leader of the Opposition, replacing Bill Shorten.
- The United States' 25 percent tariff hike on $200 billion worth of Chinese imports takes effect, raising trade tensions between the two nations

"Clive Palmer's United Australia party has taken extraordinary steps to avoid a repeat of the "Jacqui Lambie problem" by getting candidates to sign contracts that require them to return $400,000 in election support if they win a seat but subsequently leave the party." **It seems that Clive may have a new way of raising money to pay back those nickel workers.**

If I was the publisher of Clive Palmer's, corflute signs, his how to vote cards or even being paid to hand out the cards, I would want to be paid in advance and with cash. As for his legal team and the court challenge, I am sure they have already pocketed the 110% deposit.

There is so much talk of horse-trading in politics. Yet we have theoretically left the horse and buggy days behind. Is that how out of touch our politicians are with reality? Surely if a piece of legislation is assessed on its merits it is a simple case of its good for the country or its not and people would vote for it or against it accordingly. But that is not the way it works. Apparently, politicians will vote for a crappy piece of legislation so that they can get another piece of agenda. That is like nobbling a race. Doesn't lead to good and stable government. Perhaps thinking that we could change the way government is conducted is putting the cart before the horse. First, we need to make sure that those

we elect have some sort of credibility and aren't just neigh sayers content to remain on their high horse without even listening to the everyday punter.

Doesn't "My Facebook has been hacked" sound a little like "The dog ate my homework"?

Seems that section 44 isn't the only thing politicians have to worry about. Facebook, Twitter, Instagram and email will bring you down faster.

I'm a bit unclear exactly what parties have as their definition of a fit and proper person to represent them and their electorate. Seems to be up for grabs. Pauline Hanson and Clive Palmer, we thought we knew have much lower standards but it is getting harder to tell.

All those naive people spouting the "socialist" slant that Labor is purportedly taking us down should really use the words "democratic socialist". This where in which *"extensive state regulation, with limited state ownership, has been employed by democratically elected governments (as in Sweden and Denmark) in the belief that it produces a fair distribution of income without impairing economic growth."* Even that is an exaggeration of what Labor's policies are proposing.

If you pay peanuts you are supposed to get monkeys. Politicians get paid far more than peanuts and we get behaviour far worse than monkeys offer. Their attempts at humour fail. Their attempts at being serious about things fail. Politics in Australia lurches between a poor tragic comedy and an overacted soap opera. The hams who are often front and centre expect star billing but the audience is better educated than that. We would stand up and walk out but it is our theatre. Bill Shorten has been the only one this far who has stood out and it took a Q & A television program to let him show his mettle to the wider audience. His team when they stand together are also very convincing. Australia's Got Talent it seems everywhere except in politics.

There may be another UN report coming out soon that Morrison again won't have acted upon. It will be about the probable reduction in numbers post-election of well-known pests that have been at the forefront of the extinction of the million species mentioned in an earlier report. The scientific name loosely translated is *"homophobic, anti-women, climate change denier"*

When you think about it, the government during election mode has little work to do. All politicians of all persuasions are free to roam around wherever they like at taxpayer expense promoting themselves. They aren't accountable to anyone for the hours they work, although many of them are probably working harder in these three weeks than they have in the past three years. My question really is, if these people are not doing their job as elected representatives in this election period, why are we paying them?

Populism arises from the ability to get a message out that people might believe. It doesn't matter about facts in the message. There is no truth in advertising and in social media. We even have mainstream media telling untruths attempting to sway voters. Clive Palmer is the perfect example. He is spending millions to get a message out, a message that had little evidence behind it. But if you say something loud enough, often enough and long enough, it cuts through. If you are controversial, as in the case of Pauline Hanson, you will be courted by the media and thus gain some sort of credibility. It is all bait-clicking. Our awful senate quota system encourages these people to seek the limelight to gain a seat. The most disheartening thing is that the most effective people who would serve us well governing Australia, won't consider even standing for election. That is the worst thing that populism causes.

Our political system has been plagued by turmoil and trouble since the party system began. What was seen as a great constitution and pattern of government has been transformed into the backbiting and self-centred approach we have today. There should be no left and right, no dichotomy between two parties. People elected to parliament should come to represent their constituents and express a point of view that comes from their electorate and not some party machine. Sensible, sane and rational debate should provide a common direction for a parliament to take. The sheer idea of an opposition party is ludicrous. An idea, a policy, a course of action should rise and fall on its merit. Instead it doesn't. It is opposed depending on who suggested it. Australians deserve better than what the parties have turned our government into.

What was not shown on the news from the submarine that went down to the bottom of the Marianas Trench was that there weren't just lolly papers and empty chip packets found. Apparently, the Coalition's election winning formula was down there. The submariners believe it might be unrecoverable for decades to come.

Why is it not okay to call politicians sitting in the chamber, a liar? They have told so many lies this election but expect to be held in high esteem if they get elected. A lie is a lie is a lie whether it is in the chamber or on the campaign trail. Death taxes, compulsory electric charging machines??? This deceit smacks of desperation. It plays upon the fears and innocence of voters and once again leaves them thinking that there are too many snake oil salespeople pretending to work in Canberra.

When I see Morrison and Albanese together, I realise it is National Haven't Got a Prayer Day.

I am a bit concerned that the massive colonisation and pillaging by nations and multinationals all in the effort to get access to oil will be soon transferred to solar. We could be invaded for the sunshine that we have. I think it has started already. I look out of the window and can see none. It is much worse at night. Let's hope that we don't have to rely on what comes out of the rearward facing orifices of our politicians, it would be a return to the dark ages.

Keating was right about the lack of a vision by the Coalition. Morrison and Frydenberg keep pointing to the budget as saying that is the vision. The budget only supports a vision but is not actually a vision in itself. Their policies seem to be budget driven and so they have the whole forward-thinking arse about which technically means that they are looking backwards.

Are policy and budget interchangeable as both Frydenberg and Morrison seem to be mansplaining? It's like saying we can only drive to the same holiday campsite every year without aspiring for something better. Budgets can kill aspirations and dreams. So much so that if and when changes happen and you could go somewhere else, you refuse to try something else.

Morrison and the Libs don't get it. Money doesn't drive a vision of what Australia could be. Money doesn't dictate what policies are. Money doesn't dictate what is right or wrong. Money is just one tool that helps make visions and policies a reality. No vision, no policies just a bland economic statement of facts and figures. "It's all in the budget" they say. The budget is merely a mixed bag of non-cohesive statements that may lead to actions if money permits. It is not even a plan or road map to move us forward. Better to have the philosophers outnumber the accountants. Philosophers desperately needed for the Coalition. None exist there at present.

Henny Penny (Scott Morrison) and Chicken Little (Josh Frydenberg) are running around saying "House prices are falling; House prices are falling." We all know how the original story ended. Not very well for the bird brains. Perhaps Scott Morrison and Josh Frydenberg may just have to eat their own words in their own fanciful tale.

The Coalition continue to say that there is not enough money in the pie for Labor's spending. The trouble with that comment is that Labor is just evening out the same pie. Perhaps we could use John Hewson's analogy of a cake. Rich people want to have their cake and eat it too especially with things such as negative gearing, franking credits and capital gains. The wealthiest are saying to Newstart recipients who are saying they have to go without food, "Let them eat cake". It seems that the Coalition has swapped integrity, equality and small 'l' liberalism for them personally to get a larger slice of the cake.

I am a bit circumspect about a surplus given the efficiency dividend extension. I think it will be a surminus. Someone please tell Tony Abbott that is not a new knight of the realm.

"efficiency dividend extension" Now that is a term I might use to reduce the tax that I am paying. Gotta love three-word slogans. It sounds like Scomo chose randomly one word, Frydenberg the next and Cormann the third. The EDE will be entered in the Macquarie dictionary as an acronym meaning the Magic Pudding.

The government may soon be looking at taxing the air we breathe. Do we get some franking credits if the air quality is poor because of coal based power generation?

You can guarantee that if the economy continues to deteriorate, the first thing to go will be the promises made to electorates in the last election. I think the people of Corangamite must be really concerned already. Billions of dollars were promised to them if the Coalition was re-elected. It was a vote buying exercise that worked, only it didn't. The Coalition were re-elected but Labor won Corangamite. Can't see them getting anything now unless it is just before the next election.

Just can't wait until the Coalition says that there is a debt and deficit emergency because of Labor's term in office that ended six years ago. Josh's earth-shattering surplus will be in tatters as soon as the MYEFO gets tabled. It costs so much these days for smoke and mirrors. Albanese needs to let the attack dogs loose on the taxation changes the Coalition is flagging. With the economy in free fall and the Reserve Bank running out of levers to pull, someone is going to have to lose out so that the wealthy get what has been promised to them. "No cuts to education, no cuts to health, no change to pensions, no change to the GST and no cuts to the ABC or SBS" Morrison didn't quite use Abbott's words in his election spiel but it is safe to assume that to appease those who got him elected, these areas will pay a higher price.

The only hope that the modern generation and the Coalition have in the down turning economy is if we baby boomers die off quickly. Massive cuts to healthcare and massive hikes in Private Health Insurance should do the trick............ oops that is a policy that I don't want the Coalition to adopt. But am I just being selfish??

For an educated man, Matt Canavan isn't even looking at global warming from an enlightened perspective. It is obviously caused by changes over time.......... particularly daylight-saving time. For six months each year we have been banking away an hour of extra daylight each day and it has to be stored somewhere. It is definitely leaching out into our atmosphere and destroying our planet. This has been happening since the seventies so you can imagine how much heat and light has been stored away. Every science student knows that heat and light are hard to contain and too much heat in particular can be deadly. Matt Canavan can go some way to solving the issue by cancelling the use of daylight saving and finding out where all this daylight has been saved to. Perhaps he could use it to provide power and release it gradually back into the atmosphere over a long period.

Richard De Natale and the Greens have learnt nothing from their experience with Labor and the ETS. They are doing it all over again. To make a point of difference and maybe win a seat or two, they are further isolating themselves and should Labor get a majority, they will have no negotiating strength at all. This is just dumb politics. If they don't get what they want, they are like a child throwing a tantrum and will take their bat and ball and go home. The public won't countenance this anymore and the Greens may find themselves out of favour and independents may snaffle what they could have won.

You would think that across the enormous vastness of the universe, one tiny speck of dust that we laughingly think is the centre of the universe and call Earth, wouldn't matter. The life on it has been around less than a nanosecond in comparison to the universe's existence. But what if the extinction of that life upset the delicate equilibrium of the universe? What if somehow in the future, some of those lifeforms, if they had still existed would have made a positive difference to things across the universe? The idea may seem ludicrous in the extreme. It is almost like saying a small nation like Australia couldn't do something in its own backyard that might go some way to saving the whole planet. But what if it did make the difference and yet opted to do less than it could instead?

"Due diligence" How many times did we hear those words last year. Now we find that people have been endorsed by parties, have their names on ballot papers, have been spruiking their own capabilities and the party line and now found to be either ineligible or deserving to be sacked by their party. Surely the party machines are so much better than that. One would hope so because one party will be running this country. Lack of due diligence at the highest level saw us go into the Iraq war. That may be a long bow to draw but if they can't get right the people they endorse, what else are they likely to get wrong?

Just when Scott thought it was safe to go back into the water, he has to disendorse a candidate for anti-Muslim views, two candidates meet with a far right extremist and now a candidate says women are not getting pay rises because they are not interested in "money matters and other business-related 'stuff'. Just where do they get these people? The sharks are returning, Scott, and they are not your beloved Cronulla ones. These will help you snatch defeat from the *Jaws* of victory.

Just who will make up the cabinet (or shadow cabinet) for the Coalition post-election? Many contenders will prove to be many pretenders.

Things must be bad when two people, Concetta Fierravanti-Wells and Tony Abbott state that the campaign has become "absolutely disgusting" and a "new low in political life" as well as a "new level of nastiness". These two never pulled their punches when it came to head-kicking (terrible metaphor) Labor members, particularly Julia Gillard. When will civility be returned to politics? Is there a chance that we can finally elect people with some decency who won't be corrupted by the festering sore that the "game of politics" has become? Possibly when the likes of Concetta Fierravanti-Wells and Tony Abbott leave the scene. It is too late for them to try to set a better example. It is like the pot calling the kettle a deep shade of grey.

The Liberal Party with their preference deal have exposed their mantra for public gaze. They sing the same song that the Australian cricket team in South Africa sang over a year ago. "It's not how you play the game, it's whether you win or lose." Apparently, the deal with Palmer was signed on Clive's preferred yellow paper.... yellow sandpaper that is.

When will the Coalition start announcing policies and advertising the positive progressive things, they will be doing should they retain office? They have spent the whole campaign pulling apart

Labor's policies and not telling us of their own. This defensive strategy is not working and with half a million already having voted, they are fast running out of time............ assuming that they do have some progressive policies that is.

It sometimes takes a slight slip when typing to make an accurate assessment of a situation. Politicians are often said to be out on the hustings but a typo would change *husting* to *hustling* and probably give the reader a better understanding of what is going on.

The debate I would love to see is Keating vs Howard. The bloodbath would be amazing given what Keating said yesterday on the ABC. He still knows his stuff on economics whereas Howard merely trots out the Coalition line "Labor bad, Coalition good" with nothing to back up why these two statements are being made.

Amazing how well Shorten is performing when he gets some clear air. I'm sure that Morrison wishes he was in Bill's face right now but he'd be just as ineffectual at putting Shorten off his game as he was at the last debate.

Oscar Wilde said, "Imitation is the Sincerest Form of Flattery". Given that Morrison, as evidenced by last night's debate, would have been better off imitating Ardern rather than Trump. Bullying doesn't go down well. Standing up to them does. Bill Shorten would have won that debate on that alone. Whoever is stage managing Morrison needs to get him back on track. He's tried the blokey look, the vastly superior look and now the schoolyard bully look. Which one of his personalities will rise to the fore in the last two weeks? Bill may not be liked because he is boring, but at least he is consistent and you can see what you will get as a PM. You get his team, who more than make up for his "Shortencominings". What has Morrison got? Apart from possible schizophrenia, he has got a disorganised, disunited group of people behind him out to get whatever they can.

The Greens will claim that Shorten is just piggybacking on their policies but let's hope that Labor gets a clear majority/support in the Senate to back its own proposals. The climate change debate could have been done and dusted eleven years ago except the Greens wanted to flex some muscle. I hope they are not in a position to do it again. Labor has the will of the majority of people to do something positive and doesn't need to be derailed in its efforts. It is on a winner when it comes to gaining a mandate from the community. The Libs are playing catch up but are having trouble as Labor is using the Libs discarded NEG as a basis for their climate policy. It was a very shrewd move and has pushed the Libs even more to the right. They haven't released their full costings on their policy and so it seems quite hypocritical to be demanding Labor release theirs. Shorten is right to argue the cost of doing nothing outweighs the cost of making changes. I wish that he would articulate that better. We will know when the 'business end' of the campaign comes when Murdoch says which side he is backing.

Epstein's mother will run out of ink, writing the excuses for non-attendance at the Liberal Party launch.

Shorten just made the winning move in the election. He took on every question (and Tony Jones at times) and answered everyone without the glib political jargon that we thought we would hear. Morrison is the Chautauqua stuck at the barriers and Shorten the Winx crossing the line. He showed warmth, compassion and showed what a true leader could be. Let's hope that as many Australians as possible get to see tonight's Q&A. If a Preferred PM poll was held tomorrow, Shorten would leave Morrison in the dust.

Maybe with the campaign launch on Mother's Day, the Libs will actually have some policies and costings for us to look at. The have been hard to find thus far so perhaps we need a Mother look. The timing is really strange as by then a million plus voters will already have voted.

The Liberal Party launch on Sunday will be in Presidential style simply because so many of Morrison's ministers can't be let loose and actually negatively impact on the Morrison image. Many of the sitting members and aspiring candidates will be out chasing last minute votes in their electorates from Franklin in the south to Manila in the north. As for past Prime Ministers, hopefully the empty chairs will be there and not actually outnumber the audience.

I heard that with the warmth in the ground still and the late rain, mushrooms may have their best season yet. I am a sceptic. I think it is because of all the bullsh!t that has been spread in the past six weeks.

The two major party launches will actually be quite similar. Shorten has already told us what the Labor party will do and didn't really discuss what the Coalition will do. Morrison will also tell us what the Labor party will do and won't really discuss what the Coalition will do.

Up until this campaign Simon Birmingham seemed to be one of the most sensible and well-spoken of the Liberals. But having to play the repairman fixing up all the mistakes that the PM, the Treasurer and so many other candidates have made, his credibility has taken a nose dive similar to the fall in stock prices in 1929. Somehow, he needs to get it going in the opposite direction and rise as high and as fast as our accumulating debt.

If elections were decided on debates, then the Coalition need to ask for as many as they can get. They have lost all of them so far and will need to start to be more persuasive if they want to win any and indeed get voters to vote for them.

One of the saddest things surely has to be the second-rate advertising that takes place in political campaigns these days. You have the Clive Palmer saturation ones which spruik no policies. You have the Greens who have hardly made a ripple in the media. You have the ads for the Coalition that are all about running down Labor. You have Labor with their cuts and chaos. All are junk ads. They are so formulaic, so trite and don't cut through. One good high-quality ad, so good that it becomes viral, that is carefully placed, is both witty and funny and that is played a few times only will cut through all the others and be remembered particularly when people come to vote. We have had enough three-word slogans tossed around in media bites to last a lifetime. Party directors seize the day and make something that will be remembered long after the corflute signs are defaced and the letterbox dropped literature has been placed in the recycle bin unread.

With Bill Shorten responding positively to an invitation to appear on the ABC's Insiders program, I am sure that Scott Morrison will no doubt paint him as a camera hog and always wanting to seek the limelight. He will also say that Bill Shorten deserves severe scrutiny by the likes of Barrie Cassidy and that he doesn't. It used to be that politicians would take every opportunity to sell their message. Perhaps Morrison doesn't have one, or at least one that will fill the airspace of even a short interview.

For years, where I live has had little to show for the votes cast in both federal and state elections. This is not because the people who have been elected are not dedicated and honourable. It is simply because the electorate is overlooked by the party machines that have a say in the allocation of funds. While other electorates that are marginal get the visits by leaders, either trying to win or sandbag seats, we rarely see them. There are no promises made to win our votes, no big infrastructure spends like the ones offered to other electorates. Our area is one of the quickest expanding ones in rural Victoria, but not in the eyes of the politicians. It seems those politicians with the loudest voices and slimmest margins get the attention and the money; despite the two major parties both promising that they treat everyone equally and fairly. Where is the fairness when pork barrelling takes precedence? The only thing the people voting where I live can do is to try to make this seat marginal or not have long term sitting members. This in itself seems hardly just, especially to the current incumbents who have devoted so much of their lives to serving the community. However, it seems fairness needs to be thrown out of the window if you want to be even seen. Let's hope that the seat of Monash is lineball and that someone notices we exist.

We rarely see our rep in electorate of Monash in Victoria. He has his face in the paper occasionally handing out school flags or attending deb balls. He rarely speaks in parliament. Nice bloke but has exacted hardly any promises from his party (The Libs) and there's nothing really to show for all the time he has been in politics. Voted contrary to the wishes of the electorate in the same sex marriage debate. 62+% said yes and he thought he knew better saying no. Our only hope is that the seat becomes marginal or that he loses. Then we might then get something happening here over the next three years.

How often has Scott Morrison been in his own electorate? His frequent flyer miles n=must be racking up but I'm sure that there are some senior citizens and CWA events down in his electorate of Cook who would appreciate a visit or two, just to remember what he looks like in the flesh.

I have a feeling that the Liberal Party launch will be more like a faith healing communion. That might rile a couple of them though. Communionism is what Labor is taking us down the path to according to the more ignorant and illiterate Liberal supporters.

There is still the major strategy of the campaign that doesn't get discussed. The Coalition have been totally focused on discrediting

Labor and have not yet outlined what they would do in all areas. 10% of people have already voted and we still don't yet have an overall image of where the Coalition wishes to take us in the future. Surely if it was a better direction, we would have heard it by now. The latest splurge on infrastructure means nothing unless the states back it. Walking all over a state's long-term plans to try to win a few more votes in a federal marginal electorate is hardly likely to endear yourself to a state government. The Coalition think that they can ride roughshod over state and territory governments and don't realise that is not how it works.

Overheard at the preparation for the Lib party launch beforehand. "Do you want me to remove the empty chairs, Mr Morrison? You realise that the stage will be almost empty and just you will have to be front and centre. No, we haven't been able to find Melissa Price either. We have put up wanted posters but someone has scrawled 'Not' at the top of them. Your RSVP's have come back and there's a few cancellations I'm afraid. A Mr Dutton, Mr Turnbull and a Mr Abbott won't be coming. Seems to be a lot of retiring ministers also not able to attend. Mr Murdoch wishes you all the best and says he is playing his part but can't make it either. His apology was different to the others who said that they were doing something with sandbags at their electorates. Are there floods everywhere? Oh, I see... the price of climate change action is too high. But aren't sandbags expensive too? The sound engineer has said that you will be able to get by without a microphone if you just use your normal voice. No, we don't normally start these things off with a prayer, but we could if you really want to, although I have been told by many that you haven't one. Will I be staying for the performance? I thought it was just going to be a speech, not an elaborate fictional drama or we would have called for auditions. No, it is Mother's Day and therefore this is a low budget poorly rating time. Oh, I see you

are used to high budgets, high preferred PM ratings. But this is the real-world Mr Morrison. I'm sorry about the stage prop. The huge bubble you wanted is apparently still in Canberra. Introductory music.... oh, we have none that the musicians would give you licence to use. Fanfare for the Common Man? No, I don't think that's appropriate. Besides we thought you were going to blow your own trumpet. How about the theme to Q & A or Insiders? Never heard of them? That is surprising. Have a nice day. We'll have to bump you out straight away afterwards I'm afraid. We need to prepare for next Saturday night. We are catering for the overflow of Labor Party victory celebrations next Saturday night."

So far by my count in the Liberal launch, Labor has been mentioned twice as many times as the Liberals and the Coalition combined.

"Just a reminder that the advertising black out kicks in on 12am on Thursday." Does this apply to social media? Will it stop the Robocalls from Clive Palmer? How did he get my number when it is supposed to be silent?

Just how much of the proposed surplus put forward by the Coalition was actually used up in the self-promotion exercises used between the time the election was announced and the campaign launch by the party? The party only has to pay travel and accommodation costs once it's campaign officially starts.

The smell of burning autumn leaves that used to permeate the eastern leafy green seat around Melbourne has been replaced by the aroma of over cooked pork.

Ever noticed that the marginal seats get fresh pork sausages at their BBQ's on election day and the safe seats get tasteless supermarket beef ones? Seems many candidates are scraping the bottom of the barrel to get pork on your fork.

"Alan Jones went on to say that if Labor wins the election, he'll retire from radio and all public appearances."

Now there is a real reason to vote Labor!

How many trees does it take to make an election?

Based on the number of Liberal Party pamphlets and letters that have accumulated in my letterbox despite the no junkmail sign since the election was called, then I am thinking that climate change reduction is not high on their agenda and deforestation is. Daily I get a plea to vote for him. However, I have not seen the candidate in the last three years. Is there somewhere you can leave a message that you voted two weeks ago?

You know what? If the Coalition lose the election, they will say it is all Labor's fault and for once they will be right. Labor has costed policies out there. Labor has a vision. Labor has an excellent team. Labor wishes to do something effective on climate change. Labor wants to govern for everyone. Shame on Labor for not playing fair!!!!

"Labor will tax your aspiration, they'll tax your inspiration, they'll tax your perspiration." according to Josh Frydenberg. Well I think that he will be sweating over the count in his own seat.

According to the AEU stats there are 25% of voters under the age of 34 and about 30% over the age of 60. This could be the last time that baby-boomers will have the numbers to hold sway. Morrison seems to be counting on the vast majority of baby boomers' votes to fall his way. He forgets that these baby boomers have grandchildren going to underfunded schools and early learning centres. They have children who can't get into the housing market. Many baby boomers are not always guided by their own hip pocket. Many voted for Gough Whitlam back in the 70's and can remember the positive social changes that his election brought about. Scott Morrison shouldn't just assume

that just because your hair is grey that your brain has stopped functioning.

People in the Corangamite electorate are being promised by the Coalition in this election a lot of things. It amounts to $26,500 per person in the electorate. I'd like to know what the people in Monash will be getting, if anything, and why we aren't valued anywhere near as much of those in Corangamite.

Bill Shorten is trying to beat a record set by Scott Morrison. Scott was contacted by the Guinness Book of Records about a possible entry for using the word 'aspiration' in an election campaign. Bill Shorten's use of 'vote for change' is close to beating that. However, Scott Morrison has used the words 'Bill Shorten' and 'Labor' more than any other words in his speeches and that includes 'the', 'a' and 'and'.

Has Scott Morrison promised George Christensen the ambassadorship to the Philippines if he wins the election?

If the efficiency dividend extension cuts into the National Disability Insurance Agency funding how much worse off are those on the NDIS going to be? People can't get onto the NDIS because of understaffing already. As for cuts to Centrelink, cuts to staffing may see offices relocated to telephone booths. The one thing that could be cut is the use of government funds for self-promotional advertising by parties and members. Another could be the ridiculous overseas and interstate travel and accommodation entitlements of politicians.

The Age has come out in its editorial supporting Labor and justified its stance. The Australian Financial Review outlined all the good points that Labor was putting forward and then, if I am not mistaken, ignored those to support the Coalition without stating what good points the Coalition had instead. Maybe I have read it all wrong.

Imagine the number of people who will now wish to settle in the Corangamite electorate, if the Coalition get in. Per person they will get over $25,000 worth of services more than other ordinary Australians get. It cuts out vegans though. The smell of pork will put them off.

A quarter of the population have already voted, so how about the candidates back off their hard sell by 25% and let us have some peace.

When they come to reviewing the pre-poll numbers after the election, perhaps instead of thinking that the time should be shortened or the reasons people allowed for pre-polling tightened, the politicians should accept that people are happy to vote early. Politicians should modify their campaigns instead. Many people have made up their minds not on what has been promised for the future but what has been delivered in the past. Simply making the country awash with money in a three-week period is just not good enough. Money and ideas should be in play throughout any government period. Instead the way governments tend to work is that they congratulate themselves and do something in the first twelve to eighteen months and then spend the last eighteen months to two years building a war chest to defend themselves at the next election. Better off to have set election dates and a six-week period when parties can't use government funds and advertising to promote themselves. Let us have the three weeks to pre-poll and let us judge candidates on their merit and not how big their pork barrel is.

Please please make it a quick Labor win. Sydney has a chance of winning tonight and I want to watch it without channel surfing for election updates.

Please let your photographers loose in the Coalition camps tonight. I want to see smiles wiped off the faces that have egg on them.

We saw what happened when the media were embedded in the Iraq wars all those years ago. it seems the same happens in today's political wars where the media are embedded on the buses and planes of political parties. They get shown what is wanted to be shown. They hear what is wanted to be heard and they report on these things the way parties want them to report. Independent journalists should remain independent and save their money to spend it on investigative reports that expose all sides of individuals and parties to public scrutiny. If only someone had been embedded with Melissa Price and other ministers they would have been put under proper scrutiny.

Not enough money in the trust that is used to fund the busts in the prime minsters' walk in the Ballarat Gardens? Heads will roll for this.

It seems strange that Morrison will be seeking a 'mandate' if the Coalition is re-elected. I mean after all he abstained from voting in the Same Sex Marriage bill because of his religious views.

The slide down to the gutter in our political scene began after the Hawke-Keating years. It is almost as if the De Lorean was charged up and the fifties became the hipster period for so long. Now the hipster period is the Hawke-Keating times. I dread what future generations will make of the first two decades of this century.

Do you think Alan Jones will be enjoying his last day as a shock jock? I have the feeling that he will make more comebacks than Melba and Farnham combined. I'm pretty sure he won't go quietly.

Incumbent politicians are in reality seeking a rollover of their contract. They are given a huge amount of funding to promote their case. Those teachers, nurses and other people on contracts who have even less security of tenure and benefits afterwards, must be wondering why they don't get the same. Can't see any losing candidates today heading to Centrelink on Monday.

Before the Coalition talks about a mandate, they need to at least show us the policies that they advocated at the last election........ if you take out "Coalition is good and Labor is bad" which doesn't count as a policy anyway, it seems they have a mandate for nothing.

Do you think the Coalition will this time reward the electorates that have remained safe seats for them? They have tended to ignore them in the past and will probably do so again. Monash has had nothing for years and the people in the electorate don't seem to understand that a marginal electorate is a good thing.

The people in Corangamite might be wondering what is going to happen to the billions of dollars of promises they were given by the Coalition. They may actually have elected a Labor person to represent them. Corangamite could tell the story of whether the Coalition sticks to their promises or not.

"We have a mandate for all the policies we outlined during the last election....... Er. Um. Not sure we will be doing much in the next three years."

Yes, we should stop the Adani mine as this will eventually damage sea life. We need sea life and in particular sponges to grow to soak up the seawater so that sea levels don't rise.... How can the Libs miss the logic in that argument?

Regarding the Murray Darling Basin, it seems that the only answer according to the National leaders, Michael McCormack and Barnaby Joyce is to pray for rain. Perhaps McCormack should get out of his Elvis costume and do something about it. At the moment it seems the people of the basin think more like the Hunters and Collectors (slight change of lyrics)

"When the river runs dry
You will return to the scene of the crime
When the river runs dry
Castigation will rain on you one last time"

News from Hogwarts via the Daily Prophet. Harry Potter's invisibility cloak has gone missing. The Ministry of Magic are investigating and believe that it may have been taken by a Minister! They won't say which one, but cryptically they said that she has a Price on her head. Who could be wearing it?

The rare and endangered species Malicious Overpricius has been spotted in Melbourne. That is good news for the Liberals. One less species saved from extinction for now. 999,999 to go.

Scott Morrison commenting on the environmental credentials of his party is absolutely Priceless.

Is our environment minister still getting paid despite her absence? Is that just a Price we have to pay?

Melissa Price was last seen wearing a red and white hooped jumper and matching beanie. The large glasses she was wearing added to the disguise. Not sure about the name change to "Wally" as that sounds a bit old fashioned.

Statistics can be manipulated and massaged to show whatever anyone likes. The one basic statistic that people can't really argue with is that Newstart is inadequate to live on. Yet that was the one thing Labor could have said at the beginning of the election campaign that would give them so many votes. If they had targeted specific sections of the electorate such as the unemployed and others on welfare, if they had grandfathered franking credits, if they had explained their revenue streams better and curtailed their proposed expenditure until they were in office, then they wouldn't be sitting to the left of the speaker. Their lack of understanding of numbers was astounding. There is a high number of people 55 and over who may not have been affected by franking credits but who could be persuaded they would be. The census figures told us that. There are a large number of millennials who may have been scared into believing that negative gearing changes would put rents up and make

owning a house even more impossible. Politics 101 lesson 1 - Make yourself as small a target as possible. Pick your battles and wait until you have the power to do what you want to do. Mao was right. Power does ultimately come out of the barrel of a gun. The trouble was that Labor shot themselves in the foot.

I can understand how the Federal Government may want to target poor schools particularly in regional areas but they propose to hand over the funds to peak bodies to distribute how they wish..... smacks of a Barrier Reef funding arrangement. Wealthy schools will inevitable get a chunk of the pie and the government will have little control over that......... devolving accountability never works.

Tony Abbott is not about to go down without all guns blazing yet you'd have to think that his aim needs some work. *"I don't believe her, given that she's said her biggest issue by far is climate change and Labor has a much better climate change policy than the Coalition."* **This sounds like he shot himself in the foot while the same foot was in his mouth.**

A song title for Peter Dutton and for that matter any politician: Ronan Keating's 'You Say it Best When You Say Nothing at All'

According to Josh Frydenberg, Victoria will get the East-West link whether we like it or not. The idea of Federation has obviously been bypassed in his brain. The actual planning of roads and their construction is a state responsibility unless they are designated as needed for the military. The whole notion of saying a lot of infrastructure will be built is beyond the scope of a federal government especially without consulting and working with a state government. The money for the East-West link is expected to come from the surplus.... that would be the proposed surplus which doesn't exist as yet and if conditions worsen, won't exist. So Frydenberg is promising something he can't deliver using money that may not be there. I met a man in Sydney once

who was much like him. I am still waiting for that Harbour Bridge to turn up in my back yard.

Pauline Hansen apparently is not allowed to be called a liar when in parliament. However, a lyre is a type of harp. So, can we call her a harpy? Oh, but that could also be misinterpreted that she is a mean, foul-tempered woman. So perhaps not????

Just wondering whether Joe Hockey is the one who has placed a million-dollar bet on Bill Shorten. In January he will no longer be being paid from the public purse and may need some extra capital in case his foray into private enterprise sees him unemployed and unemployable.

You have to hand it to Michael McCormack who says, "I probably don't get as much cut-through as predecessors because I don't say silly stuff." and then proceeds to say some really stupid stuff. How soon will the gag order be put on him like Morrison has put on Cash, Price, Dutton etc.?

The National's leader, Michael What's-his-name is at the Lib Party launch just to help make up the numbers? But how do you pick him out from all the other faceless people?

According to McCormack, "Between 2007 and 2013, Labor did not build, install, fund, promise one mobile black spot phone tower in the regions." He forgets to mention about the string and tin can type changes made by the Coalition to the fibre to the home NBN that Labor was doing.

When is a monologue a conversation? Scott Morrison won't answer questions, respond to comments, or listen to suggestions from the media and the public.

Irving Wallace once said, "Every man can transform the world from one of monotony and drabness to one of excitement and adventure." He hadn't ever met Scott Morrison.

Morrison's one and only policy has been a rework of Psalm 56:3 "When you are afraid, put my trust in me."

After the Coalition launch that seemed just a chance for Morrison to make us watch a family slide night, I think my million bucks is safe. I just need to know if the $230,000 I win is tax-free and should I use it to buy another rental property before negative gearing is phased out.

Morrison looks like going through every person in Australia's situation one by one (Could be a long launch). When he gets to mine, I hope that he tells the truth and explains how I am much worse off now than I was six years ago.

It seems that a certain minister is infringing on Scott Morrison's copyright saying "How good is ......?". I'm not sure that Angus Taylor should continually use it with his own name at the end, or we may well answer him with 'not very'.

So, Angus was a rower, was he. Let him and his mate row down the Darling past where the Menindee Lakes were once connected to the Darling. Oh, they would run aground because someone made a fortune out of a water buy back. Who could that be?

June

- The Australian Federal Police raid the home of a News Corp Australia journalist and the headquarters of the ABC over national security and special forces stories.
- British Prime Minister Theresa May resigns as leader of the Conservative Party and PM
- Major Hong Kong anti-extradition bill protests
- Two oil tankers are attacked near the Strait of Hormuz amid heightened tension between Iran and the United States
- Chinese President Xi Jinping makes a state visit to North Korea.
- Donald Trump and Kim Jong Un agree to restart stalled denuclearization negotiations

Here's a novel form of government. Appoint a minister who:
*** knows very little about what he/she is in charge of,**
*** refuses to take advice from scientific experts,**
*** believes that self interest groups, particularly businesses, are not in it for themselves,**
*** can't see beyond the next election,**
*** believes ideology over fact**
*** will not explain reasons behind decisions**
*** hands money over to groups without public tender, business case studies or even without the group asking for it.**
This is the governMENTAL way of operating in Australia

I tried typing the words *honest politician* but my word processor rejected it saying that it was an oxymoron.

The Coalition won't split the tax changes bill and are playing Russian roulette They have just handed the gun over to Labor who have a lot to lose whichever way the barrel chamber is loaded. By agreeing to all the tax cuts, they lose credibility,

although making themselves a small target. By standing firm against the changes, they lose a chance to influence what is being put forward. It is Adani support all over again. Because the third tranche comes in after the next election, if they let it go through now then they can rescind it after the next election. They are better off pointing out the deeming rates that are eroding retirees' funds far worse than the franking dividends ever would have. They would be better off attacking Angus Taylor over his attempts to manipulate environmental regs for his own family's benefit. By backing the whole tax change bill, they take the likes of Hansen, Bernardi, Centre Alliance and Jacqui Lambie out of play. As long as they don't roll over every time, Labor can develop a more centrist stance and stop the Coalition from taking back the middle ground. The economy will tank, the surplus won't happen and the myths of trickle-down economics and the Coalitions' fiscal management supremacy will come to the fore. Play the long game, Labor.

That is where the whole 'boat people' is so wrong. More illegal immigrants arrive by plane than by boat but because that isn't newsworthy, the boat arrivals get a far worse deal. They are sent offshore for processing which may take years. If we "determine who shall come or not come into our country" then why do we discriminate against those who do it the most difficult way?

So, what the government wants us to do about our problems with a faltering economy is "build a bridge and get over it." Only they won't provide the money for construction, the money to train engineers to design and build it and the money to maintain it once it is built. They obviously think that a surplus is something more substantial. Good luck crossing the Sydney Harbour Surplus, the Surplus across the Derwent, the Westgate Surplus, the Storey Surplus, the Surpluses over the Torrens and Swan.

We have been sold a pup by master con artists. "We will meet our emissions targets. We will be in surplus. The economy is booming. Over 1.25 million new jobs." These "you've never had it so good" phrases were the backbone of the Coalition's election campaign. We bought the deceit and now we are learning the truth far too late. The growth has stalled. Wages are not moving. GDP is lack lustre. Underemployment is rife. This is the reality. The Labor party helped us stay afloat during the GFC. The Coalition are struggling to help us keep our heads above water in this minor economic downturn. So why did we elect them? They have created a myth of being the best economic managers. More importantly we have been bamboozled by graphs and statistics. What the coalition does with a line graph showing a downturn is merely turn it left ninety degrees to show an upswing. We are so inured to the swathe of facts and figures presented to us that we don't notice the details.

The economy seems to have become constipated despite Frydenberg's best efforts to 'budge it'. Perhaps a healthier diet of progressive policies might move things along?

Home ownership was once the Australian dream. For the young, trying to break into the market has become a nightmare. Many people do not wish to let go of their family home when they get old because they are concerned about the insecurity of renting. Changing the six monthly or yearly leasing of places to five or ten years may encourage more houses to change hands and open up the housing market for the younger generations.

The term 'house prices' is a misnomer in reality because the price of building a house is a constant and in fact can decline the closer you get to the centre of a city. It is the cost of the land that it sits on that rises and falls. Location is everything because transport in Australian cities by world standards is poor. Fast train and other public transport infrastructure can alter the current land cost structure. Many governments, keen to get

revenue from land tax don't worry about transportation until after the new suburb rises from the ground. Invariably it is too late or too expensive to adequately cater for those further out. This merely lessens the land value in these new suburbs and increases the land value of those with good transport already in existence. Governments should not allow land development until proper fast, economical transport links are in place.

The economy is in a downward trend and it won't be long until the promised budget surplus touted by the Coalition will be discreetly withdrawn. They have spent too much money on smoke and mirrors to secure their own jobs to the detriment of the rest of Australia as a whole. Of course, they will blame Labor as they have done for everything over the past six years. The economic downturn happened on their watch because of their policies and their inaction. If they wish to claim credit when things go well, then they should also accept responsibility when things go pear shaped.

The magic word "surplus" rang loud and clear over the enthralled few who listened to Frydenberg's budget speech. Because the Coalition have convinced the public that they are the best economic managers, his unwarranted optimism went viral and as a nation we fell at his feet as supplicants. However, a surplus is not real until it is delivered and delivery was always only going to happen one year after the budget announcement. A lot can happen in a year. Actually, a lot can happen in two months. No one knows exactly which window the surplus slipped out of or whether there was one in the first place. Frydenberg's recipe for his "books gateaux" has been used too many times before by better cooks than he. As the economy souffle loses its artificial support and the air pockets within leak, it begins to lose its shape and take on a pear-shaped look, that no master chef can remedy. There will have to be an interim budget because, otherwise, when there is no bread for the plebs and the cake suggested instead is a flop, someone's head will be on the chopping block.

How can Morrison, Taylor, Frydenberg and especially Dutton pull random figures from the ether without them being challenged, particularly by the media. Has the media called a moratorium on calling out such discrepancies? The economy is doing well according to the coalition but not according to the RBA and impartial economists. There has been an influx of Medevac applications according to Dutton but his own Departments figures belie that. We will still meet our Paris targets in a canter according to Fraser but the increase in emissions means that the nag is lame and heading to the knackery. Journalists need to lift their game or are they scared the AFP will come calling?

Now I may not be a rocket scientist, brain surgeon or nuclear fissionist, but I wonder if when we look at global warming, then rather than try to deal with the cause because no-one will ever want to do that; why don't wish just push the earth's orbit out just a little bit further from the sun. The polar ice caps wouldn't melt, cuddly polar bear cubs would thrive and penguins wouldn't need suntan cream. I am sure it could be done. My method may not be the best as it is labour intensive and involves a lot of people bent over facing the one direction. It also involves millions of cans of baked beans.

Daylight saving should not be discounted as a cause for global warming simply because all the daylight and the light and heat saved must be stored somewhere. Various environment ministers believe that it is stored underground and so they have their heads buried in the sand looking for it. In fact, Melissa Price during the election period almost did a Leichardt in her search for it. Perhaps if Queensland politicians want a coal fired power station then they should also build a vacuum sealed dome over Queensland to contain the emissions. The air quality would become so poor it would be a case of beautiful one day, imperfect the next.

If the sun is slowly cooling as the scientists would have us believe why is the earth warming up? Could it be all the solar panels sucking the heat out of the sun? Now there is a thesis worth half a billion dollars to prove! Must talk to the Great Barrier Reef Foundation about funding. They have so much government money and nothing worthwhile they think to spend it on.

There needs to be a truly fully independent panel set up that will deal with energy, emissions and climate change. It should be similar to the Productivity commission and any government that refuses to follow its suggestions should be forced to explain why. If that explanation isn't satisfactory then a joint sitting should determine the proper course of action.

Hindsight is a wonderful thing. Foresight is even better. We turn to the media for reporting of what has happened and what is currently happening. These days the media is more heavily into prediction and like the fortune tellers and their crystal balls, journalists and their poll driven opinions are often wrong. Yet we are lured to believe them, to trust in them. Sadly, political parties are too. Labor was told they couldn't lose and opened themselves up to ambush by putting out policies that might have gone through once they had taken the reins of government and earned the trust and respect of the population. The Coalition were told they couldn't win and hunkered down, closing ranks and having just the one front person and one tiny target to hit. Their strategy worked. It was a strategy that also would have worked for Labor and is often the main way governments get elected or re-elected. However, the media and the pollsters believed they knew better. They even convinced the public who rarely like being told what to do. Some voters didn't even bother voting because it was a done deal. Some went for minor parties because it was a done deal. Pollsters and some in the media now admit they got it wrong, but will they learn long term? Journalists these days prefer to express opinions instead of reporting the news, so there is little chance that they will learn. Even some of the serious and well-respected journalists are going for gotcha moments, ten second sound bites, poorly researched scoops, overblown headlines and shock jock mentality, which just further loses the public's trust and respect.

How many of us feel safer knowing that the government has brought in newer security laws that give it more power and more secrecy? Transparent government should be an essential part of democracy. FOI requests are commonly refused. Details of government deals with private companies can't be checked because of commercial confidence. Whistle-blowers are threatened with long terms of imprisonment. The checks and balances that are supposed to be in place are one by one being removed. The public has the right to know but as politicians and public servants won't tell us, we have to rely on the fourth estate. However, the fourth estate is its own worst enemy. They want the gotcha moment, they want the scoop and that seems to be paramount rather than ensuring facts are checked. Raise the tone of journalism above gutter press across the board and the public may have more sympathy. One by one our freedoms are being reduced by governments who believe they have the right to know everything but believe we have the right to know nothing. Even the comments by our PM about AFP raids have been like, "Nothing to see her. Move on!" Says a lot really for our apathy and our numbness to government overreach and the long-term possibility of government control of media.

When the choir begin singing "How Great Thou Art", Morrison smirks thinking it is in reference to himself. However, Dutton just nods knowing that he holds the power, has the most powerful portfolio and thinks the song is unworthy of himself.

Morrison may seem to be the phoenix rising from the fires of discontent in the Liberal Party but there are ashes scattered around the still burning embers that will take only a slight breath to whip them back into life. Morrison will have trouble controlling his cabinet as has been seen already. There is no 'company line' that can keep certain members' egos in check. Morrison has to tread carefully over the burning coals lest he too succumb to them as Turnbull did. Already history is being rewritten as it always is by winners. How will history judge Morrison once the flames are fanned?

July

- Japan resumes commercial whaling after a 30-year moratorium
- Boris Johnson becomes British Prime Minister of Britain
- With so much pomp and ceremony, so many speeches about doing what is best for all Australians, so much bonhomie and promise, parliament begins. The usher of the black rod will also usher in yet another three years of self-centredness, rancour and deceit. Nothing has changed. For all the piety that will be claimed, it will quickly dissolve into self-righteousness and soundbites. The bubble will continue to exist and the public can only hope that politicians will leave us alone for the next three years.

Why does the song title "Wasted Days and Wasted Nights" come to mind as parliament reopens? I mean "The Great Pretender" should be up there when I look at Morrison. And "You've Got to Pick a Pocket or Two" for Frydenberg as the new Fagin as he tries to get a surplus. Last year I went off the Wiggles as Dutton seemed to think he was the "Hot Potato". When I see Morrison grovelling to Trump, I hear "Mad World" And now with the way the economy is going R.E.M's "Everybody Hurts" is doing my head in. "Help!"

I thought the GG was supposed to be impartial. He should not have to read out the government's words. He may choke on them and then we'd have another constitutional crisis, although I am sure Tony Abbott would jump into the breech.......... And then the rest of the nation would choke on their own vomit.

Fifty years ago, humans first walked on the moon. I watched it from a vast distance sitting cross legged on the floor in a hall on a 26-inch television with five hundred other students. In a

different hall, the hallowed halls of parliament the Liberal party, was trying to disembowel itself as factions in it were at odds with each other. Fifty years on very little has changed although my body won't let me sit cross legged anymore, the TV screen sizes are vastly bigger and humans haven't settled on the moon, preferring instead to destroy their own planet first. Parliamentarians continue to play their little fantasy games but one big change for them is that they are now held in contempt by the public who now sees them for what they are.

"The Senate has adjourned as a mark of respect for Bob Hawke." What a lot of BS! The best thing they could have done to honour one of the most hardworking PM's in Australia's history would be to get back to work and on with the job they were elected to do. For Christ's sake, you would have thought that we had won the America's Cup!

Seen all the selfies in Canberra????-: self-deluded, self-absorbed, selfish, self-serving, self-centred, self-aggrandizing, self-righteous, self-satisfied, self-important, self-indulgent.......

Wonder how those self-managed retirees are doing their calculations now? Libs win and there have been two interest rate cuts. Labor was offering a reduction in franking credit offsetting. By my calculations self-funded retirees would be better off now with Labor. And the hip pocket pain caused by bad decision making isn't claimable under Medicare.

Here's an anomaly that the government could and should look at. There are so many people who for one reason or another such as disability, unemployment, divorce etc are forced to be on the old age pension AND they don't own their own homes. The majority of these are women. Those that do own their own homes get the same pension as those that don't, yet they don't have the same expenses. The pension is a social safety net for those in

difficulty. Those without their own home are in far more dire circumstances and so they don't have the capacity to boost the economy. There should be a boost in pension payments for those in that situation. The same could and should apply to Newstart!

Since when did principles and politics stand together as one? Labor made a statement about the tax cuts being wrong as far as the third tranche went. They suggested amendments and these were going to be knocked down so what would have them do? Morrison now has to live and die by the tax cuts he has put in place. The economy has all but stalled and principles won't resuscitate it. Morrison will find his bed of roses quickly becoming a bed of nails. Albo will be able to say, "I told you so" as the surplus gets clipped. The tax cuts mean a drop in revenue and to retain the surplus in a time of crisis when revenue is dipping already, Morrison and Frydenberg will have to cut services and that is also Albo's opportunity to say, "I told you so". To fight an unwinnable fight is like tilting at windmills. It is quixotic at best and Albo can throw all the supposed Labor principles at it and make not an ounce of difference. Picking your battles will get Labor back in power. The public need to say that the Coalition are not the great economic managers that the Coalition would have everyone believe.

Which group of people are most likely to put their "bonus" money straight back into the economy? It will be the ones who can least afford to, the ones who are struggling. Those wealthier will possibly pay off some of their mortgage or save it for the monsoonal rainy days ahead. Pensioners and those on Newstart, if they were given access to more money, would benefit greatly and pour their winnings straight back into the economy and small businesses would benefit greatly. But that is not the Coalition way, because pensioners and those on Newstart are leaners not lifters. Joe Hockey in 2014 was stupid enough to say what was underpinning Coalition ideology and policy. However,

by helping "the leaners", the lifters will benefit the most in the long term.

The tax cuts will see a decline in revenue. That is economics 101. It may provide a slight stimulus but much of that will go overseas as people will buy imported goods with their "bonus". There will be little left to further stimulate the economy with government spending on infrastructure AND keep a surplus. Something will have to give. The loss of revenue will mean cuts in government spending or the government going further into debt. It has nearly tripled Labor's debt of six years ago and needs to start reigning it in. This is a budget emergency of its own creation. It laid a beautifully constructed economic trap for Labor to fall into when it won the 2019 election. Labor foiled that by losing the unlosable election. Those master strategists of the Coalition who had set Labor up to fail when they took government, had only one word to say on election night. It was, "Oops!"

The magic bullet has been fired that, according to the Coalition, will resolve everything. However already they are looking at the now empty chambers in their all-powerful gun that was there to ward off an economic crisis. To say that they went off half-cocked and they have missed their target are already understatements. They have nothing left in their armoury but the power of prayer. Only now it is dawning on them that they have shot themselves in the foot and will go limping to the next election once again shooting from the hip, with loose cannons doing more damage to themselves. Maybe they should bite the bullet and try what the RBA is suggesting, although they might just shoot the messenger. So far, the Coalition's plans seem like that they are shooting blanks. Labor has them in the crosshairs, is loaded for bear, but won't be jumping the gun this time.

All those tax savings that people will be now getting will boost our local businesses as people go out and buy an Australian car,

some Australian made clothes, some Australian electrical goods.......
Just a minor detail that Josh has overlooked; we have no real
manufacturing businesses anymore!!!! Otherwise it would have been
a great plan.

**The Coalition's ideology as far as government expenditure
goes revolves around the notion that you can't spend what you
don't have. They now have a heck of a lot less.... this doesn't bode
well for any of the essential social services that the public rely on.**

Coalition's economics is based on a budget or what is often
described as a doesn't work in progress.

**I see, the tax cuts will help reduce the government debt. It's
called inverse economics. That's how the parliamentarian salary
package operates. The less work you do, the more you get paid.**

I wonder how long it will be before the Coalition decide that
they run a business and not a government. They may decide that
they have the capital to buy up other businesses; a mining company
here, a telecommunications company there, maybe even a bank or an
airline. Oh, wait a minute.... we used to own the mineral rights in our
country and we had an airline, bank and even a telecommunications
company until we sold them off because of government ideology. If
that ideology still overrides all decisions then the government will
not buy, they will continue to sell. Outsourcing the ABC, the entire
defence department, Medicare and even the Reserve Bank may be on
their agenda to achieve an almighty surplus that would make Josh's,
Mathias's and Scott's grins so much wider.

**The Coalition's election agenda has been fulfilled and like any
bucket list once done, the question must be asked, "Now what?"
Perhaps hold another election and offer another agenda? Sit back
in triumph, knowing that you have achieved everything? Or slide
away into blessed oblivion? The public accepted their bucket list,
although some people had a different consonant at the beginning
(sixth letter of the alphabet). We didn't agree to more than that**

because that was all that was on offer. The Opposition need to exploit that point for the rest of the government's term. The Coalition were given a mandate for the tax reforms and asked for nothing else. They can't take on any of Labor's policies because they decried them at the election. So, what now? They have the country's attention and only heckling will fill the empty space until they are dragged off stage.

The Coalition took one policy to the election and look like having it passed in the next week. What the hell will they have to do before the next election? Bored, they might turn in on themselves again.

When Bernardi pulls the pin, another far right-wing conservative departs. Abbott gone and soon Bernardi. Abetz, Andrews and other old dinosaurs just can't see the comet coming.

I think that the word sinecure is very apt for Bernardi as his piety is front and centre. He would cure the sins of people with whatever means were available: When Psalm 23 fails, he probably would try C4 plastic, AK47 or an FA 18.

"We are right behind you Mathias!!!"

"Why are you carrying knives?"

"Would you believe, to cut the red tape????"

James Paterson would follow Mathias Cormann into a burning house!!!!! Well hand me the matches please. This blind loyalty is what kills proper debate in party rooms and on the floor of parliament. Every individual member of parliament should be seriously studying and questioning every piece of legislation that is brought forward. They should be questioning the motives of everyone around them, and indeed of themselves. That is the best way of raising standards in political debate.

Jacqui tried wielding power like some latter day Cleopatra. Alas Octavian Morrison will win the battle, renege on any

promises and Lambie will find that she has committed political suicide, proving what a pain in the asp the Coalition can be.

Can just see the sub-editors going off with such headlines as "Senator from the Isle of the Apple crumbles". "Jacqui went as quiet as a Lambie"

August

- Hong Kong International Airport is closed due to ongoing protests.
- Fires continue to burn in the Amazon rainforest at a record rate, with more than 36,000 in the year to date, while smoke reaches São Paulo more than 2,700 km away

The Morrison ascension was a coup d'état delivered with a coup de grâce by Morrison who just earlier had put his arm around Turnbull saying "This is my leader and I'm ambitious for him!" The only thing that the picture doesn't show is the knife being embedded. Turnbull winced a little but didn't appear to feel much. He was probably numb from the Dutton attack.

There seems to be an unstated need for workers to be oppressed through stagnant wages growth, unpaid internship, underemployment etc. As the cost of living increases people will fall further and further behind and the economy already on its knees will falter. There is no consumer driven demand as people are trying to make ends meet with the basics. The Liberals who espouse a market driven economy are saying all is going well, that things have bottomed out and it is a steady as she goes approach. This is the sort of inspiration that led to the Charge of the Light Brigade. Our decision makers are safely ensconced in their bubble and oblivious of what is happening outside it. This "I'm all right, Jack" approach is not what we voted for.

Stock-market jitters, tumbling economy, recession, depression, ... these are all just words. The sad reality is that those using those words and those trying to prevent the use of those words are the least likely to face the consequences of any of these. It is the people at the bottom of the food chain who will lose their jobs, fail to adequately survive on the pittance that is

Newstart, whose children will suffer poverty, who will lose their house, their pride and their dignity. Where are our economic saviours? They have their head buried in the sand, desperate to keep the status quo and their promise for a surplus, but at what cost? The social upheaval that is taking place already will be nothing like the tsunami that will follow as Australia like other nations find that we have been sold a hoax, that the Trump vs China issue is something to worry our heads about, that free trade agreements aren't free at all, that inflated house prices aren't sustainable, that we have been living on the backs, not of sheep, but of our immigration intake, the same people we are told to despise. Heaven help Australia because our government certainly can't.

Why can't we just be neutral and offer ourselves as tax havens for the wealthy. Let's stop digging our resources out of the ground and flogging them off. Let's take other people's resources and set up minimal tax opportunities for them. Let's compete properly on this non-level playing field. Let Google, Apple and all the other big companies store their money here. We may not have the Alps of Switzerland but our coastline is better than the Cayman Islands. We wouldn't have to choose between China and Japan, we'd happily squeeze both dry of their funds. We wouldn't need to spend a fortune on defence and instead spend it on social programs. Let's remove the blue and red from our flag and begin a whole new way of operating.

The saying used to be in developing a good relationship, "What's yours is mine and what's mine is yours." It seems that the government is telling the public, "What's yours is mined. What's mined is mine" Not a good way to keep a healthy relationship going with the public, one would think.

Our economy is like the maiden voyage of the Titanic. Australia's economy has been hailed as the best in all the world and unsinkable, even if a recession hits other countries. Captain "Scomo" Smith and his Chief Officer, "Frydenberg" Wilde have no idea of the dangers that lay ahead and are incapable of turning the ship around. They will be forever remembered for the disaster that could have been averted.

Tim Wilson may well question the effectiveness of what the RBA is doing, however the RBA is only reacting to the conditions that this government has set over the past six years. If the government are the great economic managers that they purport to be, then they should be steering the appropriate course, yet they are heading into a massive economic storm and all the RBA can do is throw out a sea anchor in the hope that it will slow the vessel and maybe adjust its course before it is too late. Captain Scomo and first mate Frydenberg seem oblivious to what lies ahead. They haven't even shifted the deck chairs. The orchestra is playing on a loop "Six Years in a Leaky Boat."

"It's Tuvalu, goodbye to you,
Hate to see you go,
But we can't offend the coal lobby,
So, we'll sling you a bit of dough.
Waves will creep in; you'll start sinking
And then you'll disappear
We'll come to your aid and help you out
There's room on Manus we hear"

Australia's new defence policy is global warming. If the sea levels rise, we will have a deeper moat.

As the planet implodes, the one salient question we should all be asking is, "How much is a ticket to Mars going to cost?"

So, the family of the Pacific nations is being dictated to by an overbearing father figure who is telling them what to say and do. Morrison may think he can walk on water but that may be at the expense of those who may be soon under it. Failure to acknowledge the realities that many Pacific Islanders are facing is

tantamount to neglect. This was echoed by the inane comments of the Deputy Prime Minister. The resources industry is driving Australian foreign and environmental policy. As has been pointed out, Scott Morrison is portraying himself as the accidental leader and he hasn't a clue how to do it.

Can the crocodile tears of Joyce, Taylor and Littleproud break the drought and refill the river system?

The Murray Darling Basin plan seems just to be a Ponzi get rich quick scheme for those in the know. It has little to do with ecology and the environment. The irrigators are not only bleeding the country dry of water and money, they have created moral and ethical bypasses as well.

The Morrison ascension was a coup d'état delivered with a coup de grâce by Morrison who just earlier had put his arm around Turnbull saying "This is my leader and I'm ambitious for him!" The only thing that the picture doesn't show is the knife being embedded. Turnbull winced a little but didn't appear to feel much. He was probably numb from the Dutton attack.

Some people may ask where Trump is getting the money to buy Greenland but it is all a snake oil salesman's ruse. It is a look over hear distraction to take away from his gun law pledge to the NRA, to the border issues with Mexico, to the botching of the trade war with China. Scomo and Trump are from the same mould. He has already brown nosed his way into sending troops to the Straits of Hormuz. Scomo may well also look at doing a deal with Trump. Then we may well ask, "Australia, where the bloody hell are you?" and "How come the US flag has 51 stars on it now?"

September

- Major bushfire in Queensland
- U.S. President Donald Trump calls off Afghanistan planned peace talks with the Taliban.
- An international strike and protest led by young people and adults is held three days before the latest UN Climate Summit, to demand action be taken to address climate change.
- The Supreme Court of the United Kingdom unanimously rules that the September 2019 prorogation of Parliament by Boris Johnson was unlawful and void.
- 500,000 people march in a climate change protest led by activist Greta Thunberg and Prime Minister Justin Trudeau in Montreal, Canada. 4,000,000 go on strike around the world

The country that expects an individual to sell his soul to be president, has found the perfect archetype it has searched for. Everything for him is for sale. His soul went years ago just after his principles were traded in on literally a new model. Is Trump everything he appears to be? The sad reality is yes. Behind the fake orange tan and combover hair there is a child who is a bully and wants to be the leader of a gang. The fact that US citizens voted him in says a lot about themselves. The fact that our PM wants to ingratiate himself with a man like that says a lot about him. Scott Morrison wants the world to know that Trump is his new bestie. The fact that it puts China offside is something that he will worry about later. China is unlikely to turn the other cheek when Scott presents his second face towards it. What is this power that Trump has? It certainly isn't charisma which can be defined as alternatively "a divinely conferred power or talent" or "compelling attractiveness or charm that can inspire devotion in others". It is the uncertainty principle, the chaos factor and the ability to instil fear because people worry about what he is going to do or say next. Morrison is very likely to shortly receive a tweet saying that he has been dumped in favour of someone else. How will Morrison cope with that? He is not in the job for the money. He is in it for the power and prestige. Trump can destroy that in less than 140 characters, even faster than Rupert Murdoch. We live in dangerous times and there is no-one more dangerous than Donald Trump at the moment. Say it! Well may Jenny Morrison have been startled with the talk of nuking Iran. It is not beyond Trump to do that. He was going to nuke a hurricane, especially after he couldn't make it move to Alabama with a stroke of a pen, for heaven's sake. The greatest danger that Australia has, is that it must kowtow to this potential madman. Morrison may be quite relieved to be back in the Canberra bubble where people like Dutton, Hansen, Abetz etc look relatively sane by comparison. When Trump's tax returns finally get released, they may show that his wisest and best investment, giving him the most personal gain, was to buy the keys to a small house with the address of 1600 Pennsylvania Avenue NW in Washington, D.C. The windows may be bullet proof and the walls of the oval office need padding, but he has been unable to stop the leaks. .... And the leaks may see him want to leave that office. Then the world will breathe a deep sigh of relief.

I wonder whether Trump is going to use Pratt to recycle refugees and 'dreamers'. Trump thinks that they are garbage and we could see Pratt opening new plants in central American countries. He is flat chat in Australia recycling past promises for the Coalition.

A Royal Commission is only worthwhile calling if you know it will give the answers that you want to hear. Although the Coalition has found that this isn't the case. The RC into the unions failed to get what they wanted, Bill Shorten's scalp. The Royal Commission they didn't want to call into the financial services has opened up a huge can of worms. So, a Royal Commission into energy will have to have a very narrow focus and report before the next election to be worth anything to the Morrison government. What a shame if it proved the ETS was a good outcome or even the NEG, and how would the government react if they found that a lack of a cohesive energy policy was the main cause of the whole energy crisis?

I certainly hope that our new Prime Minister can read stats about all sorts of other things much better than he does read the stats about crime in Victoria. Stats such as the decibel level of dog whistling by Coalition politicians that seems to go up just prior to elections where Labor is in charge or a strong threat, should be something more relevant for him to comment on.

It is about time that Australia had better ways of organising elections. If a member of either the Senate, or House of Representatives, resigns, retires or dies then a by-election should be called for the first Saturday three weeks after the vacancy occurs. It should not be at the whim of the Speaker or the President of the Senate. Senate vacancies should not be filled merely by a member of the same party. That is what has caused some of the shambles we currently have. The whole state should have the right to vote elect the replacement and not just have a rubber stamp placed by the State government on the nomination of the party. Federal elections should not be at the whim of the government. What is wrong with having a set date? Surely then all the pork barrels can be put in place to match the date, candidates can be vetted properly and nominated people can be properly examined by the press and the population in general. We have an archaic way of governing our country. Adversarial politics achieves far less than the theory suggests. It stops progress and is used to avoid accountability. It also is a reason why we don't get the best people in the country to stand for election. That in itself is surely enough reason for change.

What will actually change in the financial sector post Royal Commission? Executive salaries will still be high and there will be still little accountability. The culture bred over more than half a century will still underpin the system. Any fines will be paid out of shareholder's dividends and the banks will continue to rake in billions of profit. The Royal Commission will be as ineffectual in changing the shape of the sector as a governing party toppling a prime minister.... a few changes of seats for those running the show and then same old, same old. The boards on these institutions just need to ensure profit is made and shareholders get value for money. They are not interested in customer service, that costs money and does not provide a return. Perhaps we should rename the whole thing. Let's not call it financial services sector, let's call it financial non-service vultures

If the next Victorian election is to be about law and order, why did Matthew Guy order his department to pay out a huge amount of money when the law was supposedly on his side? Is white collar crime in Victoria treated differently to black African crime. Shouldn't the law be the same for all?

I hear that the soil down at Ventnor where Matthew Guy did some strange things with planning has a strange quality. Apparently mud sticks.

People who get elected come from a small gene pool. They have only to appease the few who control the pre-selection process in each electorate. It is not only the bullies who need to be held to account but also the people who did the pre-selecting. In the AFL if the team plays poorly it is the coach's fault and not the Board's for appointing him or her in the first place. This same sort of lack of accountability carries over into the political spectrum. A few power brokers are to blame for the dearth of talent and the bully boys in parliament. Get rid of these and then democracy may actually work. The women and men who were bullied and intimidated during the Turnbull fiasco were threatened with loss of pre-selection at the next election. Just shows who is actually running, or should I say ruining, the country.

To compensate for the savings made by leaving the pension age at 67, make sure politician's pensions and perks after leaving parliament don't kick in until they turn 67.

With so few women being motivated to join the right side of politics, does that indicate yet again that women are smarter than men?

A lump of coal may have given Shorten a run for his money. Now he can casually stroll across the winning line as the Liberals keep tripping themselves up near the starting blocks.

No glass ceiling? The sky's the limit? There is a cloud scene painted on the ceiling of the 1950's styled Coalition party room. Women should be seen and not heard. "A spoonful of cement to harden up" "Learn to roll with the punches" But as the Labor party found, sometimes the best man for the job is a WOman. Julia Gillard achieved more in a minority government than Abbott and Turnbull did in a majority government. Coalition members of parliament and indeed those pulling the strings behind them need to take off their chauvinist, misogynist, archaic blinkers.

They've dumped the NEG. They've dumped tax cuts for big companies. They've dumped an increase in the pension age. They've even dumped a Prime Minister or two....... and come next election they will be down in the dumps too.

They will dump a policy they created and were trying to enact and NOW claim credit for it! That's a class act. Somehow it will be all Labor's fault that the policy was there in the first place.

Our parliament doesn't work as it should. The NEG was going to pass as Labor would have supported the compromise. However, the legislation was withdrawn because a small number of Coalition politicians didn't like it. Majority does not rule in our country.

No wonder Australia is in drought, with all the watering down of policies, there's none of the wet stuff left for farmers.

Yet another bird hits the endangered species list. It is the little-known justice bird. It's plaintive cry of ICAC! ICAC! will become just a distant memory as its habitat is taken over by twits who tweet and Indian miners.

Some people think with so many Sydney based Prime Ministers in the past few years that the capital of Australia is Sydney but even the least pedantic of us knows that the only capital in Australia is A.

The part of the constitution that Peter Dutton may run foul of reads: "has any direct or indirect pecuniary interest in any agreement with the Public Service of the Commonwealth" From my understanding of the way that politicians treat public servants, none of them agrees with what the public service says and they certainly don't have any interest in them, pecuniary or otherwise. They are quite content to blame teachers, nurses, emergency service personnel and almost any other public servant for the politician's own inept planning.... and as far as money goes, they pay public servants working at the coalface a pittance.

With Turnbull's comments, Julie Bishop chiming in and Peter Dutton trying to distract with allusions to grooming by Roman Quaedvlieg some might say the plot thickens, which is different to a couple of weeks ago when the thick were plottin'.

Perhaps the money going to research could be spent on solving the mystery as to why the general public has a low opinion of politicians, or maybe on how many election pledges actually get honoured, or even why pork barrels are causing our debt to increase faster.

At last the Coalition has recognised that climate change is occurring. The climate in the party room is toxic and people want a change of environment. Although even now they still can't agree on the correct course of action as the NEG (Need for Equality in Gender) has been dismissed.

The backroom deals between Turnbull and the right, Morrison and disaffected women, in fact Morrison and everyone need to be made public. All this horse-trading that goes on in Parliament between everyone should be made clear to the public before they vote. That way the dreamers and schemers will be shown for what they are.

When the House of Liberal falls at the next election, perhaps it will break into pieces and a new centrist party will form as a splinter group. Like a phoenix it will rise from the ashes and again fill the void that the current Liberal party has vacated. Labor has been able to move completely into that middle ground where the majority of people are. The only way that Labor will lose the next election is a self-inflicted wound....... strong possibility as they are accident prone.

Are the flat earth thinkers intelligent enough to realise that if they go too far to the right, they will fall off the edge?

I think all members of parliament and some of the ones who have been newly preselected should all front the High Court. How many are Australian or for that matter from any inhabited land on Earth? Many seem to be not of this world and on another planet entirely when it comes to understanding what real people think. When it comes to their voracious appetite for the public purse, think Predator and Alien.

"And now the end is near
And this Muppet will close the curtain
The Libs will lose next year
Leadership change again is certain"
(Apologies to Frank Sinatra)

Most of us live in electorates where we have passive people representing us. They spend most of their time sitting on back benches on either side of the floor and fail to criticise their own

party, comment on legislation and appear there, especially at divisions, to make up the numbers. These are the people that sit idly by as the frontrunners play their mind games using energy, emissions, economics etc as means to fool the public. They tell their own truths to their electorate and weave a new fairytale for each election.

If ever there was a time for crossbenchers to get deals done with the government, up to the Wentworth by-election is it. They will never have this power again! Go to it ladies and gentleman, push those wheelbarrows hard and firm!

When Scott Morrison came to power it should have been a Newstart for all (paid at the Newstart allowance rate of course) but so many people got their old jobs back again. Perhaps there should be a Sameold Allowance paid to our politicians and they should have to deal with Centrelink to get paid.

Regarding the latest call by the PM about Aged Care, to quote one of Scott Morrison's great ad campaigns when he was in charge of Tourism Australia, "Where the bloody hell" was he when Labor wanted an investigation months ago? When the banking Royal Commission was being asked for, "Where the bloody hell" was he? Perhaps he should put his own hands up and say mea culpa.

ScoMuppet is lucky that Shorten is still leader of the Opposition. Actually, if Albo was leader, then in all probability Turnbull wouldn't have won in 2016. ScoMuppet thinks that calling a Royal Commission into aged care will be his "look over here" Tampa type moment but again the Libs have been too late in doing things. Labor has been calling for an investigation for quite a while. In truth, however if Labor wants to gain a complete landslide at the next election' Penny Wong should move to the lower house and become leader of the Labor Party and Albo should become her deputy. The Libs will then have to start

looking for someone that can actually lead a united party sometime in the distant future.

We had MT as PM and his promises were empty. We now have SM as PM and they appear Sadomasochistic. What will Bill Shorten's be? BS?

I don't understand this "new government" thing. Scott Morrison may be the newer prominent head of Medusa but it is still Medusa! Electing a new prime minister doesn't change much especially when nearly all of the snakes remain there and Medusa keeps walking in the same direction (to the right). A new government will come only after an election that provides a change of party leading the government.

If there is to be a landslide as many pundits are predicting, what percentage of women will be dumped at the next election? Many are vulnerable because they are already in marginal seats, but obviously not winning will be based on merit. They will have merited a change in their financial circumstances because the public no longer think that they merited a job.

Stupid games! Scott Morrison ...... that would also include the one involving changing a leader who was more popular than the Leader of the Opposition and who was raising the Coalition up in the ratings.

Teena McQueen, the new federal Liberal vice president, said "Women always want the spoils of victory without the fight." How will that go down with female members of the Liberal party at grass roots level and in parliaments? Actually, I believe that women everywhere will be offended. Women fight battles at work, in the home and out in the community everyday just to be considered as equals to men who have no such battles to fight. What a shallow vision this woman has of her own gender. Many men assume it is their God-given right to lead. There seems to be an over-representation of them in the Liberal Party and here a woman is actually backing that philosophy.......... The DeLorean has reached the 1950's.

58% of all women who have been in cabinet are Liberal. What a great statistic to pull out at a time when numbers of women representatives in the Liberal party are in rapid decline. It shows how you can manipulate statistics. Simply by bringing different women in and out of cabinet for brief periods of time you can bump up your figures. If someone is in the job for eight years counts as much as someone who has been in for eight months. Steve Ciobo drill down your statistic and explain how that figure was attained. History is good to look back on but not something to crow about. People will look back on the Abbott, Turnbull, Morrison governments unkindly on women's issues. The ebbs and flows are within the power of the party to control but sadly the Libs don't see that the tide of public opinion is against them.

There is a danger believing in the best of people, because when we look at our politicians especially the Home Affairs Minister, we have to set the bar for "best" so low.

Apparently, the parting gift for Prime Ministers leaving office is the rest of the cutlery drawer that matches the knives in the back. Parliament House is now buying these in bulk.

People getting older and thus damaging the budget bottom line will soon be ascribed as Labor's fault.

Overall monetary amounts don't mean much when it comes to aged care funding. It is far better to use per capita of aged care users to reflect whether funding has been cut or increased or remained the same. In trying to keep the budget burden lower however that may lead to allowing more in aged care to kick the bucket sooner.

The issue the public has with the claims made by the opposition and the government in aged care funding is whose statistics do you believe? However, the fault has to lie with the government. If they have cut the funding they shouldn't have because aged care is in crisis. If they have increased funding, they haven't properly supervised the expenditure. Scott Morrison wants it both ways and the logic doesn't hold. He is making as much sense as the Swedish chef.

Oh, the irony "The future of work report is also due to be tabled at around 5pm" on a day when the Senate is finding little work to do.

Ann Sudmalis has been offered the New York UN secondment trip. When you think about it, what benefit to the Australian public will that bring? Any person who has indicated that they are leaving parliament at the next election should not be offered such trips. It may be one of the perks of office but in reality, the expensive "study" tours for people who cannot possibly pass on that "valuable" information gained in a meaningful way because they are no longer in parliament should be curtailed. Julia Banks has done the honourable thing in rejecting it. Perhaps she may be asked to be an envoy and thus also be sent to a naughty corner too.

Based on the ABC's 7:30 last night, it seems that it isn't just the Liberals who have trouble dealing with women. Perhaps Barnaby Joyce and the Nats hierarchy also have problems do too. Politicians and political parties should realise that parliament is a workplace and acceptable workplace practices apply. That prestige they believe they have, comes with responsibility.

According to Marise Payne, "Myanmar continues to face formidable challenges as it transitions from five decades of military rule." One of the formidable challenges is obviously stopping the genocide or at best stopping the world from noticing. Our government's blind eye has been forced open.

Labor needs to come to grips with the Aged Care questions. It is not the overall funding that needs comparing it is the per person funding and the continual downgrading of people's needs in aged care. To save money the rules are changed, delays in

approval are extended, different assessment tools are used, other exemptions and taxing structures such as payroll tax are altered. **This is how the government has actually cut the level of funding to Aged Care. Check with Aged Care residences and they will tell you that there has been no real increase in funding per client and in some cases a decline. Labor needs to ask the important questions**.

The responses in Question Time are called answers. There are two definitions to the word answer:

1. a thing that is said, written, or done as a reaction to a question, statement, or situation.

2. a solution to a problem or dilemma.

I am guessing that the second definition has nothing to do with what happens in Question Time

Obviously, the Aged Care Royal Commission announcement was a one day wonder as far as the parliament and the media are concerned but right now are thousands of old people in inadequately funded aged care facilities whose main two thoughts are: "What do I have to live for? What will I die from?"

Can we rename Question Time to Obfuscation Time? It is a more appropriate title given obfuscation means the action of making something obscure, unclear, or unintelligible.

No internet at Parliament House? You'd think they would have the gold plated ultra-sensitive optic fibre to the premises version not the braided cloth covered copper wire to the node some have or the two cans and a long piece of string country people are forced to use. Has Malcolm taken his bat and ball and NBN and gone home?

Morrison is running a caretaker government? You think that they are taking care? What? Of themselves maybe. Certainly not us.

Good government..... where the bloody hell are you?

Greg Hunt has just railed against antivaxers for not realising that the overwhelming amount of scientific opinion is against them and that they are using poorly researched evidence to back their claims. I wonder what Greg Hunt thinks of climate change?

Imagine the conversation at the Liberal and Coalition Spin Bank

"We've got until May to change ScoMo's image"

"And for the next impossible task???"

"Well let's try and show that the government is capable of doing something."

"You mean apart from shooting itself in the foot?"

"We haven't really done anything in five years except change prime ministers and put the voting public off."

"But we did do those very well."

"We could start a war or find another Tampa."

"What about a terrorism alert? Dutton is in charge of that and jackboots suit him."

"Sounds like a plan. Have we got enough flags for a press conference?"

"I think so..... The difficulty is... who is going to tell Rupert?"

"What do you mean? It was his suggestion!"

The old-fashioned notion, but still used by conservatives, that women should be "barefoot and pregnant in the kitchen" has been busted wide open by the likes of Jacinda Ardern. It is about time that the Liberal party in particular realised that equality is a fundamental right for all Australians. However, that realisation may only come when they understand that each woman's vote counts as much as each man's, a fact they have tended to ignore.

If merit was the sole reason that candidates were chosen and thus elected, given the standard of our politicians, surely Australia has a dearth of expertise, compassion, intelligence and open mindedness across the board.

Threatening states with the punishment of withholding funding if they don't agree to the Federal government's new funding plan is Tehan's way of negotiating and explaining. Obviously hasn't read, "How to Win Friends and Influence People' nor 'How to Win Elections by Bamboozling People'. Can't believe the arrogance that he displays. Bring back Birmingham. Tehan is making him look like a saint.

"We control how much money you get. We control who is on your board. We control who your board appoints as CEO. We control changes to your charter. That's our sort of independence."

For the blissfully ignorant, I'll translate...... Don't rock the boat.

How can there be independence in government bodies when appointments to the boards of these are done for political reasons by politicians. It is like the Supreme Court in the US. There is no merit in those appointments. The PM here is saying merit is enough to get more women into the parliament on his side. If that is the case please ensure merit is used for appointments to boards and ambassadorships......... just not the Liberal version of merit though.

If ASIO wants to know all my deepest and darkest thoughts and what I think of them spying on my phone and computer; "Call me, call me now!"

Am I being paranoid? Is someone checking up on me through my phone and computer? If so why then did we have to have a paper-based ballot for same sex marriage? Was that really a delaying tactic as the Conservatives already knew what we were thinking? Dutton certainly wasn't clever enough to use the phone back door as Home Affairs Minister. If he was, he would have known what his colleagues thought of him and never challenged to be PM.

This drug testing nonsense has got everybody talking and how Machiavellian is the idea behind it. The economy is tanking. We have just sent troops into harm's way in the Gulf. We have kicked the can down the road as far as climate change action goes. But everybody is focusing (like a person has to do to pee in a cup) on something that attacks the weakest in our community. This is a big political win for the Coalition. The worst growth figures since the GFC, spiralling debt and we jump at the distractions. Target those people who are struggling and you will always attract attention. Remember the Tampa? By raising John Setka, Jacqui Lambie shows that she has swallowed the bait. She will trade a critical vote for the scalp of one person. This just shows how little even politicians know about politics. It also shows how little everyday Australians know about politicians and politics. We would hope that the Federal Government would deal with the big issues and not paper over them. We would hope that the politicians would stand on their principles based around a fair and just society. We would hope that the media and Opposition would do its job and call the Government to account. But our hopes seem to be in vain based on the games that are being played. The quiet Australians that Morrison claims are on his side, are really not interested and who could blame them given the sham that takes place in the corridors of power in Canberra.

Canberra is often called a circus. The sideshows are gaudy and a distraction. They take our interest and our money. However, what is happening in the main tent should be the centre of attention. It isn't because we have such dull, underwhelming performers who have not enough talent to do the things that they should. Instead they just go through the motions and fail to deliver on the hype that drew us to them in the first place. As the ring empties, we see what these political animals leave behind and even the sawdust doesn't reduce the smell of the mess they leave behind for someone else to clean up.

I love the optimism about predictions about question time, however misplaced it is. We will get Dorothy Dixers. We will get shouting despite microphones. We will get people sent from the chamber. We will get non-answers to questions. We will get hyperbole and platitudes. We will get political ideology and political point scoring. BUT what we won't get is reasoned political debate and those who watch, listen or read about it will be none the wiser. It is a game for fools, played by fools and one that has no merit. Politicians call it theatre, but they denigrate the term by applying it to this display of mediocrity.

Australia needs a Canexit strategy. The idea that Canberra should no longer be part of Australia has some merit. It is already wrapped in a bubble. Can't we just stick a few stamps on it and call up Australia Post. Surely, they could manage to lose this one on route.

So, this government has been in power for six years and still thinks Labor is to blame for everything. I am not sure that I am following their logic here.... there is some sort of logic isn't there? Surely, we haven't been willing to be hoodwinked into electing a pack of political dills for three successive elections, have we? That says a lot about us doesn't it? Hang on, pass me the snake oil, I am getting RSI in my brain trying to work that one out.

Given the waistlines on many parliamentarians "fit" doesn't seem to suit them. As for the "proper", if it was based on their poor attitude to being accountable and on their language and manners in debating, then that doesn't apply either.

When a company makes a profit or performs well, a dividend is declared. When a government does well, better services don't seem to come our way. Pats on the back will be given all around in the Liberal Party room which will be quite different to the knives in the back from a few weeks ago. Turnbull was running the place when these figures were derived but Morrison and Frydenberg are doing a Steven Bradbury and claiming the prize.

Our government has changed its attitude yet again on climate change but you have to admit that it hasn't on asylum seekers. The cruel and inhuman detention lingers still and if our Home Affairs Minister had his way would continue until the water lapped at the doorways of the detention centres.

Our foreign aid to Nauru should be examined because of its links with the detention centres there. Nauru's autonomy has to be questioned when it has to bend over backwards at the behest of another nation. Forget China's belt and road influence, look more closely at Australia's cyclone fence and razor wire.

Migration high, economy grows. No causal link between the two. That will be how it will be spun.

The PM has said the economy is fine as it is. So, if the economy grows at a fast rate, then we should sack a PM. Is that how it works?

So, will this growth in our economy allow us to pay down our spiralling out of control debt? Yes, it could, but it won't happen. Investments will be made in higher quality pork and deliveries of it to marginal electorates.

Morrison/Turnbull/Abbott governments have cut funding to Aged Care. The perfect example is "The Australian Government announced the cessation of the payroll tax supplement as part of the 2014-15 Budget. It took effect from 1 January 2015". In doing so millions was cut from the Aged Care sector and providers were forced to reduce staffing levels and cut services.

One of the wealthiest companies in the world cannot afford to spend money on its core constituency? It is hard to believe that it has to go on bended knee to the Australian government for money especially as it gets the best tax relief in the country. Catholic schools should check with the head office in Rome before they beg for alms in Canberra.

Does Australia have no debt to pay off? Where did our debt and deficit disaster go? Morrison can magically pull out a few billion to satisfy the independent and catholic sector of education for his own political gain without increasing the nation's debt? How does that work? Penn and Teller would be impressed. If he can find that much, then how about some for the state-run schools or doesn't he need those votes?

The housing market needed to crash or at best slow down. The inflated prices sucked up spare cash as people struggled to pay to get into the market and were forced to take high principal amounts. This left the rest of the economy struggling. Investing in bricks and mortar actually produces nothing. It restricts our GDP and gives us an artificial understanding of what homes are worth. In the end, it became the value of a square metre of dirt rather than what sat on it. The quality of the house didn't matter, just the proximity to the CBD of Melbourne and Sydney. It began to affect regional centres an hour out of these CBD's inflating their prices and these will crash even quicker. Those on interest only mortgage payments will pay heavily for their investments as will those who jumped aboard at the peak of the market. the banks? well they never lose. Expect some mortgagee auctions soon. The crash may help drive the over inflated rental market down too and that is a bonus.

Efficiency dividends are great but imagine how much better the deficit would be and how much debt would be paid back if politicians got paid for their own productivity and weren't paid for their petty party politicking.

If the government was a publicly listed company, the Board of Directors would be changed more readily and we would get better people for the job. If Frydenberg presented a surplus by writing down assets as he has just done (NDIS for example), he would have been asked to revisit his job prescription, because the slashing expansion opportunities is limiting future growth. The prospectus offered to investors at the last election offered very

little and that is what Frydenberg and the CEO (Morrison) have delivered. With interest rates so low, why not borrow to create a bigger company with more assets? Why create a surplus to pay off debt that, although growing, is not crippling the economy? You have to spend money to make money. Sadly, this capitalist right wing government doesn't follow its own mantra and the shareholders are getting dudded again.

There are all sorts of things that will be spun about this result. *Iron ore and coal are booming.* The fact that they are keeping us afloat only just is something not worth mentioning. After all, *There are ongoing rises in employment.* The fact that the books are cooked to include underemployed, those on short term contracts and those forced to have two or three jobs to make ends meet, is nothing to concern ourselves about. And of course, *The government is steering its way through the China US trade wars with consummate ease.* This ignores the fact that we are under pressure to choose sides and we are in a lose/lose situation. *The banks are making steady profits.* As well they should because the Royal Commission findings are not being urgently acted upon. *People are earning more today than they have in the past.* Let's not even mention, pensions, Newstart, bracket creep, declining interest rates affecting those living on superannuation, and the fact that there is a growing gap between the rich and poor.

What we need is a cashless economy, a morrisonless economy, a frydenbergless economy and a cormannless economy!!

So how should we spend this surplus? This means the government has made a profit in the last financial year, doesn't it? Will it pay off debt? Will it return the profits in a form of a dividend to its shareholders, the you and me's of Australia? Will it invest in much needed infrastructure? Or will it simply spend a fortune building a statue of Josh Frydenberg to immortalize him for future generations. The current generation would merely throw crap all over it as he has cut services to achieve this great and glorious achievement. Newstart, NDIS, NBN improvement may be some areas for extra expenditure instead, as the current government has slashed/not increased these much-needed areas of national and community importance.

I think Australia, particularly this government, doesn't fully understand the implications of climate change on their neighbours. What will happen is the people on these low-lying islands will become refugees and be forced perhaps to come by boat seeking entry into Australia. What will Australia do? Turn their boats back? Pack them off to Manus and Nauru which too may be under water? Australia no doubt will be spinning things so they are seen to be taking the higher moral ground on climate change. Whereas for the islanders any higher ground would be a blessing.

I still think that the emissions targets will be reduced. Also, reduced even further are our expectations that the Coalition will do anything to address climate change. Their only climate of change is swapping prime ministers. Even when the climate is not right for a change, a change occurs. Whether it is an ETS a NEG or any other acronym, it remains as WTF until something actually gets done.

You've got to admire the architects and builders of Parliament House and their forward-thinking regarding climate. The walls are so well insulated that the people inside are completely unaware of what is happening around them.

What fires? What abnormally severe weather conditions? What coral bleaching? Politicians can't see these things as they have their heads firmly buried in the sand. Perhaps the Productivity Commission should investigate the workings of those in the House of Reps and the Senate. Their productivity surely must be called into question.

Climate action will only take place when the beach where Home and Away gets filmed gets washed away or the lifeguards on Bondi Rescue start saving people in the Blue Mountains. That way, Australians may start to notice what is happening and put pressure on politicians. The gradual rise in sea levels may have a little impact on cities, but the storm surges and changes in tidal movements are the things that will bring it home (literally) to many city dwellers.

Morrison said he did not have deep conversations with his children about emission targets and the Paris agreement but did talk to them about fossil fuels. But then went on to say "I don't allow them to be basically contorted into one particular view, I like them to make their own mind." That's oxymoronic or should I say oxy-Morrisonic.

Needless to say, while the world burns, Morrison is fiddling.... with a McDonalds menu.

Did Scott Morrison even hear or read Greta Thunberg's speech. She quoted scientific facts. It was not "needless anxiety" but perhaps he thinks he can get away with spinning it. Well it just won't wash. He is being hung out to dry and rightly so. She showed more leadership this past week than he has this past year. Perhaps there is a role for him to play in the future. Sequestration spots for carbon need to be found. With his head buried in the sand he has literally a head start on other applicants.

So, Morrison just doesn't get it. He says it is all about the economy, not about the environment. A growing economy will improve the environment, he asserts. But he fails to point out that we are growing our economy by exporting iron ore and coal. These, particularly coal, assist man-made climate change. Changes to the climate won't affect the ability for us to dig up our own backyard and sell it off, so all is right with the Scott Morrison world, particularly the economics. However, the

actions of us failing to reduce emissions, exporting climate changing material overseas does affect our environment. We can't drought proof Australia, nor prevent floods and other weather phenomena that destroy our environment, cause hardship to farmers and damage our marine parks. We can't stop every bushfire. However, we can mitigate their intensity, their timespan and the damage they cause by acting positively on what we can control. We supply nearly 6% of the world's coal. That figure should be gradually reduced. Our emissions targets are too low and are being only achieved by clever accounting tricks. For the last six years Australia's innovative outlook, its standing in the world, its environmental action have stagnated. At the same time its economy and wage growth have also stagnated. Morrison can't seem to see the connection. We protect our environment and our economy grows. Coal exports can be replaced with more tourism which provides even more employment. Australia is part of the global hothouse effect that is occurring. It needs to do its bit and lead and encourage others to do more. But leadership is what has been missing for years. Our farmers, our environmentalists, our scientists and our children are begging us to do more. To do that a government needs courage and wisdom. This government has achieved reductions but in these two areas alone.

No need to fear Russian interference in American elections when we have had an American's interference, Rupert Murdoch's, in Australia's elections for years. I bet there won't be a special investigator appointed to look into ours.

Morrison's pledge of extra money in marginal seats from the leak may seem to be signed, sealed and delivered; but that sounds akin to dead, buried and cremated to Victorians who have been short-changed in the last five years in terms of infrastructure spending.

"Prime Minister pledges to help Victorian Liberals in state campaign" by not visiting anymore???

Carrots are being dangled. Pork is being taken out of barrels and there is a magic pudding as well. Is it a Christmas feast? No, an election is coming up. Heaven help us all, nothing to celebrate. Carrots will be removed once the election is over. The only pork remnants will be the aroma and the magic pudding budget we'll find was just fanciful. But will we remember what a delightful yet ultimately illusory banquet was being put on display?

If we go to the polls on the 30th of March next year we may wake up on the following Monday, April Fool's Day, to find that the Coalition have been returned. Heaven help us if it is not a prank!

Murray Watt said, "Hope is not a strategy." Hell, it is the only thing that the voters have as they put their votes in the ballot box.

Wanted 227 people to fill vacant positions at an election. 76 vacancies are in the senate (if a double dissolution is called) and 151 in the House of Representatives. Currently many of the incumbents are underperforming and will be unlikely to have their contracts renewed. One of the key selection criteria is that you must have principles and not be willing to trade those for any personal gain, political manoeuvring or to gain a higher priority outcome. Another KSC is that you must represent the electorate who voted you in. Any affiliations you may have to a political party should not override putting the country and your electorate as top priorities.

The issue that applicants may find difficult is that the party-political machines will dominate and steamroll over any non-affiliated candidates. But please apply. You have nothing to lose except your dignity for Canberra will quickly take that away from you whether you are successful or not.

Labor took some very credible and well thought out policies to the last election and missed out on government by a small margin due to some excellent political tactics on the conservative

side, particularly in Queensland. Most of those policies should be still articulated until new policies are developed or the existing ones are developed. At the moment the Labor party seem becalmed, not knowing which way the wind will be coming from. Albanese needs to step up to the plate sooner rather than later. The election may be three years away but as it is it appears that the Labor party stands for nothing and stands to lose not only supporters but seats because it dithers on important matters. So, what if Labor missed out at the last election. There's the baby and bath water axiom although that may be seen as child abuse these days. Labor used to be the party that had principles come hell or high water. The Coalition has principles that can be bought. At least Kristina Keneally seems able to stand up for what is right and actually say something. The rest of Labor seem to have been either muted or neutered.

I miss John Howard. At least he finally admitted, if for political reasons that we needed an emissions trading scheme. He worshiped the Don. Morrison worships a different Don - Trump, not Bradman. It seems that we will have yet another three years of leaderless quagmire to endure on climate change. Political games are being played like Nero's fiddle - just ask the people of northern New South Wales and south-east Queensland.

As Sir Joh Bjelke-Peterson would say

"Don't you worry about that"

But the one to worry about is

"The greatest thing that could happen to the state and nation is when we get rid of all the media ... then we could live in peace and tranquillity and no one would know anything."

The PM is demanding choice for parents. That is fine as long as everyone has the same choice. How many people can afford to send their children to state subsidised private and catholic schools? Many of us would like that choice when you see the underfunding of state schools. If qualification for entry for all, all schools were effectively the same and entry wasn't dictated by the amount of money earned by parents, then I'd be pro-choice too. Wealthy schools are crying poor and poor schools' tears aren't even noticed by this government.

I wish I had money on the fact that the states would push for more money after the so called "sector-blind" farce that Tehan put up. Trouble is the odds would have been worse than Winx's were in her last race. It was so obvious that only the sector-blind couldn't see it, although blind Freddy was ahead of me in the betting queue. If only Morrison and Tehan didn't rely on their own perception that the public and the public-school system would be too dumb to notice. These two are always in ties and shirts to hide their lobotomy scars or maybe they are they circumcision marks? That's the problem with public education I guess from their viewpoint. Amidst all the squalor, teachers are still able to teach and students are able to learn so much more than the PM and the Education Minister think. Imagine how much better these students would be if money was spent on them!

Regarding the investigation results into the allegations against Barnaby Joyce; has anyone else noticed that whitewash has a fishy smell?

A low ATAR to get into teaching is yet just another indication what our society thinks of the value of teaching. It is a profession that pays poorly yet builds the future of Australian society. Teachers are people managers, psychologists, at times substitute parents and referees and a myriad of other professions rolled into one. Yet they are seen as the afterthought when it comes to salary, recognition and standing in society. They are blamed for the ills of society and expected to fix the failings of it. By all means seek a high ATAR entry into training but realise that you have to pay teachers more, give teachers a higher profile and remove

the blame game. Otherwise, given a choice, high scoring ATAR entrants would not even consider teaching.

An ATAR is now seen as the measure of a person's worth. It is a statistic based on mainly written information garnered in one year of a student's thirteen-year period of learning. That score can dictate what a person can and can't do for the rest of their life. What it does do is allow companies and indeed universities to discriminate. It is seen as an infallible measurement tool. it does not measure competence in many things that are necessary to function well in most jobs. Those with high ATAR's may not be the best suited for law or medicine but that is where these people are channelled. A greater amount of information gained by interviewing past teachers, interviews and some work experience would assist both the student and the university. That won't happen especially as bureaucrats like numbers to crunch and view such things as the NAPLAN as God's gift to education.

Reiterate means to say the same thing a number of times. There is no need to use the word 'again' with it. Perhaps Dan Tehan's lack of awareness of tautologies came from his exposure to the poor education he received in public schools. Although if that was the case he would see sense in improving their standards by giving them more money. So his ignorance must have been exacerbated by private schooling hence their extra funding.

Dan Tehan said his sector blind funding was not available to public schools. Therefore, logically these schools are not seen to be a sector of education. But then again, he thinks Africa is a country not a continent.

On the Lord Howe Island wind farm issue. "Frydenberg Knows Best" Wasn't that a TV program back in the fifties and sixties where true Liberal values still lie?

Apparently ScoMo is looking for a new nickname and people have suggested another abbreviation after his comment that he never used the term "Shanghai Sam". The nickname comes from taking the middle syllable ('ris') out of his surname.

Morrison has found $150 million to help fund the US Mars mission. That should buy enough one-way tickets for all the Coalition. Money well spent; I say.

We can't expect too much from Scott Morrison. At best he is just a salesman. The sad thing is that all he has is himself to sell and that is no bargain. He has sold his soul to the climate change deniers and his thirty pieces of silver have come in the form of the top job. Malcolm Turnbull was his mentor for that! So, he has the gift of the gab and offers six steak knives with his economic blather. Like some TV marketing operator, he is offering payment in small instalments over a long-time frame; $3 billion and after ten years who is going to remember what it was for and how the accountability was supposed to occur. (We can't even remember what over the $600,000 expenses special drought envoy got us.) You can bet the warranty runs out the day before things go to pot. Put him in a white lab coat and he can sell you anything and have you believe that the Ponds Institute has real merit and standing. What he can't do anymore is tell the truth from the fiction. He is so used to lying that there is confusion about what is real. He disparages the science. He fabricates his own data but does it in a very convincing way. However, he needs to be called out by journalists, scientists, whistle-blowers, the opposition and fact checkers. He has played fast and loose with the truth and with the Australian electorate. Somehow, we need some Austin Powers person to take down this mini-me Trump so that the public can see what snake oil he is really marketing.

I thought that the Tory party when they elected Boris were pro-rogue. Now it seems that proroguing parliament will cost many of them dearly.

It may be that Gladys Liu will continue on like the Black Knight in Monty Python and the Holy Grail, although that comment may be seen as racist in itself if it is twisted the way Morrison is doing with his sham rebuttal of any questioning of her credibility. Just because she is Chinese Australian doesn't mean that she gets a free pass to have her links unquestioned. In a time when Australians are begging for honest politicians, why cover up the truth with a veneer of faux smear? Even 'quiet Australians' need transparency. to be shown by the people they elect. Real time donation registering, proper detailing of candidates' affiliations and a thorough background check should be made public so that electors can choose the best person for the job. It seems that Centrelink demands more information from welfare recipients than we are allowed to ask for from our politicians. No wonder honest politician is an oxymoron.

Morrison has become a lapdog of Trump, echoing the mindless thoughts of his new "bestie". Australia is in an invidious position regarding China. If it is all about the economy, why poke the panda? Particularly Morrison's attacks on Chinese emissions and the trade imbalance. Closer diplomatic relations with our major trading party won't be helped by Morrison deriding them in public. If he wants China to move towards better emissions then perhaps, he needs to try behind closed doors diplomacy. Now he has put Australian trade at risk at a time when we are relying on the good will of China to bring in the much-vaunted surplus. Trump has basically invited Scomo to be in his gang and on behalf of Australia, Morrison has agreed. So much for independent thinking. He is so out of touch with climate change issues and as much out of his depth in international politics as Harold Holt was when he said, "All the way with LBJ". To quote Forrest Gump's mum, "Stupid is as stupid does."

Strange bedfellows that Morrison has. He receives praise alternately from Xi Jinping and also Trump. Perhaps the whole US China trade war is solely a bizarre love triangle with Scott Morrison being wooed by the other two. Scott may have to choose between the two and I hope he has the wisdom of Solomon. How will the spurned one take it? Will Xi Jinping see it as a (land) bridge too far? Will Trump call Scott "nasty" and build a wall on the west coast of the US? If only Shakespeare were alive and writing today. It could be a cross between many of his plays: Romeo and Juliet, Henry V, Hamlet, Macbeth. But we normal folk would really see it as a bad Midsummer's Nightmare. "The course of true love never did run smooth." "Lovers and madmen have such seething brains"

October

- Climbing Uluru is banned
- Royal Commission into Aged Care Quality and Safety interim report is published
- After the withdrawal of US troops, President Erdoğan[1] of Turkey[2] announces a military invasion of north-eastern Syria, targeting Kurdish militias
- Typhoon Hagibis makes landfall in Japan, the biggest storm to hit the region in decades, with over seven million people urged to evacuate
- An estimated one million people march through London to demand a second referendum on Brexit
- U.S. President Donald Trump announces that the leader of the ISIS Abu Bakr al-Baghdadi, was killed in a U.S. special forces operation
- Heavy rain and flooding leave 32 dead and 230,000 people homeless in Somalia and Kenya.

We have allowed governing to become all about the economy. It never used to be that way. It used to have social elements to it. It used to be a way of improving society for all. Now it is all about money and greed. Greta Thunberg shone a light on it with her climate action speech. We have the finance and mental capacity to solve many of the world's major problems such as climate change, poverty, disease, racism etc but not the willpower to put the good of society above the economy. It seems that we need to amend the constitution to add a chapter that explains the purpose of government............ e.g. the purpose of government is to maintain and improve the Australian society for the betterment of everyone. No one person

---

1. https://en.wikipedia.org/wiki/Recep_Tayyip_Erdo%C4%9Fan

2. https://en.wikipedia.org/wiki/Turkey

or one group is to be seen to be better than any other. The aim is to produce a cohesive society that works towards the common good etc.

In a classroom on a planet in a distant galaxy, a teacher had students studying another planet. It was found that the dominant creatures needed water to survive, but would pour toxic chemicals into it. They also needed oxygen to breathe, but polluted the air with fumes and also tore down forests that would have cleaned the air. They needed sustainable food sources, but their actions on the environment changed weather patterns and ruined vast areas of productive land. The teacher asked the students to assess the intellect of the creatures and was unsurprised when the creatures were seen as low functioning beings. One student however pointed out that the creatures had developed explosive devices that would allow them to blow up their own planet many times over. After some discussion, it was agreed that being able to destroy one's habitat, either slowly or quickly, was not a sign that these two-legged upright standing creatures on that blue planet showed signs of intelligence.

Two cockroaches were quietly chatting when one asked, "How was it that mankind was seen as the superior being on this planet?"

"Were they really that superior? They changed the climate to make the planet slowly uninhabitable for their own kind," came the reply.

"They elected a madman to sit in the White House who picked fights with North Korea, China and countries in the Middle East," the first responded.

"Cleverness and humans don't go together. Even their pesticides, we became used to," the second pointed out.

"They were also the ones who pronounced that only three things would survive a nuclear holocaust," the other replied.

They looked around at the desolation of what was once the great and bountiful planet Earth.

"Yes, but what the hell are we going to do with all this Laminex and Tupperware?"

Labor's self-examination to the tune of the Gambler by Kenny Rogers

They study mind reading, and crystal ball gazing
They play with tarot cards, and are good with tea leaves
They foretell the future, by using necromancy
And there's palms and star signs, that they choose to read
They seem to tell everything, by who holds all the aces,
And knowin' what's in their minds, by the way they hold their eyes.

I hear they check entrails, for affirming traces
And use a Ouija Board, to add more insight
When you hear they're all knowing, your mind goes slowly hollow
And you wonder where they got their, mystic second sight
They've used clairvoyance, and come to a decision
Some say Bill's to blame, and maybe they are right
Policies have been sold out, because of what's unfolded
Policies are a blank canvas, while people rage and vent
Labor may wither away, caused by too much harping
All this self-examination, ain't worth the time that's spent

Shooting the messenger is a sport that has become the favourite of our politicians and those overseas. Trump is a master and we have been following suit. Democracy is about the right to speak freely on issues. It is not about shutting down the voices that politicians disagree with. We can protest about the treatment of asylum seekers. We can protest about our involvement in wars. And we can certainly protest about the direction our government is taking on climate change. Fake news, distraction and shutting down conversations are the signs of a totalitarian government. Perhaps we should protest about the direction that our government is taking us to. We don't need an authoritarian government. We need one that will address the concerns of the population and will engage with the public. Taking welfare off those who protest, naming and shaming them, then isolating them are the tools that were used in Germany in the thirties and forties and Italy in the twenties, thirties and forties. We are seeing this sort of malignant disease spreading again. Perhaps Australia will not be caught up in the pandemic but even the mildest symptoms can destroy the sort of democracy we had.

I am concerned about the Canberra bubble. It should be inspected by Workcover as the fetid air inside the bubble appears to be starving politicians' brains of much needed oxygen. They sound so plausible with their arguments prior to elections and once they get to Canberra, they change their minds and show no logical reasoning at all. This may be just circumstantial of course and they just could be lying to us in election periods.............

Politicians sipping tea in the dining hall. Sipping tea? Immortality is just immorality with T.

Has the government announced a review of the reviews it has started and will it shelve that one's report just like it has shelved nearly all of the other reports? The government is seen to be doing something if it announces an inquiry. That's how this government works...... by being seen to be busy. The fact that it might actually get something done is an accidental by-product and a statistical anomaly.

"The bells are ringing for the beginning of the parliament session.

This is what doom sounds like." Perhaps there should be other ways of calling parliamentarians to the chambers. I can think of some very good movie themes such as Jaws, Darth Vader's theme from Starwars etc but the one the most appropriate is the Monty Python theme.

It has been said that there is too much polyticks in Canberra and one cannot disagree when "poly" means many; and "ticks" are small minded parasitic creatures.

The government may be floundering but what the L! It is foundering and in the annals of history it will sink without a trace.

The Coalition had effectively tied up the education fund not allowing any of it to be spent where it is much needed and Labor has decided that the money should be in circulation in some form. It is going towards drought relief and so will serve fewer people. I can understand why Lambie and Plibersek are exasperated. They obviously believe that one should stand on principles. Labor caving in has shown it is quickly throwing theirs out. The Coalition may have had some once.

There are times when I despair about the lack of leadership in Australia and the rest of the time, I go beyond that. Apparently being in government is all about getting in and staying in power and nothing to do with policies and what is best for the country. This has been the case since the Gillard years. Populist governments are do-nothing and bland. We have a PM who can't articulate a policy without prefacing it with what Labor did almost seven years ago. He is beige in a baseball cap. Hot air coming out in gusts with a guttural shout and with nothing of any substance behind it. To paraphrase the great VFL/AFL coach, John Kennedy's famous half time speech, "Do. Don't think, Morrison, don't hope. Do. At least you can say, 'I did this, I tried, I made a decision. At least I did something for the sake of Australia. Do. Act. Don't think, act. Eye on the ball. The contest is still the same. You must know what you are doing to win over the people. And more than that, when you lead you must cooperate with those around you. And you must be desperate enough to stick at it. The opposition might laugh. It might go wrong. Are you game enough to try? Are you game enough, Scotty?"

Parliament seems devoid of leadership, both in the government and in the opposition. This turns the public off even further. Policies don't exist; therefore, they are not talked about. 45 days this year the parliament will actually sit, so people have little to go on except the sound bites that are on the news. Whoever can create the most spin, steal the most limelight and be seen for what they pretend to be, grabs our attention. Charisma seems to have been sucked out of everyone who enters the place. We leap from one crisis to the next with no forethought and even afterthought. Morrison is overseas seeking to strut the stage with the big boys and girls. You can guarantee he will make announcements over there because he will come under less scrutiny here; not that he can be pinned down on anything here. Weasel words, obfuscation and distraction are his shtick and really all he has. Parliament should attract our best and brightest yet from what we see it attracts just pests and lightest. We laud our democracy but we certainly don't applaud it these days.

Every fourth word ... redacted by the .... government. We should .... back and give .... a taste of .... own medicine. election time by .... out every fourth ...... of the Coalition.

Any self-respecting totalitarian government would be totally remiss if they didn't control the media and what the population got to hear, see and read about. It is a case of "What they don't know won't hurt us". There is a thin veneer that they have spread over the whole media to make it look like there is freedom of the press. What we actually need is freedom of the oppressed.

Journalists used to report the news, now a lot of what we read is opinion and conjecture. Is this because the government is regulating to remove transparency or because it is easier and cheaper for media companies to employ fewer people to trawl through the data that is available? It helps the government hide more things if opinion pieces are written so that only contributes to the secrecy. Governments who claim to be open are often the ones who are the most closed to scrutiny. A simple stamp of secrecy and redaction of documents along with the lengthy FOI process makes one wonder whether the fourth estate has any potency anymore. We are supposed to live in a democracy where people have a right to know what the government is doing on their behalf and where the money goes. Each day our freedoms are chipped away. The press should tell us what is being held back from scrutiny and the government should be continually challenged as to why. Don't write based on conjecture, write based on fact. If the facts are missing, say so. Tell us what the government is hiding or lying about.

The government is calling documents privileged, is delaying FOI requests and not answering questions by the media and in question time. Does that make them arrogant or unanswerable? The first is a huge concern. The second smacks of a dictatorship.

It would be wonderful if the Senate held those Ministers and public servants who didn't properly answer questions in Senate Estimates, in contempt rather than just admonish them. Heads of Departments and government ministers think that they are above the law and prosecution. Better to make an example of a few of them rather than let them ride rough shod over our democracy.

A lot of this argy bargy between Hanson, the Nats, Morrison, John Laws and Alan Jones is all about the glory seeking, be they politicians or the radio announcers. It is more important that the job gets done. Give us some quiet hard-working people in the media and in parliament who actually achieve something with their day. They get paid heaps to it seems achieve nothing substantial. What a waste of money. What a waste of time. What a waste of space. There should be a sign at all media doors and the doors to Parliament House which reads "Get down off your high horses. Park your wheelbarrows outside. Leave your egos in the cloakroom. This is a place of work not self-worship."

Strangely it isn't all about the economy. Government is about people. The economy is a tool to manage to get the best outcomes for the people. Governments lose sight of that. Human services, health and education should be the main action plans for governments followed by defence and infrastructure. The treasurer should not have such a high profile and dictate what policies are. His/her task is to ensure that money can be raised to support the policies. Morrison took very few policies in human services, health and education to the election. All he had was the economy and a promise of a surplus. Now it seems he may fluke a surplus based on the mining sector but then have to spend it on the issues caused by the extreme drought caused by climate change. He will be just shuffling the money around to be seen to be doing something. Morrison is a 'look busy but achieve nothing' PM.

Amazing how much Labor can stand out as a progressive party when it starts to look forward rather than inward. The Coalition would have us recast to the sixties, which would be good only because I was younger, fitter and had more hair then. It is time to take some of the main players down too. Morrison for example has been able to get away with too many things Labor should start showing him up to be the hollow man he is.

Time to really hold Ministers to account especially the PM. Seriously ask questions in parliament and question them outside of parliament. A yes/no question is useless. It is a political waste of time. Senate estimates questioning is so much better than House of Reps Question Time. Ministers get better questions on Q & A ad are more uncomfortable. The smarmy point scoring in Question Time won't win over the public. Make it real and not some schoolboy gotcha moment.

If we had to cast our parliamentarians as people in the Harry Potter series, I am thinking Morrison would have to be the very thin veneered seeking attention Gilderoy Lockhart rather than

Voldemort as there's not enough of a strong character in the Coalition to play him except Dutton and I wouldn't want him to have star billing. Can't see Albo as Harry though and saving the day. Perhaps Albo is more a Seamus Finnegan. Penny Wong would be easily cast as Minerva McGonagall, Kristina Keneally may be a good fit for Hermione Granger. Maybe Hunt and Frydenberg as Crab and Goyle to Joyce's Draco. Michael McCormack is nearly headless Nick who is very transparent, says nothing of interest and is very transparent. Any suggestions for the others?

Do we have to get to negative interest rates before the government acts to stimulate the economy? People will not leave their money in accounts if it gets too low. They may decide to buy things and as such more money may flow around the community. The sad things though are that:

People will have money tied up in investments especially housing and will probably reinvest in the housing market as it may make gains. This will further disenfranchise young home owners.

People will invest in overseas markets and stocks and not Australian ones.

The Morrison government should forget the surplus and invest in infrastructure to create more employment and thus more spending by the general public. The ones who will spend it more readily are not the affluent who are getting a substantial tax cut, but those who are struggling. A raise in Newstart would be a marvellous stimulus. Changing the deeming rates to match the actual interest rates would also free up money as those in retirement are now hoarding cash reserves to try to pay an unfair impost. Those in retirement are also reluctant to spend because their own investments have taken a hit as the interest rate has dropped. The government seems to be in a state of narcolepsy. Perhaps it should itself be deemed dead, then buried after being cremated.

The government is trying to add some stimulus to the economy through infrastructure building. The latest is to have a rail tunnel from Melbourne CBD to the airport. A really good notion except they want a private company to do it and run it afterwards. Victoria would be signing away its rights to its railway and could easily be held to ransom by the private company. Why should a state or for that matter a government outsource funding and infrastructure when borrowing costs are so low? It isn't logical unless someone is getting a kick back somewhere.

The government thinks that we can mine our way out of recession. Mining is a primary industry that has a limited supply of raw material. the mining companies are making the money and quite rightly are using whatever tax loopholes they can to ensure they give back very little. Mining is not all that valuable as an income stream long term. We lose so much of what we own and get a pittance in return. The fact that the government spruiks how much we get back indicates just how much is leaving our shores as raw material and money for overseas shareholders. Not sure that our economic managers understand the true situation.

A surplus has taken on a God-like quality. It is chanted by the happy clappers of the Liberal party and everything else is seen as paganism. The idea that people must suffer for the sins of this almost religious belief seems unchristian. The poor, the disabled, the unemployed, those most desperately in need of some charitable assistance are cast aside by those who would chant the mantra 'surplus' as if they had no other understanding of the world. These zealots have created their own cult with little understanding of the realities of the world and what impact their fanaticism has on others. It is an uneducated, ill-informed and dangerous pontification they are preaching and our PM is at the pulpit crying fire and brimstone will befall all those who don't believe in what he is saying. Australia is being crucified by such dogmatism. Come election time however those who practise this doctrine may find that what they sow they shall also reap. Amen to that!

If we need to be back in surplus to make our economy work better, there are a few solutions

1. Tax us more

2. Spend the money more prudently

3. Cut back on the social support which is the reason why we need taxes anyway

4. Cut back the profligate spending by people in government

5. Stop supporting businesses that aren't profitable. (This was done to the car industry but not so with agriculture and horticulture

6. Stop pork barrelling

7. Collect the taxes on incomes that are earned by big business in Australia

8. Choose policies that will benefit all Australians, not just one ideological bent.

The only way that we can rescue the economy is to use it strategically. That's what big business does. That's what banks do. They buy a government with donations, lobbying and advertising. Scruples get replaced with lies and deceit. Clive Palmer and Rupert Murdoch are just more open about it. The behind the scenes lobbying takes place and the public isn't aware of it. Businesses don't give money away without getting something in return. Public companies would be remiss if they didn't do anything and everything to make a profit for their shareholders. So, unless the general public don't buy their democracy back, things will continue as is. People come election time are bombarded with slanted truths and think that their vote won't mean much. It is worth so much and perhaps it is time that they stood together and lobbied on their own behalf.

We are told to blame our fall from economic grace on overseas issues, global downturns, China and the drought. We have elected a government who promised to deliver on the economy. There were no caveats, no exculpatory clauses just a promise that they knew what they were doing. More fools us for believing them I suppose because we have a downturn in our economy, rising actual unemployment and underemployment, poor wage growth and a welfare system that is bearing the brunt of this government's mismanagement of the economy. Instead of finding excuses, the Coalition should just do what they promised. If it means going against their entrenched ideological principles, then so be it. A surplus means that even more money is being taken out of the economy. It would be far better to raise Newstart because those on it are the people who will spend it rather than store it away in non-stimulating investments such as property. When money flows around then small business survives and employs more people who may be able to get off Newstart. Simple economics 101. The action by the Gillard government during the GFC is proof that a stimulus works. We didn't bottom out like many economies. We are now tumbling down the world rankings on economics because creating a surplus is the only game in town. Ideology wins over practicality and everyday Australians are the losers.

The only signs of inflation that the public are seeing are in the size of the Canberra bubble and in the egos of the Coalition who want us to believe that they are the best economic managers. Their 'levers' are to hit those who are the most vulnerable in our society, give tax breaks to big businesses in the hope they will reinvest and not say thank you very much and take the money offshore, and to protect the surplus which they see as the shining light. That shining light is an oncoming train that will plunder through our stagnant economy which has been propped up with false projections surrounded by smoke and mirrors. If the

government could just effectively market deceit to the world, our burgeoning debt would be wiped out overnight.

Morrison and Dutton have decided that global warming is good for the country. Rising sea levels will further geographically isolate Australia and our "moat", in which we are girt, will be much wider. Less chance of people coming by boat they think or more potential for them to drown at sea, maybe. What they don't realise is that we will become the favoured destination of climate refugees whose Pacific and Indian Ocean island homes are lost.

The life of mankind and indeed the life of the Earth itself doesn't even amount to a grain of sand in the hourglass that records the course of the universe's history. I wonder somewhere within a galaxy in the future, some knowledge will be passed on between generations about a far less intelligent life-form that, despite knowing the consequences, decided to do nothing about its own wilful destruction of its own planet.

The continual exporting of coal and the refusal to do anything substantial to mitigate climate change will see at least one job lost......... The PM's!!

Climate science......???? That's climate silence if you are a Coalition supporter. It's only one little letter you change and that's a simple thing to do. Simple things for simple minds.

Greta Thunberg has just turned down an environment award. She said, "The climate movement does not need any more awards. What we need is for our politicians and the people in power start to listen to the current, best available science."

In this parody of The Living Years by Mike & the Mechanics, I echo her sentiments.

Every politician
Blames who came before
With all their indecision
The can's kicked down the road some more

They don't do what they promised
It soon becomes quite clear
So, the country's held hostage
To blind eyes and deaf ears
I wish that they'd do something in their elected years
They shuffle lots of paper
Once the election has been won
It fills us with frustration
As nothing ever gets done
So, we don't believe them
As they shout in parliament
They don't seek agreement
But they still call it government
They speak a different language
And they make no sense
Do something now (yes right now!), not next year (oh not next year)
Climate change is something to fear
So, don't wait (so don't wait) The nation's dry (oh the nation's dry)
Denial will just see the world die

The drought is Labor's fault. Why don't they just come out and say it! Moral cowards, that's what the Coalition are. However, on a more serious note, why are the Coalition not being held accountable in the parliament and in the media for what is happening now? They are in their seventh year of power and allowed to get away with denying anything bad is caused by their management. Where does the buck stop? The opposition can't enact anything in reality, so why are the opposition asked what they would do? With great power comes great responsibility. With the Coalition accepting little or no responsibility that indicates they are powerless. Such stagnation on their part is what is heading the country towards recession.

The Minister says that the government responds to drought. That is a cause and affect scenario. There is little being done to change the antiquated use of the land. Massive clearing is taking place which stops moisture being retained in the soil and the soil gets blown away to boot. We are growing the wrong crops. Eternally thirsty ones such as cotton.... why? If David Littleproud doesn't want the next generation scared off agriculture, he'd be better off providing money for people to change crops and farming techniques to ones that are actually sustainable and suitable for the current and future climates.

I think that Morrison has just said that he will save Albanese's offer of help with the drought, for a rainy day.

Albanese is hoping that Scott Morrison will look at the drought offer from Labor and will change horses midstream. Sorry, Albo the stream's dry. You are up a certain creek without a paddle and water. It has all been syphoned off to cotton farms and to dams whose ownership can be traced to various politicians.

All those cotton farms still have huge amounts of water syphoned off from rivers before those downstream could even get a small trickle of it. What are they doing? Saving it for a rainy day?

What did our drought envoy achieve? Our resources minister justifies land clearing. Our politicians accede to the demands of large landholders who use massive amounts of water for unsustainable crops. The water buy back scheme has become a farce and profiteers have moved in.

The following is to the tune of Fire and Rain by James Taylor.
You know every morning, there is nothing but sun
God damn, not a cloud on the horizon too.
Despite all our efforts, all our feed has now gone
And the politicians say there's nothing they can do
We're in drought, years with no rain.

Upstream the water's been syphoned off again
And photo ops with pollies won't break that trend
It's about time the Nats were on our side again
I'd like to give them the Bejesus, they've forgotten us on the land
Their mates have stockpiled the water for a rainy day
It's now we need it, but they don't understand.
Cotton farming companies have won the day
We're in drought, years with no rain.
Upstream the water's been syphoned off again
And photo ops with pollies won't break that trend
It's about time the Nats were on our side again
Land clearing all the time is such a crime,
It leaves the ground baking in the sun
God knows when the hot wind blows,
There's no soil left on the ground

Labor lost the last election. Statement of fact. It was not a rout however. The Coalition have a slim majority. The baby doesn't need to follow the bath water down the gurgler. Expectations were raised so high for a landslide Labor victory that people have decided that everything needs revamping. Take out the Clive Palmer millions of dollars in advertising. Take out the character assassination of Bill Shorten and you might have had a closer and more positive result for Labor. The settings were not wrong except may be franking credits should have been let go until Labor was in power. There is a danger that the public will not even know by the next election what Labor stands for anymore. It seems that the MP's don't know. It was a poorly run campaign that exposed Labor to too many attacks on too many fronts. Morrison's was far better. It was all about the economy and his personality. That was all he had. The selling of those two things and the denigrating of Labor on so many fronts was the cause of the election loss for Labor. Lies and deceit in election

campaigns will win the day. The election strategy by Labor and the analysts who misread the mood of electorates are to blame. The vast majority of policies were accepted. If they weren't, then there would have been a landslide against Labor.

Whitewashing history is all to do with winning. You win, you can rewrite history as you see it. It takes a lot of gall, a lot of balls, a stubbornness and determination that is ongoing, and a disregard for the truth and the people who elected you in the first place. The Libs fit the model. What GFC? It never happened. Labor came in and frittered away all the money that Howard and Costello had saved. One wonders whether if Labor wins the next election, they will say there was never a drought in the same way that many in the coalition decry the thought of man-made climate change. Who can the general public trust? There are so many truths out there. In a certain country in the 30's and 40's starting with G, truths were lies but the propaganda machine informed the population there that everyone was against them. The press was shut down and so was any dissension. The public were fed just one story. Any opposition was not countenanced, eventually in the most serious of ways. How far in Australia are we from that. Morrison's "on-waters" way of avoiding the truth has progressed to "Canberra bubble" and outright deception. Only when the media, the opposition and the public call the Coalition on it like they are doing with Angus Taylor, will there be a chance that the winners at the last election will seen to be the losers they really are.

That Banking Royal Commission has shown us one thing only and that is just how much pain a wet lettuce can cause. Business as usual for the banks as they refuse to pass on the full interest rate cut. Big business is running the government and the economy. Canberra is just a sham.

The ones investigated by the Royal Commission will always make huge profits in their four-way cartel. You can bank on that!!!

Ever noticed that the warranty on election promises runs out as soon as the election is over?

I wonder if the government intends to make Newstart people wait three months before being able to claim, then will it apply to farmers? Will Robodebt also apply to farmers? Makes you wonder who are the second and third-class citizens in our country.

So, to all the people who are unemployed, underemployed and struggling because of lack of wage growth, is it right just to point at a graph and say that we are doing well? In their bank accounts, in their wallets and in their fridges and cupboards they do not see how well they are supposed to be doing. If the graphs and data say that we are doing well, then a certain select group must be doing excessively well because a far greater number are slipping backwards.

I'm not sure what conflating means when Cormann uses it. I know condescending is when a person named Con goes down in a lift. I know that if Mr Foot was an optometrist and my podiatrist was called Iris, that would be a pair o' docs (paradox) but what is conflating? Is that when Con pumps up his own ego? Wouldn't it be more appropriate to say Mathias was Cormannflating then?

Is it just me or is it that Pauline Hansen's mouth and brain are getting further and further out of synch?

We have a minister for drought? An envoy obviously wasn't up to the task.

Given Lambie's rollover recently and her bragging about the improvement in Tasmania's housing crisis, we all know that she can be bought. That her vote is for sale is an abhorrence to democracy but not unexpected. It seems every politician has a price. Honesty and integrity are tradeable and disappearing commodities in those that we elect to represent us. Just what Lambie's going rate is, will be only understood after the deal is done and we are floating down the river which we have been sold.

The word lie according to Morrison doesn't apply to him and even if it did, according to his religion, a venial sin is a lesser sin that does not result in a complete separation from God and eternal damnation in Hell as an unrepented mortal sin would. Maybe he misheard, misspoke, circumstances changed, was wrongly quoted, was in the Canberra bubble or was taken out of context. He is very careful with the truth. That is why pre-election, his policies were so narrow and thus we find that what we have been gifted post-election wasn't what we thought we were getting. Policies to win an election don't need to be followed after an election. They are merely sales-speak. Morrison played fast and loose with the truth when it came to Labor's policies, appealed to the hip-pocket nerve of electors and did one of the best character assassinations seen in Australian politics. His own policies were scant and he relied us to trust him about what he would do post-election. We gave him carte blanche to do as he liked. We may complain that the big end of town is getting the goodies. We may wonder why the tax benefits for the poor are not forthcoming. Those in retirement may wonder why despite the franking credits being saved, they are worse off. However, it is not Morrison's fault. We elected him and his cronies based on what we were led to believe. How stupid are we?

Morrison is out of his depth in foreign diplomatic relations. His siding with Trump over China is a sad indictment of this. His supposed assistance withe Mueller report interference is yet another. He stands in awe of Trump and is digging himself a hole which will make Trump look even more almighty. Sadly, that hole is full of excrement that Morrison can't see or even smell. We do not need to be the laughing stock of the world, let Trump have that on his own. We do not need to be drawn into American politics nor 'back a winner'. That is just bad diplomacy and could come back and bite us in the posterior. This is what happens when we appoint ex politicians as ambassadors. They are

often ill-equipped for the role, have a slanted view of politics and do not give clear and well thought out diplomatic responses and advice to the government. We have trained, independent people in the diplomatic cops whose opinions are being over-ridden by show ponies.

Morrison from the very beginning of his tilt at the leadership has shown the same Machiavellian approach based on one consistent mode of operating - distraction. When he put his arm around Malcolm Turnbull, it was to distract him. It made Morrison seem to be wearing the white hat and made out Dutton to be the baddie. Then in an instant the knife was plunged into Turnbull by Dutton and then Dutton by Morrison. What was his first act as Prime Minister? Was it to solve the economic woes? Address climate change? Resolve issues about detention of asylum seekers and unite the country? No, he chose a distraction. He took on the strawberry problem caused by a disgruntled employee and passed laws that were probably covered by others, both at federal and state levels. When it came to the election, did he offer a swathe of policies for the betterment of everyone in Australia. No, he distracted us with character assassinations of his opponent and gave us the notion that Bill Shorten was worse than "Scott Who?". Now as the economy tanks, he has done it again and he has ventured into foreign policy, denigrating concerns of our islander neighbours, sidling up to Trump and offending China. He is telling the world how it should be run and absolving Australia (and his government) of any blame for what is happening politically, economically and environmentally. In yachting terms, he is too busy tacking to make any forward progress.

Angus Taylor has got a heap of questions to answer on a number of issues but so far has gone relatively unchallenged. He rarely gets tested and is able to let things go through to the keeper. So much so in fact, he could even be selected for the Australian test team. A recent review of his past nine months

shows that he is known to be a top spinner and aggressive in delivery. Won't admit to a "wrong 'un". When not bowling, likes to be in the game and often opts for a silly point position. As a batsman he is a flat track bully and prefers a drop-in pitch rather than a natural one. He always has an eye on cow corner, as he is a bit agricultural in outlook. Known for the occasional ill-informed sledging too, so that could be a weakness to exploit.

One Australia sank without a trace off San Diego in California. As people look back in years to come, they will probably not even reflect on One Morrison suffering the same fate.

I wonder if Scott Morrison's mentor/pastor accidentally misquoted Romans 6:23 and said that the wages of spin is death, perhaps Scott might actually answer questions properly without obfuscation or changing the topic.

Morrison has raised the spectre of chaos (Kaos?) in the Opposition. When it comes to actually answering questions from the Opposition, the media and the public, he insists on the cone of silence.

If Morrison claims to represent the quiet Australians, why does he shout so much?

It is about time that Angus Taylor admits that meeting the Paris commitments in a canter refers to the gait of Chautauqua. Stuck in the Kyoto barriers and refusing to move.

"Great beef barbecue at parliament today, supporting Australian primary producers and the tasty Angus beef we get to enjoy!" Well I have a beef with Angus but it is about water scams and clearing of land!

It seems that Angus Taylor's response to helping prevent the impacts of drought is to clear away all those pesky native plants that may use up valuable water.

Angus Taylor, how black is the pot you are in? I assume that you do not travel by air to conferences, political ones. Put down

that stone back on the pile and look at your own sins. Reflect on the native grass clearing, the selling of coal overseas, the sidling up to mining companies, the syphoning off of water by profiteers. You are certainly not one of Morrison's quiet Australians and definitely not a quiet achiever; neither quiet or achieving much. Get on with your job, which I'm sure doesn't have in it a descriptor about denigrating others.

At their meeting at the White House, Trump was probably asking Morrison how to deal with whistle-blowers. Obviously, he has heard about the East Timor bugging where the crime that was committed by Australian spies was taken to the world court and Australia lost. However, through clever politics the whistle-blower and his lawyer are the ones who now face massive criminal charges and are seen as the villains of the piece. Politicians have been able to sweep under the carpet an international crime by seeking to punish those who exposed it. Morrison is the man, Trump thinks, who may have the answers to his own current problem.

November

- Three people are killed and 150 homes are destroyed by a large number of bushfires burning across New South Wales and South East Queensland
- The United States formally begins process to pull out of the Paris Agreement on climate change.
- 11,000 scientists from around the world publish a study in the journal BioScience, warning "clearly and unequivocally that planet Earth is facing a climate emergency".
- Air pollution in parts of India hit record levels.
- Israeli Prime Minister Benjamin Netanyahu is indicted on charges of bribery, fraud and breach of trust
- The World Meteorological Organization reports that levels of heat-trapping greenhouse gases in the atmosphere have reached another new record high of 407.8 parts per million, with "no sign of a slowdown, let alone a decline."

What does Donald Trump think about climate change? Too many letters in it for tweeting purposes.

"Suicide, aged care............ they are social issues! We are not a socialist party. We are the Liberal Party where it's every man (not woman) for himself. We cut red tape. We let the market dictate. We do not have a social agenda. We don't and won't have those communist leftie discussions let alone actions such as caring for the elderly and those with mental health issues in our party. The strong must prevail!"

It will be Labor's fault that very little has happened, despite the fact that they haven't been in power since 2013. The aged care inadequacies and the rise in mental health issues are nothing to do with this government because they have done nothing whilst in office. That will be their argument. They have done nothing wrong. It must have been the other lot. Choosing to do nothing is

an act in itself. More importantly it wastes time; time that could have been better spent fixing issues, not creating smokescreens and holding yet another review. Where is the accountability? If a government lets things slide, they are responsible or in this case irresponsible. How many people could have had better treatment for their mental health during the period of the Coalition government? How many people could have lived a dignified life in an aged care facility in that time? It seems that the Coalition's policy is to outsource what should be done by them and in doing so outsource their responsibility too.

The middle ground is getting quite crowded. This causes stagnation of ideas. Luckily Morrison is moving further to the right as is his wont and this may give Albanese some breathing space. Who will take "the quiet Australians with them is another matter? The only chance it seems to have some progressiveness in Australian politics is for someone to gain power and then head down a path afterwards. Labor tried the progressive politics at the last election, promising things that made a lot of sense and offered a vision, but politically was very naive. First gain power and then lead. You can't lead from behind. Labor may learn a lot from the last election loss. Hopefully the baby isn't going down the gurgler chasing the bathwater. It needs to re-establish its identity, market its brand and when it comes around to the next election, not do politically dumb things. I have a feeling however that the last thing is beyond them.

Okay the fossicking through the entrails is over. Labor needs to draw a line in the sand and move quickly on lest the line become a chasm and they fall headlong in it. Labor needs to revisit a number of policies, not rewrite them all. It stood for something a while ago and was elected to power in the seventies with Gough, in the eighties with Hawke and in the zeroes with Rudd because people could see that it wasn't wishy washy and just a pale imitation of the Coalition. Stop looking in the mirror, stop

talking among yourselves. Meet with the electorate, look them in the eye, listen to them and then talk about what you will do. The clock is ticking almost as fast as the national debt is rising.

If Labor is to walk two sides of the street, have a foot in both camps, straddle the fence or whatever other analogy it is to be called, then it will have more issues than just splinters in its posterior. No-one will know what it really stands for. It will have chameleon like qualities and be so well camouflaged that it will be indistinguishable from other parties. Labor was essentially on the right track but played pathetic politics at that last election. If it gets drawn into seeking the populist way of gaining votes it will lose another election. Cormann was right with "vibble vobble" but not jelly, more like blancmange. By trying to wear two faces, one for Queensland and its mines, the other for the southern states and its environmental concerns, it came across as schizophrenic and no-one knew what it stood for. The public are looking for leadership and someone they can believe in like Whitlam and Hawke who were known commodities. Even Howard was eventually. Until a strong leader emerges, Labor will remain in the wilderness, plucking the lint from its own belly button again and again. Kristina Keneally and Penny Wong are stuck in the Senate but they are far more presentable options to lead Labor unless Albanese can extract the digit and really outline what Labor actually stands for. It is so hard to do that when you're stuck on the fence.

'thoughts and prayers' from politicians aren't useful. A genuine thought among them is as rare as rocking horse poo. As for their prayers, not sure that hypocrites' prayers are worth much.

The so-called advocates of free speech, the Andrew Bolts and Alan Jones of this world should be out on their soapboxes with what Scott Morrison and Michael McCormack have been pedalling. Morrison wants more quiet Australians who won't speak up and he seems to want to pass laws to achieve this. McCormack wants to howl down the Greens but in doing so he is also criticising his own constituents as farmers are beginning to speak up strongly on climate issues. Brush in hand McCormack is painting himself into a corner and hasn't realised it yet. We have a right in this country to believe what we believe and despite not having a bill of rights, we can generally say what we want to say. The Coalition appear to want us merely to say what they believe.

We believe ourselves to be the most educated, most self-aware and most technically superior creatures to have walked this earth. In comparison to previous generations, cultures and societies, we believe that those alive today are so far more advanced than any others. Isn't it strange then that we are still waging war on each other, are creating huge gulfs between rich and poor, and are destroying our own environment far quicker than at any other time in mankind's history? Intelligence and wisdom are two different things. We expect our politicians to be intelligent and they prove us wrong. As for them having wisdom, that was always a forlorn hope.

God visited ten plagues on Egypt according to the Bible. First came the blood. After that it was frogs, lice, wild beasts, pestilence, skin disease, hail, locusts, darkness and the slaying of the first born. We should be grateful that we just have a plague of unlistening, ideologically fixated, science ignoring, pontificating politicians. However, the country will be destroyed just the same.

Parties that appeal to the hip-pocket rather than doing what is right have forever been part of this archaic political system we have. Electors are bought off with promises and many of those promises are never realised, but we don't learn from our mistakes. It is to do with our gullibility and the type of media and advertising we are exposed to. The electoral commission should be empowered to remove ads, media reports and internet posts

that are flagrant lies. There should also be a set standard of a prospectus that parties should send to the public. Costings, policies etc should be set out in an easy to read form that enables proper comparison between parties. The prospectus becomes a binding contract with the electorate once the party is elected. Thus, we would have a warranty and faulty goods would mean another election. If such rigidity was put into the system then watch how carefully parties would advertise, set policies and do costings.

What is the difference between opaque and transparent? The answer is: one will win an election and one will lose an election. To their moral credit, Labor tried to be transparent, publishing detailed policies and costings so that people could see what was on offer. The Coalition, to our eternal damnation, chose to be opaque and we were unable to ascertain just what was on offer. Capitol Hill in Canberra is not the moral highground. Labor should have realised that. The Coalition prove it every day and their actions on climate change are just a very good example of opacity.

How does the Canberra bubble stay so full of hot air with so many pricks in it?

Can we impeach the government or at least get the ACCC to investigate them for false and misleading statements?

Sometimes politicians should remember that just because a microphone is placed in front of them, it is not a command that they have to speak. Indeed, vitriol can be done with body language, eyes and by what is not said. Then it doesn't get printed, doesn't become a sound bite and you can't be misquoted. Politicians need a proper synchromesh between brain and mouth because for many there is a distinct grinding of gears in some which produces a raucous sound and a lack of forward momentum.

The issue that concerns me the most is that the politicians are able to lie, be selective about data and aren't being held appropriately to account by our democratic system. Like blind sheep they follow the party line whether it be the correct course or not. They are beholden to the party that preselected them and not to the people who elected them. They are content to whitewash history and promise things they can't deliver. If we agitate, we are shouted down, called ignorant or our timing is poor. Climate change has been an issue for forty odd years but it goes against the ideology of certain parties. The GFC has almost been wiped from people's memories and is now portrayed as a tiny ripple that Australia rode out but the Labor party is disparaged for keeping our economy going with stimulus packages. History is being rewritten and science has been ignored. Amazing how these same people are decrying our education system when they themselves appeared to be in need of some tutoring in such things as civic responsibility, interpreting data, community relations, economics and listening skills.

What qualifications do politicians have to be the decision makers in our society, apart from being able to be pre-selected by a few people in a political party and then being able to fool an electorate? Ministers often have little knowledge and experience in their portfolios and all too often ignore the opinions of those who do know and instead rely on political ideology and advisers. What we need is innovation in how our government is organised.

I am reminded of the walk in the Ballarat Botanical Gardens where the sculptures of the heads of prime ministers are displayed on plinths. One day Morrison's will be there too once they catch up with the numerous ones that have to be done in recent years. To save money perhaps instead of a plinth, a pike might suffice for Morrison. I don't understand why we laud our prime ministers as we don't vote them in to the position. Sometimes there is a free for all in a party room and the one with the sharpest knife is put forward as our prime minister. The only qualification needed is having the most dirt on someone else. Morrison is of that ilk. He is not a great orator. He is no deep thinker. He does not bring with him a wealth of experience in managing a nation or a business. He has shown that working with people is not his forte. He is a salesman and the only thing he sells is himself, if you don't count the selling out of Australia and his principles. And he is not a good salesman. When leadership, statesmanship, visionary thinking and diplomacy are desperately needed around the world, we have Johnson, Trump, Duterte, Erdoğan, Xi Jinping, Putin, Netanyahu, Abbas, al-Assad and others. Our offering of Morrison just adds to the list.

Looking at the political circus we have, I would have to say that there are far too many clowns and that they are the scary ones particularly on the far right. Josh is walking the high wire without a safety net as he tries to get to the other end where the surplus awaits. So, who would be the strongman? Dutton? No-one is sure what Angus Taylor is doing but his pockets seem to be well lined. Cormann is busy juggling the accounts. Everyone appears to be adept at knife throwing. McCormack is handing out peanuts to the crowd when he finishes his sideshow act of putting both feet in his mouth. You gotta love their gall but how we wish they'd move on.

If the flat earthers on the far right go further to the right, will they fall off?

If the House of Representatives should be more appropriately named the House of Misrepresentatives, then what should the Senate be renamed as?

What is worse? To have your guilty conscience pricked by public pressure, or to be seen by the public as a prick under pressure with a guilty conscience?

I don't understand why politicians when they open their mouths fail to put their brains into gear, especially their political

brain. The likes of Fraser and Joyce are prime examples. Do they listen to what they say or is it just a case of any sound is a good sound? More importantly, how do they get elected in the first place?

It seems that this government gets its most satisfaction from closing stable doors. Another thing let loose on the unsuspecting public and all the government can do is to try to put the latch back on an empty stall. Sadly, like a number of racehorses, Australia is heading to the abattoir and we will be knackered like other countries who have a reactive rather than proactive government.

Surely our politicians (current and ex) should seriously think carefully before agreeing to do television interviews. They could easily make a right royal mess of things. (a la Prince Andrew)

All politicians and those thinking about going into parliament should be given an education and sanity tense and if they still wanted to go into parliament after that, it proves that they were either ill-educated or insane and possibly both.

In the great time and space of the universe. In one little galaxy there is one tiny solar system. Within that solar system a blue planet orbits around a sun. In one small country, at one certain time in the planet's existence, in one small chamber of a building, a person lied. Is that going to change the whole universe? Given the vast complexity of everything that has happened post big bang, does one small lie matter?............... Yes, because it is wrong!

With all these motions being moved in the House, maybe that's why parliament and politicians are on the nose. Something stinks methinks.

So many 'gags' in parliament. It would be laughable if it wasn't so serious with these clowns in charge.

A definition of a politician: Anyone who thinks that a whole lot of words that say nothing, or a whole lot of promises that amount to nothing, make them superior to the rest of the population.

Hasn't just been a terrible week. Soon there will be talk of an anus horribilis and we will immediately think of Scott Morrison. (Yes, the spelling is deliberate)

The Coalition have had a disastrous week so much so that the government has decided that they qualify for relief and millions will head their way, along with thoughts and prayers as many of the public think that they haven't a prayer at the next election.

Income averaging should be conducted on all politicians. They should get the average wage of all Australians. Their income should also be tied to their productivity similar to the way it is with the "quiet Australians". You never know, Morrison might find an even bigger surplus.

It seems any policy, program or failing minister will be supported at any cost and for as long as possible to save the government from being proven wrong. There is nothing wrong with making a mistake. Failing to acknowledge it, apologise for it and remedy it, are the areas where this government falls down. First comes the ideology and then the policy and programs are forced to fit around it. If the ideology is flawed never admit to it. Find an echo chamber, no matter how small and continue on. What would experts know? What would the person in the street know? It appears that politicians believe that they are the repository (or suppository if you like) of all knowledge. Saying, "I don't know" "I'll ask for help" "I don't understand" are not signs of weakness. Believing you know everything is though. Politicians will be lodging WorkCover claims over having to carry their egos around with them. They would be better off leaving them at home instead. That excess baggage must be costing the tax payers a fortune.

They won't repeal Medevac as it will be used to relocate Morrison and Taylor to a much safer place than the House of Reps where they lie battered and bruised.

What an expensive present the government has given a young family from Biloela. Months of free accommodation and food on a remote tropical island, aptly named Christmas. The value of their winning prize is about $27 million and they hadn't even had to buy a ticket in this lottery. Some people just don't seem grateful!!!

If a small business struggles and fails, does the government step in like it does for the mining, large manufacturing and farming sector? No, it doesn't. The Coalition believe in free enterprise but are pretty free with taxpayers' money when it comes to handing it out to enterprises that are failing (car industry excepted). This allows unsustainable businesses and farms to continue unchanged and unchallenged. It smothers the hopes of new innovative businesses. It would be far better for the government to buy farmers out and return the land to its natural state. As far as big businesses and mining are concerned, we sold most of these and cut royalties during the eighties and nineties because private enterprise would be better able to make them work efficiently and effectively. Now certain chickens have come home to roost. The government and big business's solution is to just throw more money at it.... our money!

It seems that Morrison makes a special Christmas Pudding that is Magic. You dip into the budget and take money from somewhere and that doesn't affect anything especially the surplus. He must be closer to God than we reckoned and will make a certain person's miracle of the five loaves and two fishes seem pretty arcane. There is no denying that extra money is needed to support those in aged care. The same goes with the drought. He has spent a fortune on keeping Christmas Island open for four occupants and there is Manus and Nauru of course. Something mystical about the man. The Mid-Year

Economic and Fiscal Outlook (MYEFO) may bear some scrutiny or it might get released as a fiction book.

The simple solution to the decline in everything under the economic management of this government is to "spin" the downward trending graphs...... ninety degrees to the left would do! Things will then look up and will show an exponential growth. This right leaning government initially may have issues with turning to the left, but they can achieve the same result by turning to the right even further...... 270 degrees. Doing this will show, without close examination, that their tax cut, red tape cut and wage cut policies are working.

If wage rises were only 0.5% and inflation is running at around 1.5% then that seems to be a negative in terms of liveability. I'm sure Cormann however will be spinning like a top over these figures. He's better than Warne, Grimmet, Lyon, Benaud and MacGill combined. Put him in the test side!

Frydenberg's federation talk is all about shifting the blame for a tanking economy onto someone, anyone else. He can't blame the unions. They have been decimated due to laws. He can't blame Labor who haven't been in power for over six years. He can't blame global issues because things are on the improve elsewhere. He can't of course blame himself or his government.... so, it must be the states fault. Accountability is not something he will accept. He won't account for his lack of ability!

What is the going rate for a government these days? Trump leased one for four years with an option of another four. Ours was up for lease and it seems that coal companies and mining interests averse to the damage to their businesses by doing anything about climate change, have been the winning bidders. They will of course be able to write the investment off as a business expense and no takes will be paid. So, the Morrison government is now a shell company allowing these large businesses to freely strip the assets of the nation.

Perhaps when the lease comes up for renewal, the general public should develop a cooperative and buy back the lease so that the best interests of the nation are served. The current board of directors would be ousted and new ones appointed. Taking back the government off our country seems like the only way that we can make progress on climate change.

It seems that in trying to achieve a surplus, many things had to be cut. A realistic workable policy on climate change was deemed surplus to requirements. Or was it too hard to sell to the coalitions right wing and the mining companies? Or was it just beyond the capacity of the Coalition's elected representatives? Who knows? It certainly isn't worth the paper it was not written on.

Australia, it was once said, rode on the sheep's back. Now we ride on the stuff we dig out of the ground that can't be replaced. Once that has gone, we will have nothing left to sell except our souls. However, the government has put those in hock anyway in the likelihood that the planet will be destroyed by climate change around the same time as the minerals run out.

When it comes to the economy, the phrase, "When it's all said and done" will never be uttered by the current government. This is because they will never stop talking about it and nothing ever gets done.

Who is going to front up and take the blame for the flatlining economy we have? There are a number of candidates who should, including 'Wozzinme' Morrison, 'Sumwunelse' Frydenberg and 'Blaimlayba' Cormann.

If you are poor, if you are defenceless, if you don't understand how the system works if you are already downtrodden, if you lack the education to understand things, if you are alone and in need; then you are likely to become the target for scammers. We have learnt that the scammers now include banks and our own

government. Our government will target the weakest because.... well, because they can. Says a lot for the humane society we call Australia where the rich can get off scot-free, pay bugger all tax and look down on those below the poverty line caught up in a downward spiral not of their own making. Makes you feel proud to be Australian.......... NOT!!!

"Well may we say God Save the Queen, but nothing will save the surplus," (apologies to Gough)

Everything seems to be trending downward for the Morrison government from public confidence, through to employment figures. However, on the bright side, the national debt remains on an upward trend and the disappointment levels of Christian Porter are increasing exponentially.

If Pauline had waited another twenty-four hours, she would have had another reason to not back the IR laws while businesses are being let off scot-free. Bunnings has acknowledged it stuffed up salaries for workers to the tune of $6.1 million. Accounting errors never seem to overpay, do they? Businesses are given a lot of tax incentives but are not held to account. Unions seem the only ones who are willing to hold them to account. Yet it should be the government that does. This is just another example of the captain having no idea where he is going and his hand off the tiller.

"Large business found to have accidentally overpaid staff millions due to an accounting error"

.... Sorry, got Black Friday and April Fool's Day muddled up.

Apparently, the treasurer wants older Australians to start singing, "Hi Ho, Hi, Ho. It's off to work we go" but there are no jobs. Meanwhile back at the cottage, the head dwarf is no longer Happy, he's Grumpy because Dopey has got him into trouble.

Our $50 billion dollar submarines are now expected to cost $225 billion including ongoing maintenance. That represents a

450% increase. Now how much better could that money be spent? The current expert economic managers should not get a free pass on this. 12 submarines we get at $18.75 billion each including maintenance. Do the navy really need them or is this just a case of big boys and their toys. The toys being phallic in shape and possibly ordered to compensate for something. Who is going to attack us that we can defend against with these submarines that will be out of date when they arrive? The idea of even considering them from the clowns in Canberra would seem laughable if it wasn't for the waste of taxpayers' funds which could be put to better use fixing the NBN, providing social housing, raising Newstart, getting the NDIS properly done, fixing mental health shortfalls.......... you name it the list goes on. In twenty-five years, these subs will only be suitable to take tourists down to look at remnants of the "not so great anymore" barrier reef.

The so-called debts were outsourced which is the point that is hard to understand. Compassion and understanding are not traits that are associated with private enterprise.

Forget Nigerian princes' schemes. We have Australian Ponzi schemes proudly brought to you by the Australian government.

Canberra is adding to the emissions too. All that hot air is fanning the flames of political cowardice.

One would have thought that water was a human right, but apparently it isn't. It is a saleable commodity available to the highest bidder. Instead of evenly distributing water in the Murray Darling Basin, it has become part of a bidding war. The buyback scheme is a farce as people are being paid for excess water that might come on their land in flood time. People are harvesting water rather than crops. Those downstream seem to be dependent on how much water is left in the river after the water cowboys have had their fill. Our river system is fragile, too fragile

to be left in the hands of privateers intent on stockpiling it for their own rainy day. Morrison is too busy praying for a miracle while people are preying on water. Independent water bodies reporting to government are the answer. Ministers should not be able to interfere in the distribution as that can and has led to quid pro quo favours to friends and lobbyists. As rivers dry, as droughts deepen and as more knowledge of the sham that has been going on come to light, it is time that the government set up an independent body to manage our precious resource.

Plausible deniability is Morrison's answer for everything to do with climate change. Unseasonal fires, ongoing drought, floods, ever increasing more volatile cyclones, coral reef bleaching, dust storms etc are all acts of God and are not man made and have nothing to do with man except he says are signs to change man's ways and focus on faith. Sadly, for many of the dead, injured and those driven from their farms and homes they never had a prayer. If indeed they are acts of a punishing God, and Morrison is sounding more like an actuary for an insurance company these days, then perhaps we do need to change. That change is not to meekly kneel down in a subservient manner but to rise up and demand real action takes place to alter what mankind is doing to the world. Spurious emission targets, massive ground clearing, giving private enterprise government money to save the reef, subsidising farmers to stay on the land and grow crops and farm animals that are unsustainable, treating water as if it is a saleable commodity and selling it to the highest bidder, will not change anything except for the worse. Anyone who openly states that climate change is an existential threat, who backs that up with evidence, who protests at the lack of interest by government are howled down and Morrison would change laws to prevent such "untruths" being spoken. The sin that Morrison should be highlighting is the pursuit of money for short term gain that also means long term destruction of the current environment and lifestyle we now lead. Morrison may well pray for rain to end the drought and to douse the bushfires but his God isn't listening or is just being vindictive.

Australia has a choice to either say it is too hard to change the world and whatever we do will be insubstantial, or to do what it is within our power to do and perhaps model what can be done. Given the emission target settings of the Morrison government and the use of Kyoto credits, it appears that it is they who thinks that there is no climate emergency. Australia should take into account in its settings what emissions the coal it is exporting makes as it is burnt overseas. If it doesn't, then it is like an arms manufacturer who says that the guns they are selling are no danger to anyone as they are just an inert piece of metal. The world is staring down the barrel of a gun by the use of too much coal fired power generators. I would prefer that Australia's name was not on that barrel.

The world has more than tripled in population in the last seventy years. Emissions per capita on 2.5 billion people in 1950 did not have the same effect as those per capita today at 7.7 billion because the sheer numbers are higher. Yet if good environmental practices had been put in place and extended into the culture back then, we would be better off now. They weren't and we can't change that. We cannot drastically reduce our population growth without a war, famine, mass sterilisation or something similar. Reducing our emissions even further is a pathway ahead, but sadly so many people aren't capable of looking far enough down the existing pathway we are on and so aren't willing to make the sacrifice of the here and now lifestyle to change direction. We do not have the leaders willing to take us there, leaders who are willing to fight against the entrenched capitalist culture to secure our future.

De Nile is de river that flows through Egypt and the LNP party room it seems.

I think that the only way to get any action is to sue the government. They have continually deferred any action on climate change. They have no drought plan. They provide Band-Aid solutions for drought and bushfires along with thoughts and prayers. Yet it is their thoughtless inaction that is at the base of the drought and the bushfires. This is a case of neglect on a national scale and someone, even if it has to be the courts, has to hold them to account. The government ministers fly in for photo ops and then move on. Recovery will take years and years. They won't be thinking of those affected by this devastation beyond the next news cycle.

At least we know that our politicians aren't selling the country down the river. With all this inaction on climate change, the river has run bloody dry!!!!

All these nay-sayers about climate change that are in parliament, especially our PM must be on another planet where it is pristine and euphoric. If that is the case beam, us all up Scotty!

Under the proposed new laws to do with protesting, I wonder if climate change denialists took to the street, whether they would be facing the full force of the law. Centuries ago, Galileo was censured, arrested and placed under house arrest for proving the Earth wasn't flat and thus going against the religious based law of the time. How far actually have we come these days?

I don't know why Morrison is telling us to shush about climate change. It is not as if he is listening.

Morrison's climate change policy is based on smoke and mirrors........... actually, just smoke these days.

We may have 1.3% of the world's emissions but as we have 0.33% of the world's population, we are per capita one of the highest emission producers, even before you take into account that so much of our coal is sent overseas to be burnt.

Fancy us thinking that our views on climate change are going against government policy. They don't have one!!!

The government has set perdition targets......................

The issue of climate change is not a (pardon the pun) hot topic among the generation who are currently in power. Once they leave this mortal coil, many will have another type of heat to deal with, so they aren't too fussed about creating a hell on Earth after they've gone.

Morrison's new ad campaign on climate change has been held up by copyright laws. Simon and Garfunkel are refusing the use of "The Sounds of Silence"

Tourism Australia may need to look at their ads for this year and go back to "I'll put another shrimp on the barbie." and add, "Bloody big barbie here for you."

If Morrison actually had an agenda, he should ram it through parliament now while everyone is distracted by the fires. He has the smoke. Is he lacking in mirrors or a policy agenda?

All this water to fight the fires in the drought, where does it come from? Surely the cotton farmers and the almond tree orchardists haven't missed out? Or have they sold it back to the government at a profit?

If hyperbole and hot air put out fires, we could send our politicians to the fire front. But alas they just fan the flames.

Scott Morrison has said that the army will be deployed in the fire areas on request but they haven't had any training to work at the firefront. The question needs to be asked, why not? There are many things that our soldiers have been readied for and drilled for in preparation for war. Why shouldn't firefighting be one of them. it would add to their skills and allow them to better mix within the community especially in dangerous situations. They are very well disciplined and used to following commands. As a supplement to our volunteers and professionals, they would be invaluable. It would be a wonderful PR program. Currently we are waging a war on the natural disasters that have increased

in number and intensity over the years. It is an all Australian issue and our soldiers would earn extra praise for offering their services.

Queensland, beautiful one day, burnt the next. Rainforests, that records show have never burnt, are burnt out. Queensland and NSW are becoming parched deserts. Come to tropical Victoria!

Interesting use of stats with "four of the past five worst bushfires in Australian history occurred between 1910 – 1980". Is it based on loss of life, area burnt out, loss of buildings? If you look at the history of bushfires you will see that the frequency has increased in the last thirty years and the severity has remained high even though we have better evacuation plans, firefighting capabilities and awareness. Random stats are just that, random.

There will be a coronial inquest into the fires. I am betting that Barnaby, McCormack and Craig Kelly will insist that it was started by a wind turbine or a solar energy panel.

Some thought it the sound of Bogong moths hitting the glass of Parliament House in Canberra. Others were sure that it was the weight of public opinion coming down on the government's lack of climate change policy. A few thought it was the mournful wail of a dingo echoing the sentiments of first nation people. They were all wrong. It was the sound of a wet lettuce striking a number of bank executives.

The penalty for having 23 million suspect banking transfers go through is a little loss of dignity, a huge payout and the opportunity to retire in a style that befits a king. Oh, to be a bank executive!

Apparently when one bank's CEO stepped down, he accidentally slipped on some wet lettuce leaves. I wonder whether he will sue for damages.

The treasurer's latest utterances are just another example of just how out of touch, the government politicians are with what happens out on the street. They are too busy talking, fighting among themselves and planning for the next election to even listen. We have a growing unemployment especially in real terms if you take into account under employment. The economy is tanking and yet the treasurer is telling older people to get a job. The experience, maturity and education don't seem to count as much as youth and vigour, when it comes to employment. Lose a job in your fifties and it is really difficult to get back into the workforce. This is just another case of blaming the victim. The treasurer and members of the government should sweep the smoke away from the mirrors they employ and reflect on just who should take the blame for a stagnant economy. But which face of the two that look back at them will they blame?

Cash seems to be saying that the rise in unemployment is nothing. She should tell that face to face with the people that her government's inept managing of the economy has just put out of work and onto the unsustainable Newstart. Let her read their lips instead of the other way around.

Now that Pauline has destroyed Morrison's IR laws, how long will it be before Morrison dumps her from the parliamentary inquiry into family courts? Someone might have to explain to her what quid pro quo means.

Barnaby Joyce is protesting that man-made climate change doesn't exist and that fires are caused by the sun's magnetism. If he continues to speak out as he does, will his electorate finally dump him before he falls foul of Morrison's proposed new laws about protesting.

I learnt an interesting fact from Craig Kelly today. There are even more ways to be stupid than I thought. His ability to interpret facts accurately has declined 24% over the years and it wasn't very high to begin with.

Doesn't Craig Kelly know that 110% of statistics aren't accurate?

Michael McCormack and Barnaby Joyce.... what a prickly pair. Noxious weed!

When Barnaby Joyce fell foul of the public, he created a vacancy and true to form, the Nationals found the most vacant member they could to fill that space.

Any truth in the rumour I am starting that Michael McCormack mistook the word *satellite* images for *set alight*?

There may be a few spot fires that the Prime Minister is trying to put out, but there are glowing embers of discontent in the backbench all watching and waiting for Morrison to crash and burn. Scott knows that where there is smoke that there is fire and he is using a lot of smoke with those mirrors. He may find it too hot in the kitchen as that prime cut Angus is slowly roasted. Watch out Scott, you appear to have jumped from the frying pan into the fire for now the heat is on.

We are not allowed to talk about <u>fires</u>. On <u>water</u> matters are off limits. Saving the <u>earth</u> is taboo. <u>Wind</u> generation can't be discussed. Yet these are all natural elements. There is something unnatural about Morrison's agenda.

If we are relying on prayers to get us through then I have to question whether Morrison's God is not benevolent or just has too many things on his plate. (yes, for Morrison, God has to be male)

How does Morrison get more of his 'quiet Australians'? He effectively gags them. He is doing it unions, to retired firefighters, to climate change scientists, to first Australians and is doing it those who wish to raise issues in his own party room and in parliament itself.

I just wonder when the plastic surgery will take place and whether Medicare will cover the costs. Morrison's forked tongue is quite distracting.

I don't understand. How can politicians stand for election when we have no idea what they stand for? Morrison is the "prime" example. He got his seat by standing and now sits in parliament, but we can hardly call him an upstanding citizen. I wonder how many in his party can't stand him and will try to unseat him in future. While we wait for this to happen, he sits on his hands and does nothing.

Apologies to Stephen Sondheim for this version of Send in the Clowns.

Turnbull was rich
But got nowhere
They tore him right down,
Scott took the chair,
Another clown?
Next on the list?
Next to remove?
He's on shaky ground,
And dare not move,
Another clown
There's too many clowns
Just who is Scott, no-one is sure,
He's something he's not and nothing more
Playing salesman again. He doesn't care
Spouting his lies
Going nowhere
It's just a farce
Our fault, we fear
We thought that he'd want what we want
It's now quite clear!
All we got was a clown
Another clown
And someone to fear

Why do I get the feeling when I look at press conferences with Morrison, that is the same when a call centre rings up wanting to sell me something? "No, I don't want to listen. No, I am not buying anything (including what you say). And no, I don't care what other piece of junk that comes 'free' with it. My time is valuable. My hard-earned money is valuable. Yet you seem intent on robbing me blind of both!"

Seems that Scomo was talking rubbish back when he and the Police Commissioner were neighbours. Little has changed.

Scomo's antics in parliament are gifts for us all: coal, nonsense and mirth.

With Morrison's fabrication now being exposed regarding Julia Gillard, he may miss out on presents from Santa. But hey, I don't think he'll mind the coal in his stocking.

Anyone surprised that Christian Porter said that Morrison wasn't in the House because he had a matter outside of Canberra AND then in walks Morrison!!! Did he walk across Lake Burley-Griffin? Does he have a magic carpet? Did someone beam Scotty up?

I'm not sure whether Morrison's Pentecostal god uses bolts of lightning for sinners and whether lying is deemed a huge sin; but I wouldn't be standing too close to the PM for a while!

Deflect, deny, distract are all strategies that this government employs to cover up its lack of policies and its sheer incompetence. if you throw in other 'd' words such as deceitful, duplicitous, dumb, disorganised, disingenuous, deceptive etc.; you can understand why their erstwhile leader's description should begin with a 'd' It is a wonder that Abbott didn't knight him when he had the opportunity.... Sir Doofus seems quite appropriate.

The DSA (Doofus Society of Australia) are protesting as they wish that they not be associated with Scott Morrison in any way shape or form. His application for membership was declined as

he didn't even attain the low bar of qualification. They have officially barred him along with other would be members, Onions Abbott, Wazzanme Taylor and Vibble Vobble Cormann. The latter displayed major adding up problems that makes even the worst doofus seem like a Mensa star.

If Morrison had spent more time selling his IR package to the cross benchers in the senate and not allowed the banks off the hook, he might have got the IR package through. Instead he chose to defend Angus Taylor at great cost. His political judgement needs to be called into question surely.

Scott Morrison is seen as a political animal but then which sort of animal would best match a description of him?

* Something that attacks from behind,

* is rat cunning

* is intent solely on his own survival

* at times is very naive and gullible bordering on stupid.

* An animal that proudly displays itself in public but when challenged cringes away in fear.

* Survives on carrion and indeed does carry on too much.

* Has a raucous voice.

* Is easily provoked

I could go on but I think it would be an insult to match a real animal with him.... an insult to the animal.

Scott Morrison may believe in 'the quiet Australians' but turns a deaf ear to them. This week he has just shown that he is dumb as well. I wonder whether his deaf mute NDIS package has been processed yet.

What has Angus Taylor got on Scott Morrison? It must be something substantial as Morrison has been drawn into the quagmire, instead of just cutting Taylor free. Taylor has had numerous strikes against him and he remains as a minister

serving at the prime minister's pleasure. I'm not sure how much more pleasure and enjoyment he can take at the moment.

Seems that the excuses that Morrison is offering about his Energy Minister are Taylor made.

Why isn't Angus Taylor answering questions about his latest scandal? It appears that he has the speaking skills of Prince Andrew, but just a little more sense than him and so, has chosen not to expose those to the public.

What's the beef with Angus?.......... Really? No bull?

If Taylor has been found to have misled parliament, it may give cause to argue what he has also lied about? Energy emissions? Perhaps the emissions target won't be a canter but the horse is already in the knacker's yard. Land clearing by a company he is associated with? Perhaps that is why he isn't too fussed about global warming as these may be just the tip of the iceberg and every day the earth's temperature rises, the iceberg gets smaller.

Taylor is seeking immunity for his actions yet he thinks he can continue along with impunity as well.

Was Taylor lying when he was standing at the last election? Now is he sitting in parliament and lying? Such great gymnastic feats! He can contort the truth as well! Wait for the backflip though. It should be most entertaining.

"The Labor Party has a track record of using police referrals as a political tool, Mr Speaker."

Angus Taylor should be able to recognise a political tool simply by looking in the mirror.

Morrison's political advisors would be well advised to look for a new career given what he has been through this week. He backed the wrong horse in Taylor. He compounded it by misquoting information himself and by ringing his old neighbour, a police commissioner who is in charge of

investigating Angus Taylor. I'm sure Scott will right now be thinking "How good are my advisors?"

"Almost 7 million people watched Johnson/Corbyn debate, says ITV" proving some people need to get a life or better streaming services. However, on the plus side, the vast majority of the population (more than 60 million others) did have better things to do.

Latest news (that may need to be fact checked) has stated that Kanpur in India briefly lost its title as the world's most polluted city. A place called Salford in England overtook it for one night. There is some concern that it happened at the same time as the Johnson Corbyn debate. All that hot air and bullsh!t released may have just tipped the balance Salford's way. Residents of the city are hoping that no more debates will be held but if they are, then perhaps another UK city should be chosen. A massive expensive clean-up is currently underway.

December

- Eight people are killed, hundreds of homes are destroyed and the Royal Australian Navy is mobilised to assist evacuation efforts following bushfires on the New South Wales South Coast and in Victoria's East Gippsland
- Scott Morrison spends time in Hawaii with his family as fires burn on the east coast of Australia
- The United Nations Climate Change Conference takes place in Madrid
- Speaker of the U.S. House of Representatives Nancy Pelosi asks the House Judiciary Committee to begin drafting the articles of impeachment against U.S. President Donald Trump
- The World Anti-Doping Agency votes unanimously to ban Russia from international sport for four years for doping offences
- The World Trade Organization is left unable to intervene in trade disputes after the U.S. blocks the appointment of new panel members
- Boris Johnson wins Britain general election.
- A volcano erupts on White Island in New Zealand, killing 20 people and injuring 27 others
- Pope Francis abolishes pontifical secrecy in sex abuse cases
- The U.S. House of Representatives approves two articles of impeachment against President Trump, making him the third president to be impeached in the nation's history

There is a god complex when it comes to parliament it appears. The government believes it has all the knowledge and that crossbenchers and the opposition are there merely there to thwart any progress. That is not what the Senate is there for. It

is a house of review where amendments can be put forward to improve legislation. The opposition's role is similar in the House of Reps. It may be the alternative government at election time but in the intervening period, its responsibility is to improve legislation not automatically oppose it. This god complex of a government with a majority of one is unfounded but it is apparent. They think they know best and have the numbers to prove it (along party lines of course). Until the system and culture within change, we will continue to have dysfunctional governments. Let's get back to the way the constitution sets out our government. There is an overview at the beginning that is more a statement of what conventions apply. However, the actual constitution does not mention a Prime Minister, an Opposition or even political parties. These are hangovers from conventions from the British way of operating. Get rid of the god complex and have each representative and each senator vote on each piece of legislation in the best interests of their constituents rather than their political affiliation or their own self-interest.

Glad question time is over. Can someone please tell when answer time begins?

(**With apologies to John Lennon**)
Imagine there's no Senate
No House of Reps too
Just a known consensus
Of what we all must do
Imagine there's no pollies
And no more of their lies
Just human kindness
And all that it implies
Imagine all the people
Caring for the world
Let's get rid of the schemers

Every last rotten one
We would save lots of money
And lots of good things would get done

The Senate chamber quickly emptied when someone's pants caught fire.......... again!!!

Expect all matters now to labelled as "national security" in the same way "on water matters" was used to not have to explain anything. Government responses to questions by journalists and even in parliament itself will come out as visible verbal redactions. Don't we have a right to know? Or is that just something for the ruling elite? The government's transparency has now just gone from opaque to a one-way mirror.

A government is seen to be a reflection of the country itself. So many ugly uncaring inhumane Australians will not help our tourist industry.

I am in a scientific dilemma. How does the Canberra bubble still remain intact with so many pricks in it? Are there special properties of moral vacuums?

The new department of prayers and promises; where is that to be located?

Regarding the stopping of discussion on bills, the government's gag isn't very funny.

It seems that the biggest piece of infrastructure that the Coalition have achieved since they have been in office has been the moral and ethical bypass around Canberra.

Perhaps we should set key performance indicators that are linked to politicians' salaries and super. These would be published before an election and politicians would have no excuse for not meeting them. Failure to get a satisfactory rating from a truly independent review would cause a by-election. How many politicians would put themselves under such scrutiny? This might flush away some of the dross that ends up in Canberra.

The whole idea is to stop the public talking. We can't talk about climate change. I may have mentioned asylum seekers once but I think I got away with it. Argument, protest, debate is all being shut down. The Canberra bubble is so big it has covered the whole continent and has the word gossip painted over it. Government is apparently all about secrecy and the need to know.... and the public don't need to know. A perfect example is that we know that currently there is a royal commission into lawyer X. We also know that there is a witness K who, along with his lawyer, is about to undergo a secret trial over the whistleblowing of the Australian government's illegal spying on Timor-Leste. There is also a witness J who has had a secret trial and has been secretly incarcerated. My concern is for thirty-two others, the lawyers A to W and the witnesses A to I, whom we have not heard anything about. Are they safe? Have they faced court? Have they suffered from our inadequate whistleblowing legislation?

We have been told repeatedly by the Coalition that the first responsibility of a government is to ensure the safety of the public. It is the reason given for offshore detention of asylum seekers. It is the reason given for the purchase of soon to be outmoded fighter jets and submarines that we haven't even got yet. It was the reason Howard used to get us involved in the Iraq war. Vast areas of the country are on fire. Because of the drought, farmers are going under and the suicide rates are abnormally high. Safety is a relative word. Apparently, it applies only to influences outside of Australia. Within our own borders we have thoughts prayers and a surplus to keep us safe.

My understanding of the Medevac legislation as it stands is this. A layer was inserted into the process when the original bill was passed. That layer meant that a team of independent doctors would assess the need for a person to be brought to Australia for medical reasons. That person would still be in detention but able to have treatment not available on Manus or Nauru. When well enough to return, the patient would return to Manus or Nauru. In the past that decision was made by bureaucrats. The Minister still kept the power to veto that transfer but would have to explain to parliament why. At no point were people going to be released into society willy nilly as the Home Affairs Minister claimed. There was no threat to our sovereign borders. It basically gave what was essentially a medical decision to people who were more capable of making it. It was logical. It was humane. However accordingly for the Home Affairs Minister it meant for him a loss of power. It meant that he would also have to explain himself to parliament. Now I am a lay person who may have this all wrong, but surely a humane government interested in the welfare of all people in its care (and no matter what they say or what outsourcing is involved, the detainees seeking asylum ARE in our care) would take their responsibilities seriously and not see the original Medevac legislation as a loss of face.

Over 2000 years ago, it is said that two refugees made their way to a tiny town where they were made to feel unwelcome. A local innkeeper offered only the use of a stable, despite the woman being heavily pregnant. Compassion was missing all around. No mid-wife was called. No-one came to help. Based on what we have just witnessed in parliament with the Medevac repeal, not much has changed in two thousand years, despite the birth of a child to that couple so long ago.

Thirty pieces of silver was the price for which Judas Iscariot betrayed Jesus, according to an account in the Gospel of Matthew 26:15 in the New Testament. There are 31.1035 grams per troy ounce. At spot valuation of $25.18/oz at today's price, 30 "pieces of silver" would be worth around $300. I assume Jacqui Lambie is getting more than that for her sellout on Medevac and betrayal of those ill people on Manus and Nauru.

The audio in the Senate chamber must be faulty. There is a hissing sound when Lambie is speaking. It's almost like that

of a snake in the grass. Is that a forked tongue? Well it seems those on Nauru and Manus who are in desperate need of medical treatment are "forked" anyway.

Morrison has chosen just one family to bless this Christmas. And it is not even his own! He has given one family free accommodation on a tropical island appropriately named Christmas Island. How many of us are so glad that we didn't get a ticket in that lottery? Today I am thinking about them, about those on Manus and Nauru, those who are fighting fires, those who are homeless, those who rely on charity to survive. I choose not to think about the thoughts and mean spiritedness of our politicians and the way that the proselytize. They can keep their religious hypocrisy to themselves.

What is the point of saying "Growth is forecast to return to 2.75% next year and 3% annually by 2021-22, which the government says will be driven by this year's personal income tax cuts and investment in productive infrastructure." when forecasts have never been accurate with this government? Their crystal ball has a rosy tint to it. They spin the figures, finding ones that they think will somehow rationalise their implausible policies. It is a wonder that they don't hiss when they talk and their noses don't increase in length. How much flame retardant is being used on their pants? Morrison talks about the quiet Australians yet it is his quiet Australians who are suffering the most. They are finding their energy and health care cost increases exceeding inflation. They are finding that wages growth is below inflation. Even if these quiet Australians start to speak up, it is very probable that this government aren't listening.

Do the treasurer and Finance Minister actually believe what they say when they address the public? Are they caught up in their own spin? Someone shoves a graph in front of them that looks like it has an upward trend and that is all they need? Is it that they don't see that someone has transposed the titles of underemployment and household disposable income? Do they just tilt a graph to the left so that it looks like growth has occurred? It would be more honest if they showed us what they actually saw and not just what they wanted us to see. When I shop, when I look in the fridge, when a bill arrives, I can't find my pair of rose-coloured glasses similar to the ones they wear.

Climate and weather are two distinct, but not mutually exclusive notions. Climate is the long-term view of things and dictates to a certain extent how we manage our lives and our environment. Weather is the short term and we generally only look as far as today, tomorrow and the week or so ahead. Our politicians are not looking at the long term either in most things. The trend today is to look at the short term and what will be needed to win the next election. That appears to be their focus. A promised surplus is more important than ending homelessness or converting military aircraft into water bombing ones capable of extinguishing fires.

(apologies to Paul Simon)

Here's to you Mr Morrison
Jesus loves you more than you will know
Farmers on their knees Mr Morrison
But you won't talk about climate change
Not today. There's no way
Is there an evil cunning behind your smirk and smile?
Do you just allow your friends to help themselves?
Do you just follow all those scripted party lines?
And help friends bring their bins in when they're not at home?
Here's to you Mr Morrison
Jesus loves you more than you will know
Farmers on their knees Mr Morrison
But you won't talk about climate change
Not today. There's no way

"Don't mention the words climate change. Be vewy vewy quiet, Morrison is hunting wabbits (dumb bunnies who speak out of turn)"

Just imagine how swift the action would have been by our politicians if the smoke affected flights out of Canberra on the last sitting day and if Canberra was ringed by fire and they couldn't get out for their long long summer break. There would be money to convert RAAF planes to undertake water bombing. The lack of water to put out the fires might make them think and act far more swiftly on water conservation and the environment. The Murray Darling Basin issues would be solved overnight. We'd be allowed to talk about climate change. The Paris emission targets would be made real and possibly even raised. If politicians can't get to where they want to be, they'll try to move hell and high water to change that.

Scott Morrison seems to be taking a different stand to Israel Folau's reasoning. Morrison's explanation of the bushfires, drought, wild storms, coral bleaching, possibly even the deaths on White Island in New Zealand along with their floods is the Latin, stercus accidit. Or to those less learned like me and able to use google, "sh!t happens". Except that Morrison doesn't recognise that all but the volcano deaths have causes that we can address by doing something about climate change. Morrison seems content to do nothing and the sh!t that is happening is taking on diarrhoea-like dimensions.

Surely there must come a time when a government becomes accountable for its own failings. Litigation by people affected by the lack of action on climate change may make this government more circumspect about caving into ideologues and the coal mining industry. This government treats parliament and the electorate with disdain and should pay a price personally for their arrogance. Australians are not fussed about fudged figures that will create a surplus. They are more concerned about the fudged figures that will be used to falsely show we have met our emissions targets.

Climate change doesn't affect many people who make the decisions in this country. Therefore, it seems, that what we need to survive the effects of climate change is a Canberra like bubble that covers Australia, or better still the whole world.

Honest politician - oxymoron. Brave politician - oxymoron. Climate change denying politician - moron.

The federal government wants to build a lot more dams to store water, presumably not for a rainy day. However, in times of drought, dams actually impede the river flow, syphoning off water that is needed by the environment and farmers downstream. The needs of farmers upstream compete with those downstream and the upstream ones have a significant advantage called gravity. Trading water as a commodity does not work as the rich get richer in literally liquid assets and the poor go thirsty. The river system can only take so much before it becomes nonviable as a system at all in drought times. Water caps should be based on water flow not some arbitrary level decreed. If the levels are to be set, then they must be set at the worst possible scenario and people should manage their farms accordingly by destocking and planting only what the land can carry in times of drought.

(Apologies to Midnight Oil. To the tune of Beds Are Burning)

Our cities shrouded in smoke
Deputy PM just says it's woke
And climate change is just for lefties
But we bake in forty degrees
We choke on smoke, that fills the air
The government won't, do its share
The time's well past, for us to act
The future looks, exceedingly black

We've reached the point of no returning
How do we sleep while our forests are burning?
We've reached the point of no returning
How do we sleep while our forests are burning?
We choke on smoke, that fills the air
The government won't, do its share.......

Climate change is CRAP! Constantly Raising Australia's Profile as the worst polluter per capita in the world

God alone determines what happens to the Earth or so religions would have us believe. It is our so-called sins that determine God's blessing or vengeance. If humans try to do anything about climate change they are interfering with God's will. Thank heaven (pun intended) that we don't have a religious zealot as a PM!

Both new coal fired power stations and new solar and wind farms will take years to construct. We need to phase out coal and increase renewables over a proper balanced timeframe. It is not one or the other but a phased transition that should start sooner than later. Business want it to happen and for a so-called liberal government that supports business, they should be listening.

Time's Person of the Year is a sixteen-year-old female who has risen to fame by speaking out on the most challenging problem that mankind faces. For once Time Magazine has got it pretty right. Trump complaining that it should have been me is in character but out of step with what normal people think. Jacinda Ardern is another leader people could follow. It seems to me that perhaps we should look for young females to lead the world out of the crises we are facing. Old mostly white males have done a pretty crap job up until now.

Platitudes, prayers and thoughts will not douse the fires that are raging across the country. Nor will they end the drought that is tearing at the livelihood and life blood of our farming areas and our natural environment. Blinkered ideology and dodgy

accounting of emissions will not alter the fact that the Australian climate that we knew last century has changed for the worse in the new millennium. It is not business as usual and 'nothing to see here' as much as climate change denialists would have us believe. The new norm involves more severe weather events, a drying out of our continent and a gradual warming of the atmosphere and the sea over a relatively short space of time.

More and more, the community at large has become aware of what is happening. Politicians are losing the esteem that they once were held in and still covet. They are being seen as duplicitous, ignorant and irrelevant. In times of crisis, we look to our leaders for guidance. These days that leadership, like the parched earth, has dried up. One thing that we have learnt from all this is that there is no need for further experimentation or even blind trials. The truth is now obvious and incontrovertible. It is impossible to see things and hear things if your head is buried in the sand. I'd like to thank our politicians for their research into that particular matter.

What would happen if insurance companies began to sue governments for the inaction by politicians on climate change? Bang goes the surplus! The taxpayer would have to foot a hefty bill but that may make us realise that we are electing the wrong sort of people to what is effectively a Board of Directors.

Australia would be so much better off if politicians reduced their own emissions as many of them talk through the wrong orifice. They pollute the truth with spin and have decided their contribution to the energy debate is to conserve their own and do nothing.

It is the severity of the bushfires that is a concern. These types of fires are not started by climate change but the drought riven land caused by climate change has led to the early start to the bushfire season; rainforests, previously almost immune to fires, being burnt; and the enormity of the fires themselves. Playing games with semantics and pedantry, as well as saying that we have

always had fires merely tries to normalise what is something far from normal. Sadly, however what we are witnessing may become the new normal.

Joyce and Morrison are saying that what we are enduring is God's will, almost as if man is powerless to stop or mitigate what is happening. This is a cop out or palming the blame off to a greater being than can't be seen or heard and as such he/she/it can't respond to the charges labelled against he/she/it. I am not sure that I believe in such a vengeful, merciless god that indiscriminately targets the innocent and the guilty. They should explain that to the families of firefighters who died, never able to see this Christmas, to those caught by a volcanic eruption, for those imprisoned on Manus and Nauru and those who are homeless. Accountability and action are the province of our government, otherwise why have a government. We all have one life. We all have one planet to live on. What we do in that time and in that place matters. Our government should not just shrug its shoulders indicating it is not within their province or it is all too hard. Doing nothing is a choice and they will be judged accordingly by the electorate and, perhaps if they are correct, by a higher order being.

(With apologies to Australian Crawl and to the tune of Boys Light Up)

Let me tell you how big's the fire zone
And how many have lost their homes
As all the volunteers join the fight
Our PM tries to hose things down
Saying time for talk's not right
As massive fires all combine
He still says that it's not time
To talk about climate change
Offers thoughts and prayers for rain
He won't let truth and facts get in the way

Saying that's all baloney
For he thinks he's God's gift only
And that the answer is to get on your knees and pray
What a sing song dance
What a performance
What a cheap tent show
Oh no no no no no
As the bush lights up
As the bush lights up
As the bush lights up
As the bush lights up, lights up, lights up
As the bush lights up
As the bush lights up
As the bush lights up
As the bush lights up, lights up, lights up

All those thoughts and prayers from Morrison have just gone up in a puff of smoke.

The government seems to think that firebombing with thoughts and prayers will extinguish the fires. If anything, their benign comments are inflammatory. Rain is the answer but it seems that normal rain isn't coming because of climate change. The government can't make that simple connection. I hear Angus Taylor has some left-over carbon credits that he will try to smother the fires with............

Perhaps when parliament sits next year, an opposition member might bring in a lump of burnt wood and show Morrison. However, Scott may say that he sees nothing different to that and a piece of coal. Reality is not something he grasps well, a bit like subtlety, irony and compassion.

Not only are the politicians on the right aiding the things that are making these blazes much worse, they may actually be inflaming the situation with the fires emanating from their pants.

Why did Morrison eventually fly back from Hawaii? Probably for the same reason that McCormack suddenly began to say that we needed to address climate change, and that because their political advisors got wind of the likelihood that they would lose votes. That wind was around laden with smoke for a long time, but the politicians still couldn't see it until now. If it was John Howard, he would have more politically astute and as a cricket tragic would have picked up on the idea earlier especially when that Canberra Big Bash match was stopped because of the smoke from the fires.

We will grow tired of it. The horrific fire season will eventually pass. Politicians will just sit this out and the media circus will move on. Climate change and the fires will be glossed over in the same way that mass shootings in America don't make headlines over there. We have become decatastrophised, our senses numbed and eventually we will become immune to it all. Journalists will find a different sort of carrion to feed on and the politicians will smile because it is a long time until the next election. The scarred trees and burnt forest floor will sprout new leaves and growth and people will forget that our PM was on holiday, that politicians bickered while firies toiled for months on end. Spin merchants will take over and the spring and summer that the nation burned will become just an obscure footnote in history. Families who lost loved ones and property will remember, but others who were inconvenienced by poor air quality will soon forget. What will have been experienced in the spring and summer of 2019/2020, will soon become the norm and be deemed by some as "God's will" and seen to be unable to be mitigated again in the future. The human mind is a wonderful thing. It has inbuilt safety mechanisms that prevent it from sensing that all hope is lost. It locks horrific memories away lest they interfere with day to day functioning. It reacts to the

environment around it and normalises it. Politicians rely on the way our minds work. It keeps them in power.

Victoria hasn't escaped the fires despite the rain and cool temperatures. There are massive fires out of control in East Gippsland, north east of Bairnsdale and north of Orbost and at Nowa Nowa. Combined damage so far is over 20,000 hectares. Should they link up in the coming weeks as is expected, then expect nearly 200,000 hectares to be burnt out and towns in the area be placed under threat. Victorian firies will sadly be called back from Queensland and NSW to defend their own properties. So, when will Scott Morrison meet with those fire chiefs? When will he allow us to talk about climate change? I've looked on my calendar and still can't find the 12th of Never.

There is one policy that is being enacted and that is the one on smoke and mirrors. Morrison, the master illusionist, appears only good because we are the master delusionalists. We are incapable of failing to believe a convincing liar...... do we really get six steak knives with that? Oh yes please.... The postage and handling is three times the value of the product.... never mind I'll take one. This government should be taken to the ACCC for misleading advertising. I read their prospectus and it's a tissue of lies and a web of false promises. Can I get my money back!!!!! What do you mean the warranty runs out a millisecond after the result of the election is announced!!!! As a shareholder when can I vote the board out? Another three years!!!!

Australians showed many things last May. One was that they can be bought and their hip pocket is more important than their conscience. Another was that they have difficulty discerning lies from truth. It seems detailed policies aren't necessary when short sound bites and slogans will do. We have been given the government we voted for. We voted for them out of ignorance. If the May election is seen as a turning point, then hopefully it would will be a turning point for creating a more politically educated group of electors.

A leader's job is to lead in the good and bad times, to accept responsibility on behalf of the nation, to listen and to learn and provide a focal point for the community. A leader needs to speak genuine words of encouragement, promote resilience and to bring together a nation. Do we have a leader as a PM? Is he actually capable of fulfilling those duties? Sadly, we have no-one at the helm who can do that. Scott Morrison appears to not want to take responsibility, to answer questions and is too intent on political brinkmanship to even look at what we want from him. Compare him with Jacinta Ardern and he falls way short. We are not in a time of war, so we are lucky we don't have him leading us into that. However, we have other battles with drought, fire, climate change and with improving our reputation overseas, that he has no idea how to lead us through. Our democracy is under direct threat by his stifling of debate in parliament and he seems to be hell bent on a dictatorial role. Heaven help Australia.

What we need in Australia is strong leadership, not a government riven with its own in-fighting, not a government that flip flops according to the latest trend. We had John Curtin who led us strongly through World War two. We had Gough Whitlam who led us finally out of Vietnam. These were great leaders. Now we have a Scomo who doesn't know his arse from his Albo. He can't see that we are at war. However, that war is against global warming. Anthony Albanese seems cut of the same cloth. There are few in either of the major parties who have leadership qualities that will inspire a nation, support a nation and be front and centre and represent what our nation stands for. It is about time we got rid of these middle-aged men in their suits and let the ones who demonstrate capacity to lead to come to the forefront. Wong, Pliberseck, Birmingham, Payne,

Keneally all spring to mind but there are so many others not in parliament who would do a better job.

Hell hath no fury like a public scorned.

We don't need to worry about overseas threats. The threats to our lives, lifestyle and economy come from within. They are omnipresent in the form of droughts, floods, storms and fire like we have not witnessed in our lifetime. Predictions are that they will get worse. Why are we spending a fortune on subs and planes when we have to rely on volunteers to go into battle for us. We spend billions on keeping people out but not on putting fires out. The cost to Australia is phenomenal but our wonderful economic managers can't see it. I suppose with your head in the sand, you really can't see much.

Accountability seems to be the word that was left behind once we hit the year 2000. Maybe the Y2K bug ate it. From those in government to those on company boards and quite rightly we who elect them, the move is on to shift accountability to others so that it dissipates entirely Governments commit to reviews and royal commissions and rarely publish the results of the former and fully implement the recommendations of the latter. Company boards oversee losses, ethic and law breaking but still get re-elected and the CEO's retain their bonuses. Everyone tries to blame those who have been in charge before them even though they have been in power for over five years. It has become a farce that we have come to accept. We have also come to accept leaders who can't lead but who can use three-word slogans to obfuscate, deny and yet somehow woo us. Accountability should be front and centre in the next decade. We should not accept anything less from those who seek power. Nor should we accept the lesser of two evils. We deserve better than that. In a democracy, demanding accountability and using the power of our votes are the only weapons in our arsenal. It is about time that we got off our collective posteriors and did something.

If I go and rob a bank, then when caught, I am gaoled. If a bank however robs me and gets caught, the local greengrocer runs out of wet lettuces. How does that work?

Why does Morrison want to launch his new religious laws at the height of the bush fire crisis? Bushfires are God's punishment (ask Folau) and fire and brimstone come from the pulpit. Morrison is just doing his perceived Christian duty.

If the Union busting bill gets passed, through whatever means in the Reps, will it have to be reconsidered by the Senate before the Senate closes down for the year? If not, this is just arrogant petulance by the schoolyard bullies of the Coalition. Perhaps they don't mind coal in their Christmas stockings.

Bill Shorten tried to straddle a fence and now is sitting on the sideline pulling splinters from his posterior. Albo saw it happen but has refused to learn from what he saw. The fence now has razor wire on it and the damage might be too great for Albo to survive. He needs to plan a future employment strategy for those in a dying coal industry. He needs to give them hope if he wants to win their vote. Economics will shut down coal and he needs to offer something for these people when that happens. Don't plan for the next two years, plan for the next decade.

Yes, Dutton is the face of EVIL. We should also remember that an anagram of EVIL is VILE and that we have to LIVE under a VEIL of secrecy.

Did Lambie get one of those "Read my lips promises" a la George Bush senior? Did she check to see whether Morrison's fingers were crossed? Did she check for timed invisible ink? Did she have a witness? Did Dutton promise something possibly sinister if she didn't vote his way? How heavy will the guilty conscience be that she has to carry around now if a refugee gets really ill on Manus or Nauru? lots of questions but as it is in Question time…. no answers.

If Jacqui Lambie has indeed done some horse-trading, then expect her horse to be at a Coalition owned abattoir as soon as this Medevac race has been run.

Mirrors are shattering in the room of one crossbencher as she reflects on what she has done. Don't worry, Jacqui, now you are ScoMo's friend, he has plenty to lend you, even if they are a bit smoke stained.

If Lambie received an agreement from Morrison to a deal so that she would vote to repeal Medevac which of his two faces was she looking at?

If only McCormack's IQ matched his level of shouting, he would be admitted to MENSA. Unfortunately, it is in inverse proportions.

McCormack broke out into song again forgetting the script which called him to have a non-speaking role. He started out with a classic

"They asked me if I knew
The Sydney fires were true
Oh, I of course replied
Looked them in the eye, and just asked them why?
They say truth is hard to find
That I've lost my mind
Or, of course I'm a liar
But I can't see the fire
'cause smoke is in my eyes"

McCormack, so well-known as an Elvis impersonator, sings unthinkingly, "Wise men say, only fools rush in" as he hastily tries to cover his tracks.

Apparently, according to holy scripture, only god is above the law. Is Michael McCormack god?

Michael McCormack doesn't seem to have the nous of Morrison who refuses to answer questions. McCormack answers

them and gets caught up in his own web of lies and deceit, leaving us to question how vengeful Morrison's god is to leave McCormack in charge of the country in a time of crisis.

We saw yesterday Michael McCormack getting a verbal serve from some of the Nationals' constituents. We then heard his lame excuses back to them and then his petulant tirade in parliament. It is hard to believe that Scott Morrison is our Prime Minister, but what is more disconcerting is that Michael McCormack assumes the role when Morrison is out of the country and could be Prime Minister should something happen to Scott Morrison. Is Michael McCormack the second best we have to offer?

Remember when Morrison asked his colleagues all those questions and they had to put their hands up? People laughed at the Hitler like moment. Now he has the policies to go with the salute.

Will Morrison have a proper gander at what his Medevac repeal will do, or does he just think that propaganda is how to run the country?

Morrison seems to be glad the parliamentary year is over especially with his experiences trying to shore up Angus Taylor's credibility. He is seeking some clear air and time to suck in a few deep breaths. As the smoke from the haze of the climate change caused bushfires rasps his lungs, perhaps he is thinking that he hasn't quite got himself out of trouble yet. Unlike Joan of Arc whose last words were "Hold the cross high so I may see it through the flames!" he may be wondering why God is forsaking him at the moment.

So, the focus is on the religious freedom bill. The union busting bill gets a guernsey. The surplus is front and centre. But the climate change debate seems to have gone up in a puff of smoke. However, Scomo the illusionist is far from an expert because that smoke is lingering and the public can see the mirrors behind the ruse. Morrison is not magic. He is tragic.

Morrison may begin to wonder what he has done wrong and how he has offended his god. In his short term of office, he has had to deal with a plague on strawberries, the plague of drought and now the plague of bushfires........ Should he heed the warnings or wait until the next seven plagues run their course. Why has his god forsaken him?

Take a deep breath, everyone. Well maybe don't, as it is hazardous to your health all along the east coast and over in WA. Morrison, like everyone deserves a break. I mean the parliament sat for under fifty days this year. Some of our fire fighters have done fifty days straight and the fire season is just beginning so the government tells us. What if our PM wants to chill out in Hawaii? It's getting a bit hot underfoot here. New Zealand could have been on his itinerary to thank those who rescued Australians and recovered bodies, but he probably had pre-booked through Helloworld and wasn't going to get a refund. He has left us a surplus and some tax cuts. He has met our emissions targets admittedly through accounting fudging. That was all he promised before the election. He has done his job. Leave him be.

The only difference there is between Morrison in action and Morrison inaction is a vacant space. Which reminds me, where is Michael McCormack?

Scott Morrison has added a last-minute award for the Australia Day awards similar to Abbott giving out knighthoods. He will be the first recipient of the Medal of Inclusive Australians. It is likely to get the backing of everyone as Scott Morrison MIA has a certain ring to it. Not sure he has thought it through well enough, as MIA is well known as Missing in Action. It could also be seen as Morrison Is Absent.

"Morrison, where the bloody hell are you?"

Morrison is lei-ing low in Hawaii!

Scott Morrison could have met with the fire chiefs - didn't.

He could have attended the UN environment in New York - didn't (went to McDonalds)

He could have gone to Madrid to put his case on emission reduction - didn't. (Angus Taylor went later.)

He could have been continually out encouraging and supporting the firefighters - isn't (Postcards from Hawaii)

He could have gone to New Zealand after the White Island volcanic eruption - didn't (Marise Payne was sent)

Master politician? Somehow, I don't think so. If we are invaded and someone says, "Take me to your leader!" Just where should we look for him?

Was Scott Morrison really overseas? Maybe he was here all the time and it was just his action that we couldn't see.

Can we impeach a Prime Minister for I dunno... say...dereliction of duty? Perhaps a petition signed by half or more of the population might send a message.

Years ago, Scott Morrison severely criticised Christine Nixon, the Victorian Police Commissioner for going out and having dinner when Black Saturday was on. I hope humble pie is on the flight menu as he jets home.

MORrisON has only one thing he can sell to the public and that is his image. No wonder he was sacked as an ad man.

Scott Morrison returning from a poorly timed holiday in Hawaii while the nation burned and chickens coming home to roost, any connection?

The difference between 'in action' and 'inaction' is often just a typo. However, for Morrison, it seems that it depends more on your ideology.

Think back to Morrison's first challenge as PM. It was the massive emergency over needles in strawberries. He was action man then, bristling with energy and speed. Now he is inaction man and not even wearing his underpants on the outside will convince us that he has superpowers anymore. Maybe he used them up on the strawberries and is now feeling a bit burnt out, like so many people caught in the national bushfire emergency.

All this secrecy with Scott Morrison and his time in Hawaii, makes you wonder whether it was cloak and dagger or smoke and mirrors.

Was Scott negotiating a trade deal in Hawaii with Trump? Perhaps he offered Australia as the 51st state and in return would get Brian Houston an audience with Trump. Trump might not be happy with a fire sale offer though.

Now that we really aren't at war with anyone (Afghanistan, ISIS and the climate excepted) now would be a good time to invade New Zealand. Then we could encourage Jacinda Ardern to stand for parliament of Australia and we could have a PM who leads and cares.

The real reason why Morrison cut short his holiday was actually a phone call from a certain red-haired senator. There she was decorating her tree, humming her favorited Christmas song, "I'm dreaming of a white Christmas...", when she misheard a news item that said half of New South Wales was blackened. Immediately she rang Morrison and told him he had to come back and fix the problem if he wanted her vote on any legislation.

Apologies to the Sanford Townsend Band for this parody of their song Smoke from a Distant Fire.

You left us here for a Hawaiian paradise
With fires burning and some were losing their lives
Didn't know you were going; thought you'd stay and help us fight
But you casually dismissed all the smoke from the distant fires.
Lord, we were stung shoulda seen it come a long time ago.

That you weren't suited for this PM role
Then you tried to explain why you had chosen to go
Saying that you were incapable of even holding, a fire hose
This lying, and denyin', is upsettin' and gettin' us nowhere
It don't stack up, our back's up so rack off
'Cause you don't care
We can't talk climate change while fires are about
Nor even say what's behind this awful drought
You keep telling us that fires and drought happen all the time
And with thoughts and prayers everything will be fine
It just seems that your beloved God isn't on our side
As you casually dismiss all the smoke from the nearby fires.
As you casually dismiss all the smoke from the nearby fires.
As you casually dismiss all the smoke from the nearby fires.............

Morrison crosses back and forth between denialism and denihilism. The former is how he is prepared to deny truths and overwhelming evidence if it doesn't match his own ideology, political ambition and those whom he owes favours. The latter is about how everything and everyone must fit around his religious and moral principles which define his view of the world. He is a dangerous person to be leading our country.

You don't need to be a Rhodes scholar to work out that Angus Taylor has done the wrong thing.... actually, it doesn't help if you are!

Angus Taylor seems to think that the only way to get out of the hole is to keep digging it deeper. Can't he hear the reversing beeps of the sewerage tanker reversing up to fill the hole FULLER.

(With apologies to Rodgers and Hammerstein II)
to the tune of My Favourite Things
Doing favours for friends not forgotten
Doesn't matter if they're good or they're rotten

Brown paper packages tied up with strings
That's the reward for doing those things
Change the course of an investigation
At the request of the leader of the nation
When asked, just deny everything
And get a reward for doing those things
Hide the misdeeds of a boy called Angus
Tell others to forget that someone rang us
Make up a joke and offer a grin
Saying that you didn't say anything
Put the bins out
Bring them back in
That's what neighbours do
Just remember to deny everything
And there's something in it for you

Angus Taylor is probably sitting back and laughing right now as he is not the centre of attention and the most hated person in parliament at the moment. No prizes for guessing who is.

Angus Taylor is so used to dog whistling about so many things that he fails to understand the danger posed by a Wolf whistle. She all but used the words of Monty Python, "He's not the Messiah he's a very naughty boy!"

That hole Angus Taylor has dug himself into must be giving him ideas about how to sequester carbon miles underground. The trouble is that he is so far down towards the earth's core that he is really feeling the heat.

Morrison's "I have full confidence in Angus" If Angus was an AFL coach, he would know that comment meant that he was about to be sacked.

Despite the fires burning all over the place, Scott has decided to slash and burn the public service. Fraser probably helped him as he thought that might be better to do than attend the climate change summit in Madrid.

Angus Taylor in Madrid has explained that we are controlling our emissions with special means. He won't tell the people there what those means are but word has it that Morrison has borrowed some police crime scene tape from a former neighbour to gag any protest and to keep people away from the truth. He quite rightly says, when asked about the smoke pollution in Sydney, "Nothing to see there, move on."

Our energy minister is finding out that with hubris goes karma.

The Australian Characters

Tony Abbott
Anthony Albanese
Cory Bernardi
Bronwyn Bishop
Julie Bishop
George Brandis
Michaelia Cash
Mathias Cormann
Peter Dutton
Josh Frydenberg
Julia Gillard
Pauline Hanson
Joe Hockey
Barnaby Joyce
Craig Kelly
Jacqui Lambie
Michael McCormack
Scott Morrison
Clive Palmer
Christopher Pyne
Kevin Rudd
Bill Shorten
Angus Taylor
Malcolm Turnbull
Penny Wong

Tony Abbott

Tony Abbott was a very divisive person who rose to Opposition leader after being a minister in an earlier Coalition government. He rose even higher to become Prime Minister. As Opposition leader he was masterful and opposed almost everything that the government put forward. He was also very divisive within his own party ousting Opposition leader Malcolm Turnbull who repaid the favour by ousting him after Abbott became PM. A member of the right wing, Tony Abbott opposed Marriage Equality and Climate Change, denying the later saying that it was 'crap'. He defended big business, refusing to call a Royal Commission into banking and saying that 'Coal was good for humanity'. One of his strangest decisions was to reinstall knighthoods and knight Prince Phillip. After losing the Prime Ministership, he moved to the backbench promising not to undermine and snipe, yet that is precisely what he did and assisted in ousting PM Turnbull. Eventually he was beaten in the 2019 election and his blue-ribbon Liberal seat became an independent one.

Anthony Albanese

A very popular member on the Labor side of politics, Anthony Albanese was narrowly defeated by Bill Shorten as he attempted to become Opposition Leader. After Bill Shorten's defeat in the 2019 election, he was elected Opposition leader. A normally quietly spoken person some believe that he does not have the strength to win an election.

Cory Bernardi

Cory Bernardi as a senator from South Australia for the Liberal Party helped swing the party even further to the right especially on such issues as marriage equality and acceptance of any gender issues including the teaching of sex education in schools. He made the statement that homosexual relationships were just a step away from having sex with animals. A strong fundamentalist Christian he was against abortion and railed against Islam and the immigration of Muslims into Australia and met with ultra-right-wing advocates from overseas. He believed that the ABC as a broadcaster should have its funding reviewed if it continued to express views other than his own. In 2017 just after winning his seat as a Liberal, he split from the Liberal Party to form his own Conservative Party. This party of one eventually failed and he returned to the Liberal fold before announcing his retirement from Parliament in 2020.

Bronwyn Bishop

As Speaker in the House of Representatives who is supposed to be unbiased when making rulings, Bronwyn Bishop ruled with an iron fist and that fist was always on her right hand. The left side, the non-Coalition one, took the brunt of the force she exuded in the position of power she held. She set a record for the number of people she ejected from the chamber. Her position became untenable however because she claimed travel expenses of $5000 for a private helicopter flight to travel 80km to a Liberal party function.

Julie Bishop

Julie Bishop held the deputy leader position for the Liberal government from the time it went into Opposition in 2007 and saw four male colleagues come and go as leader of the party. She was a Minister between 2003 and 2007 and again from 2013 to 2018 when she was Minister for Foreign Affairs. A forthright speaker, she was known for her 'death stare', fashion sense and rarely seen dry sense of humour.

George Brandis

Known as 'Bookshelf Brandis' because of the very large and expensive bookshelves he had installed in his parliamentary office to store all his legal books, George Brandis served as a minister in the dying days of the Howard Government in 2007. From 2013 to 2015 he was made Attorney-General and Minister for the Arts, during which time he cut $105 million from the arts budget. He was left out of the ministry in 2015 but became Leader of the Government in the Senate. He was given a retirement gift of the High Commissionership in London in 2017. He was hailed by all sides of politics for the speech he gave condemning Pauline Hanson's wearing of a burka in the Senate.

Michaelia Cash

Michaelia Cash has seemed out of her depth in whatever portfolios she has been involved in. Accident prone and lacking in the understanding of what her powers are, she has been involved I many gaffes and abuses of power. Prime Ministers have nt known where to hide her. In one case, her staffers did their best and shielded her from questions by the media with a whiteboard. She has beautifully coiffed hair that shows that she is ding her best to delete the ozone layer. As speaker she is very good for the deaf as her lip movements are exaggerated. George H Bush may have said "Read my lips", but with Michaelia Cash, her lips seem to work on their own.

Mathias Cormann

Mathias Cormann held many positions in government and in opposition. His Belgian accent made him sound like Arnold Schwarzenegger but his dry wit and intelligence easily surpassed anything Schwarzenegger had to offer. He was articulate as Leader of the Government in the Senate and often called upon to argue strongly in the public arena on money matters. He served time as Finance Minister and was caught out smoking cigars with Joe Hockey at the time of the budget from hell. When leadership spills occurred as Malcolm Turnbull jockeyed to keep his position, he misread the situation and changed sides which ultimately led to the ascension of Scott Morrison.

Peter Dutton

Unfortunately blessed with the face of a funeral director, Peter Dutton has wielded power in the immigration/home affairs portfolio with the same compassionless façade. His ministry's powers have grown as has his standing within the Liberal Party despite his often poor timed and poor choice of words. He challenged for the leadership against Malcolm Turnbull and on the second challenge felt confident he would win and become PM, only to be undercut by Scott Morrison. A member of the right wing of the government he still manages to steer the government away from a centralist course and often is accused of speaking too much outside his portfolio.

Josh Frydenberg

As a relatively young person Josh Frydenberg moved up the ladder quite quickly to the point where he became deputy leader of the Liberal party and the country's treasurer. His main claim to fame he hopes will be delivering a surplus. However, he should be credited for the work he did to almost secure as Energy Minister an agreement between all parties for an emissions and energy policy. This was ultimately rolled when the right wing of his party forced a spill of leadership and Malcom Turnbull was dumped.

Julia Gillard

Julia Gillard became Australia's first female Prime Minister after Kevin Rudd lost in a leadership spill. She was also one of the most successful ones, managing to pass a lot of legislation despite having a hung parliament and relying on independents to get things through. Her biggest lack of success was in getting an emissions policy through and the scheme that was put forward was blocked by the Opposition who thought it unnecessary and strangely by the Greens who said that it didn't go far enough. Her statement that "there will be no carbon tax under the government I lead" gave the opposition all it needed even though her proposal wasn't a tax at all. It was believed that she was a lame duck going into the next election and a spill saw Kevin Rudd return as PM. She is credited for her beginning the Royal Commission into child abuse which saw many changes in society and ultimately the gaoling of priests and even a cardinal, George Pell. Her misogynism speech in parliament in 2012 aimed directly at Tony Abbott was lauded by women and many men all around the world.

<u>Pauline Hanson</u>

Originally elected to the senate in 1996 as an independent after being earlier taken off the Liberal Party ticket because of her racist views, Pauline Hanson is very right wing and accident prone when it comes to speaking and stunts. She lost her seat, was gaoled and then returned to the senate in 2007, this time not targeting Aborigines and Asians in her maiden speech but instead Muslims. She has been able to manipulate governments as her party One Nation has had balance of power opportunities in the Senate. Her party has had members come and go, some being more outlandish, some finding her views and control too hard to take. Her biggest and strangest stunts, gaffes and speeches have included responding to a question on xenophobia with "Please explain?" indicating she didn't know what it meant; wearing a burka into the senate; having her party associated with the NRA; speaking at ultra-right wing rallies; and releasing a video saying that she had been murdered.

<u>Joe Hockey</u>

Joe Hockey served as a minister in the Howard government from 2001 until 2007 and then became treasurer when the Coalition resumed power in 2013. His handling of the treasury portfolio and the 2014 'horror' budget in particular when he described Australians as 'lifters or leaners' saw him lose his portfolio when Malcolm Turnbull became PM. He retired from parliament only to become Australia's ambassador to the US in what seemed a payoff for services not rendered and also something he was not really qualified to do. Nicknamed "Smokin' Joe" by his enemies after he was caught puffing on a huge cigar with Mathias Cormann, this shadow treasurer who claimed that there was a debt and deficit emergency prior to the 2013 election managed to increase that deficit and debt in his short reign as treasurer.

Barnaby Joyce

He started as a senator in 2005 and in 2013 moved to the Lower House. He was often described as the best retail politician in the Coalition but when he became a minister in 2013 and then leader of the Nationals in 2018, things began to go awry. As a senator he threatened to and did cross the floor but as a cabinet minister he was not supposed to. His maverick persona was dulled. From a rural electorate he was supposed to represent what rural people wanted but that wasn't always the case because he towed the Coalition line. Caught up in the dual citizenship issue he had to recontest his seat and was successful. Best known for his ability to shout, his beetroot red face and his extra marital affair that cost him his position, he was one of those who undermined Malcolm Turnbull.

Craig Kelly

A person with strong right-wing views, Craig Kelly wields a lot of power from the backbench. An avid climate change denier and supporter of coal mining, he speaks out on these issues much to the annoyance of his fellow members of the Coalition. He threatened to join the cross bench if he was challenged for preselection and this bullying tactic worked as he was not challenged and held his seat in the 2019 election.

Jacqui Lambie

Jacqui Lambie is a former defence member and was elected to parliament under the Clive Palmer United Party platform as a senator. Following a fall out with Clive Palmer she became an outspoken independent senator who held the balance of power in the Senate. She had to recontest her seat after being found to have dual citizenship and was successful. She shoots straight and from the hip and horse-trades to get her way on many things.

Michael McCormack

He would rather be known as an important politician than an Elvis impersonator, sadly he is good at neither of those. He was the bland leader needed for the Nationals after the demise of Barnaby Joyce. His vacant look and his boring monotone seem to be a genuine reflection of his personality and his Coalition colleagues and indeed the Opposition as well as many members of the public are genuinely concerned when the PM leaves the country and Michael McCormack is left in charge.

Scott Morrison

In 2018, Scott Morrison seemed surprised when all those around him fell and he became Prime Minister. However, some say that it was heavily planned by his supporters. He set up a masterful campaign, creating himself as the person front and centre, and had few policies to criticise thus he was able to narrowly win the unwinnable election in 2019. Having worked in the tourism industry in New Zealand and Australia where he "left" both these positions before his contract was up, he moved into politics in 2007 and made his way quickly into a shadow ministry position. He became Immigration Minister in 2013 introducing sovereign borders policies and denying the media and public to information on asylum seekers and their detention on Christmas Island, Nauru and Manus Island. In 2014 he was moved to Social Services Minister and then when Malcolm Turnbull became PM, Morrison became Treasurer, a position he held until he became Prime Minister. One Question time in Parliament he brought in a lump of coal as a prop and told the Opposition not to be scared of it. His Pentecostal faith he has raised front and centre and this has left him open to criticism. He made horrendous errors of judgement at the end of 2019 and at the beginning of 2020 when the whole east coast of Australia was hit by bushfires. Taking a holiday to Hawaii at the time seemed to show lack of leadership and even on his return his performance was gaffe ridden. A strong supporter of the coal industry and a climate sceptic, he continues to paint a rosy picture of the country's ability to meet emissions targets. Any criticism of him or any of his colleagues he takes the line of "that's just the Canberra bubble" or he obfuscates, changes the topic, won't answer the question or lies. He has earned the nickname as "Scotty from Marketing" but he much prefers Scomo.

<u>Clive Palmer</u>

Clive Palmer first captured the centre of public attention when as a millionaire with mining interests he decided to splash out on building *a full-sized working replica of the Titanic in 2012. Before that he opened a dinosaur theme park with huge models overlooking a golf resort. To say that the public thought that he was eccentric was an understatement. They thought much less of him when he had cashflow issues with his nickel business, owing massive tax debts, making a whole lot of workers redundant with wages, redundancies and leave owed and at the same time heavily investing in his quest to become a political player in federal parliament through his newly formed Palmer United Party. He achieved success in the latter and had to be taken to court over the former issues where he sought continual delays and then somehow negotiated deals that were very much in his favour. His PUP rose like a phoenix in 2013 and he became a member of the House of Representatives along with four others who became senators but two soon left his party because of his dictatorial approach. By the time the 2016 election came the phoenix was in ashes. It rose again in the 2018 and one sitting senator from Pauline Hanson's One Nation party defected to the UAP. In the 2019 election, under the banner of the United Australia Party, Palmer invested $60 million and succeeded in swaying voters to the conservative side of politics without any of his candidates winning a seat.*

<u>Christopher Pyne</u>

Christopher Pyne came into federal parliament as an MP at the age of 25 in the safe Liberal seat of Sturt. He moved into shadow cabinet in 2008 and when the Coalition came to power in 2013, he became Leader of the House and Minister for Education. He then went on to other ministries before retiring in 2019 having spent 33 years in parliament. He is best known for his dry wit, slightly effeminate voice and for being well liked by all sides of politics. His speed at leaving the chamber when he didn't want to have his vote counted was evident when he and Tony Abbott raced to the doors before they were shut. Christopher proved far too fast for the more athletic Abbott but that was due to his nimble, highly intelligent mind which also left Abbott in its wake.

Kevin Rudd

Kevin Rudd was a Labor leader who had no union affiliations or factions to be beholden to. He had come from the diplomatic corps of the public service and took over as leader of the opposition from the much-liked Kim Beazley in 2006. He took Labor to a landslide win in2007 which saw the sitting Prime Minister, John Howard lose his seat. However, his dictatorial approach to leadership rattled his colleagues and in 2010 Australians woke to find that they had a new PM in Julia Gillard and a new foreign minister in Kevin Rudd. When she looked like facing defeat in 2013 despite having won the 2010 election, she was dumped and Rudd returned as PM in 2013 only to lose the election. Not long after that election Kevin Rudd resigned from parliament. He is best remembered for the apology speech he gave to the indigenous people of Australia and his work in foreign affairs. He remains bitter as to his dumping and regularly adds his voice into the public political discourse.

Bill Shorten

He lost the unlosable election in 2019 because of some very clever campaigning and advertising. As leader of the Opposition for six years until that election he had united the Labor party but hadn't been able to win over the public. His involvement in the removal of Kevin Rudd as PM as well as Julia Gillard as PM didn't help. However, he was a numbers man and had grown up in the union movement and thought he saw the writing on the wall for his party. A Royal Commission into the Union Movement orchestrated by then PM Tony Abbott in an attempt to besmirch Shorten, found no wrongdoing, but it tarnished Shorten's reputation. He is credited with designing the National Disability Insurance Scheme as one of his greatest achievements.

Angus Taylor

The Energy Minister, Angus Taylor has found himself in a lot of hot water. Once seen as future PM material his stocks have fallen low. He has questions to answer on a number of fronts including water buy back schemes where a company he had an interest in made lots of money from the government; doctoring of a document detrimental to the incumbent Sydney Lord Mayor, a position his wife coveted; naming in his maiden speech a well-known author he knew when he was a Rhodes scholar at Oxford even though she wasn't there at the time; possible unlawful land-clearing on his property. As a strong supporter of coal mining he vigorously defends the government stance on the use/misuse of carbon credits left over from over 20 years before to say that targets will be met.

Malcolm Turnbull

A merchant banker and self-made millionaire, Malcolm Turnbull entered parliament in a blue-ribbon liberal seat and rose through the ranks despite him leading the push for a republic. He played the numbers game after the 2007 election and eventually ousted the newly incumbent leader of the Liberal Party, Brendan Nelson. He was too removed from the job because of his stance on the need for action on climate change, by Tony Abbott. Many years later he would replace Abbot as Prime Minister due to the falling popularity of Abbot. In 2016 he took the government to an election win but was ousted once again because of his climate change stance. He eventually retired from politics and his blue-ribbon seat was taken over by an independent for a short period.

Penny Wong

She is the antithesis of what once was the norm in Australian politics. She is educated, well spoken, surprisingly honest, of Asian extraction and a lesbian. Any of these as well as her gender would see her as the target of political bullying, yet she has risen to Labor's Opposition Leader in the Senate because of her stance over many things including the denigration of women. A strong positive advocate in the Marriage Equality debate, she pulls no punches when she needs to call out bullies, spinners of the truth and outright liars. If she was in the House of Representatives and not the Senate, many believe she would become Australia's second female Prime Minister.

The Overseas Characters

<u>Jacinda Ardern</u>
    <u>Boris Johnson</u>
    <u>Kim Jong-un</u>
    <u>Theresa May</u>
    <u>Barack Obama</u>
    <u>Xi Jinping</u>
    <u>Vladimir Putin</u>
    <u>The Royal Family</u>
    <u>Donald Trump</u>

Jacinda Ardern

New Zealand's young PM who gave birth while in office, will be remembered for her humanity, stoicism and honesty in really difficult times. She came to world attention after a shooting massacre which ended up with 51 innocent people dying at mosques. Her warmth and sincerity helped heal the country. She was also exceptional when a number of tourists were killed during a volcanic eruption on White Island. Her independence and willingness to speak from the heart at major leadership conferences has been widely acknowledged.

Boris Johnson

Former Lord Mayor of London, Boris Johnson became known as a blond headed fool who sought the limelight, made extravagant promises that he couldn't deliver. Logic said that he was playing well above his capacity and as is the British way, they elected him as PM replacing Theresa May. His rash promises on Brexit and during the election confirming his position may come back to haunt him.

Kim Jong-un

He is the supreme leader of the poor nation of North Korea that has had a succession of leaders all from the one family. Kim Jong-un's rivals from his family seem to mysteriously pass away or disappear. Rather than spend money of feeding the population, Kim Jong-un has spent money on the development of nuclear weapons and ballistic missiles so that he can become a main player on the world stage. He has attracted the attention of China, Japan and the US in particular who have applied trade and other sanctions on North Korea to keep Kim Jong-un in line. Unfortunately, the impact is far more felt on the poor people of North Korea who now have the state-run media telling them that the country is being victimised and oppressed by these countries so North Korea has to fight back. Kim Jong-un seems very artful in wooing attention and exacting promise in return for ones he has no intention of delivering.

Theresa May

May took on the role as PM after the resignation of David Cameron. She had to fight those in her party and those in the Opposition to try to get somewhere in the ongoing saga that was Brexit. Ultimately, she was tossed out by Boris Johnson who said that he had the solution, but has ended up with less than what May had negotiated.

Barack Obama

Spending two terms as president of the US, Barack Obama was the most statesman like president for many years yet it was the downward turning economy that would see his final term being less fruitful. He constantly had to fight battles with the Republican dominated congress and his health care plan that so many poorer Americans would benefit from was a real struggle. In the end a Republican president would dismantle it almost completely.

Xi Jinping

Xi Jinping is the leader of the most highly populated nation in the world and now as President for Life he continues to bring China closer to being the most powerful country in the world. His belt and road policies in poorer countries where he offers infrastructure for influence are getting developing nations on his side. China's expansion into the South China Sea through the creation of artificial islands has caused diplomatic uproar in other nations but Xi Jinping seems unperturbed by that. Rapid expansion has caused difficulties but China is now no longer a developing nation but a major exporter of goods throughout the world. Xi Jinping keeps a close watch over it all and as the companies are largely state run, his leadership decisions are implemented quite quickly and without question. Hong Kong was drawn back into the Chinese control in 1997 and is an essential element of Chinese access to and influence in world trade and affairs. There are major riots occurring in Hong Kong as people are protesting about the crushing of their freedoms. Xi Jinping may be wanting to avoid another Tiananmen Square situation so they haven't been fully crushed as yet.

Vladimir Putin

He took over as President of Russia from Boris Yeltsin in 2000 and through careful swapping of positions with his colleague Dmitry Medvedev (Prime Minister elected in 2000) Putin has led Russia from 2000 through to now. A fitness fanatic and careful diplomat he has improved the circumstances for many of the people in his country whilst still retaining influence in what were states and satellite countries in the old Soviet Union days. Russian military strength is still evident under Putin but also is the use of cyber attacks on countries where Russia now tries to influence election results, most notably the 2016 election in the US. He has often been seen as backing leaderships in countries that are contrary to the ones the US is backing, Syria is a perfect example. This potentially leads to confrontations between the two super powers of Russia and the US and with a diplomatically unstable President Trump in power, the intelligence and guile of Putin in avoiding a conflict has won out so far.

The Royal Family

The royal family began this period with the strange situation where Prince Phillip was given a knighthood by the Australian Prime Minister, Tony Abbott. There have been royal marriages and births as well as scandals involving Prince Andrew and Prince Phillip. The future king's brother, Harry, now married and with a family has asked that he become independent from the throne as another sign that the monarchy is a frail relic that somehow Australia still wishes to cling to.

Donald Trump

Donald Trump was elected president of the United States in 2016 despite his strange behaviour. He defeated Hilary Clinton after bullying and intimidation and a smear campaign. He somehow managed to do the same thing to other Republican candidates and win the candidacy and then the presidency. He has had a high rotation of staff and has put out fake news and uses twitter to state new policies. After seeming to threaten Ukraine with blackmail in order to get information on his own potential opponent he eventually was impeached by the House. He has been continually mocked by world leaders and has met with the president of North Korea among others in what now appears to be a waste of time. He has withdrawn troops from the Middle East leaving the countries there open for more warfare. He has also pulled out of climate change agreements, trade agreements and nuclear agreements.

Lacking diplomacy, economic vision and the ability to communicate with women in particular, he has walked the world stage with the world half in fear that the ignorant spoilt brat of a buffoon may one day begin a nuclear war simply because he can.

The issues

Asylum seekers/Immigration
- Banking
- Border Protection
- Brexit
- Bushfires
- China
- Climate change
- Defence
- Drought
- The economy
- Education
- Elections
- Environment
- First Australians
- Leadership
- Marriage Equality/Gender Equity
- The Media
- Middle East
- North Korea
- Religious Freedoms
- Russia
- Unemployment/Employment
- Unions
- World trade

Asylum seekers/Immigration

Australia has had a major issue with asylum seekers. It has taken over five years before so many of them have been processed. They are incarcerated in concentration type camps in foreign countries including on Nauru and Manus Island. These camps have been funded for by Australia but Australia claims no responsibility. It seems it is an out of sight, out of mind policy that is being enacted. At the end of 2018 moves were afoot to allow asylum seekers trapped in concentration camp type conditions to be assessed by independent doctors and if treatment was needed, they were to be transferred to Australia. This was successful but quickly repealed after the May 2019 election.

Banking

The Australian economy remains reliant on the four-pillar banking system. Four privately owned banks, two of which were once owned by the government, remain dominant and the government seems to be at their beck and call. In the Global Financial Crisis of 2007-2008, the government was forced to underwrite these banks because the banks were so intrinsically part of the economy that if one or more failed the nation would fail. These banks because of their size, power and reach were often seen to be making their own rules. After years of being asked, the Coalition finally called a Royal Commission into the banking sector and the rorts were revealed. However, it seems little has changed.

Border Protection

The Australian government dramatically beefed up its border protection after 2013. Special units of armed "Border Force" personnel were formed and some government departments and spy agencies were melded into one super ministry called Home Affairs with special powers and controlled by one minister, Peter Dutton. Australia had gone from a friendly welcoming place to what some people described as a police state. Freedoms were slowly being eroded, including those of the media.

Brexit

In 2016 There was a referendum in Britain about whether Britain should leave the European Union. The Leave vote was heavily reliant on the push factor of immigration and the loss of jobs and didn't really discuss the consequences of such a departure. The Prime Minister David Cameron resigned when the Brexit result was announced. Theresa May was appointed his replacement and set about working through all the conditions to achieve a Brexit deal and avoid some of the ramifications. In the end it cost her her job and she was replaced with Boris Johnson who called an immediate election to ensure that he had the country's backing. Postponement after postponement had taken place since the referendum but a final date was set when a whole new set of border and economic problems would change Britain forever and perhaps disunite the United Kingdom completely as Northern Ireland and Scotland voted to stay in the European Community.

<u>Bushfires</u>

Australia's climate continues to change for the worse. We have always been a place of 'drought and flooding rain'. After years of drought, massive bushfires hit Australia in the last months of 2019 and the early months of 2020 killing many, destroying homes, livestock, forests and wildlife. Many parts of the whole east coast, parts of Tasmania, South Australia and Western Australia were ablaze and attracted worldwide attention and support. Prime Minister Scott Morrison was loudly and strongly condemned for taking a family holiday during that time and not providing the leadership required. Firefighters, mostly volunteers had not had a break for months because the fires were so severe and were unable to be put out. The navy stepped in and rescued people in isolated towns who had fled to the beaches trying to survive. Months and years before government bodies had asked for more money to buy more equipment but the government had denied their request.

China

China's rise to power as a nation has had major implications on trade with Australia and on its diplomatic defence strategies. It is a major importer of our minerals, especially coal, which China consumes 13% of our exports. We, in turn, import 25% of our goods from China. Australia also provides many opportunities in its universities for Chinese students. Concern has been expressed over the purchase of properties, businesses and opportunities by China in Australia and also China's expansion into the South China Sea. There are also signs that politicians have been influenced by Chinese 'gifts'. Senator Sam Dastyari was forced to resign over his links with Chinese moneylenders. At the moment Australia is caught in the middle of a trade war between the US which sees itself as the leader of the world, and the upwardly moving China that will soon dislodge it. Defence ties with the US and trade ties with China make for awkward negotiations for Australian diplomats and politicians especially as the state-owned Chinese company Huawei wish to become involved in the expansion of Australia's telecommunication network.

<u>Climate change</u>

The vast majority of the population acknowledges that there is global warming caused by increased carbon in the atmosphere and that man through its use of fossil fuels contributes heavily to that carbon. There are people in parliament in Australia who deny such things and are at the beck and call of the mining industry. These same right-wing people have controlled any possible position that the Australian government can take to reduce the emissions. Twice Malcolm Turnbull has lost his position because of it, one when he was Prime Minister. Kevin Rudd and Julia Gillard both lost their Prime Ministerships because of the stance and Tony Abbott rose to power because of it. The Coalition government, with a wafer-thin majority could lose power if some of the ultra conservatives withdraw their support. It is a case of a few controlling the vast majority and Australia and the world suffers because of it.

<u>Defence</u>

Australia relies heavily on the US alliances for defence. This has led us into wars however including Vietnam, two Iraqi wars, Afghanistan and against ISIS. The country spends about 2% GDP on defence. In 2020 this is about $40 billion. Very little equipment is made in Australia and our once great shipyards and other defence industries are just shadows of what they used to be. Major contracts have been signed for submarines and planes that will be delivered many years in the future and possibly by then will be out of date and inferior. For many average Australians who see the photo ops of politicians doing their big boys and their toys routine, the expenditure seems unwarranted and money would be better spent on the homeless, reducing the crippling debt that we have. The military in peace time have done us proud in East Timor and assisting with recovery in disaster situations. They remain independent of the government and the Prime Minister is not the Commander in Chief.

<u>Drought</u>

Australia has been enduring more frequent drought periods of late. They are more widespread, lasting longer and having a bigger impact on the country's ability to grow sustainable crops and to farm traditional livestock. There is a growing belief that the foodbowl that we once were, is becoming a thing of the past. Changing away from traditional methods and recognising that there is a water shortage may help stem the flow of farm foreclosures, farmer suicides and small towns shutting up shops. There are rorts in the Murray Darling water catchment and water allocation. Those downstream suffer the most. Droughts are linked to climate change and the federal government has been slow to act. They are more likely to pout an ambulance at the bottom of a cliff than fence off the top of the cliff.

The economy

Australia has a preoccupation with the economy and that drives policy more than the needs of people. We have ever mounting debt and our GDP has fallen because we rely heavily on mining. Our manufacturing industry has all but stalled. Low wage growth, excessive government spending and poorly funded community service programs like aged pension, unemployment benefits and disability and aged care sectors, mean that the people who need help the most become the first casualties of a stagnant economy.

Education

Australian runs a private and state-run school system. The state-run one is supposed to be free and secular, but that is a matter of debate. By comparison the state-run system is poorly funded compared with the private one as federal government funding flows fairly freely to the private system. This has a real bearing on the social strata that lies under the surface of the egalitarian life that Australians believe they have. Introduction of and publication of testing across schools has not properly assessed student outcomes and instead has set up competition between schools and widened the divide between rich and poor schools both in the private and state-run system. Religious groups such as

Catholics run separate schools in the private/independent system and are heavily reliant on federal funding. Come election times, whichever party is in power, school funding is used to benefit the party and its ideology. All schools are having less time to do their basic work as more and more of society's ills are blamed on the school system and schools are forced to add "fix-ups" into their curriculum.

Elections

Australians seemed to have a revolving door of Prime Ministers from 2007 onwards. Four times the Prime Ministership was changed without an election. This was very destabilising. After one merry go round ride of Prime Ministers, Tony Abbott swept to power in 2013 only to be part of a domino chain of Prime Ministers leading to Scott Morrison thrust into the position just before an election. He won the unwinnable election by one seat. Many of his counterparts left parliament altogether choosing not to stand rather than lose their seat.

Environment

Australia has a unique environment. It is extremely fragile however and for centuries the indigenous population have managed it. Within the last two centuries since the arrival of Europeans and their land and marine management, there have been massive changes, most of them negative. Entire species of animals have been wiped out and native vegetation has been lost. Heralded all around the world is our Great Barrier Reef but the global warming that has changed the temperature of the water, the use of fertilisers that get washed downstream into the ocean and the introduction of non-native species such as the crown of thorns starfish have decimated a large extent of the reef. Tourism has suffered accordingly. The Reef is a prime example of what is happening across Australia. The Greens political party was set up to provide arguments for a better awareness and management of the environment but they have become just another party, but one of the far left. The public are often left with the feeling of helplessness as the people they elect don't seem to care because the economy is seen to be more important than the environment. Melissa Price was appointed Environment minister by Scott Morrison but had no qualifications apart from a mining background. She made many gaffes and went MIA around election time in 2019.

First Australians

When the Europeans arrived in Australia, they declared the land Terra Nullis indicating that no-one lived there. In doing so, they were stating that the indigenous population were nothing more than fauna, which also meant that the Europeans effectively stole the land from those who had come before them. No treaty such as the one in New Zealand was ever signed. Aborigines became slaves, were conscripted into the army, had their children taken from them to be raised "properly" and were given very few benefits and moved out of productive land. In 1967 they were finally given the right to vote. Under a Labor government in the 1970's they were also allowed to argue for their land rights. For a long period under a conservative government there was little progress made. In 2008 they were finally given a much belated apology about the stolen generation (children taken from their families). In 2017, the celebrated Statement from the Heart was made recommending changes to the way the indigenous population could have a voice about their future. The Coalition government rejected it out of hand.

Leadership

Australia had been devoid of strong leadership since around 1996 in the early days of John Howards prime ministership both in opposition and government at a federal level. The state governments had a number of effective progressive leaders in that time but there was not the quality coming through at a federal level who were willing and capable of leading. Some were trapped in the senate and couldn't become a prime minister. With so many factions in the major parties, would be leaders needed to spend more time unifying their party than unifying the nation. Oppositions and governments were at loggerheads just to prove that there was a point of difference. The image of politicians and indeed leaders went on a downward spiral and may not have bottomed out yet.

Marriage Equality/Gender Equity

The idea that LGBTQI people should be able to legally marry had been the bone of contention for a long long time. Some states wished to make it happen but were wary because the federal government had power to override state laws. It was determined that a law had to be enacted federally to guarantee people the rights that others took for granted. There were all sorts of delaying mechanisms put in place by right wing parliamentarians, media shock jocks and by religious groups. One of these was the introduction of a plebiscite which was a very expensive, non-binding and unnecessary act to slow down the momentum. It was very divisive, yet in the end proved to the politicians that the vast majority of Australians wanted marriage equality to happen. The passing of the law on Marriage Equality was celebrated by LGBTQI and heterosexuals alike and the ultra-conservative politicians when asked to vote in parliament defied their constituents by abstaining or voting no. They proved to be only a minority.

The Media

The media in Australia used to be quite diverse and rules were put in place so that no one person or media company could dominate. However, under changes by the Coalition these rules were relaxed and the Newscorp companies have begun to dominate print, radio and television media, squeezing out the smaller players. The owners of large media companies have extraordinary access to and influence on politicians and policies of parties. Rupert Murdoch is one of the owners who has more say than most. Politicians have been stretching "in confidence" aspects of the law to stop or delay Freedom of Information requests by journalists and when information has been released it has often been heavily redacted. Pressure has been placed on journalists and media groups to reveal sources through the use of Federal Police. Politicians however use the media for the purpose of deliberately leaking of information and have become very fussy whom they will be interviewed by on radio and television. Door stop interviews to create sound bites suitable for the evening news are often held but politicians are finding it difficult to adapt to the 24-hour news cycle and the rise of social media.

Middle East

The Middle East has been a hot bed of uncertainty and division from the earliest of times, some of it religious based, most of it economic. With the rise of the need for oil products, it became and remains a powder keg. At the end of World War 1 artificial lines were drawn on a map separating tribes and families. At the end of the Second World War there was a need to create a Jewish state and the nation of Israel further divided the area. War after war has been fought non-stop between a host of nations. Interference by multinationals and backed by European and US governments has not helped. The ever-present threat of a nuclear holocaust exists and when one renegade Arab group took on the US on US soil causing the 9/11 events, the world held its collective breath. Strategic withdrawal of US European and Russian troops seems unlikely as this led to the rise of other groups such as Al-Qaeda and ISIS. Underlying all this is the world's need for petroleum-based products.

North Korea

This poor impoverished reclusive nation has been under the rule of one family since 1948. Money is spent on developing nuclear capabilities and missiles to strike countries. Surrounded by China, Russia and South Korea, its leaders have been able to get the population to believe that they are under imminent attack. Widely seen as a renegade state, it manages to strut a high profile and threaten countries around it.

Religious Freedoms

Australia has a good set of discrimination laws despite it not actually having a bill of rights. After the religious community were rolled in the Marriage Equality discussion, plebiscite and vote, voices were raised about enshrining discriminatory rights for religions into law. Australia is supposed to have a separation between church and state, through secular governments. This is more in name than in deed as the religious lobby groups wield a lot of power and influence despite a steep decline in the number of people practising any religion. The

Coalition government has been pushing for a revamp of the religious discrimination laws to allow religious bodies to have special dispensation to discriminate.

Russia

Since the end of the Cold War in 1991, Russia has loomed large in Australia's foreign affairs as Australia walks a tightrope of increasing its trade with Russia but also aware of Russia's expansion plans through influencing other countries. Tony Abbott once threatened to "shirtfront" Vladimir Putin over Russian involvement in the downing of a plane and its use naval ships north of Australia. Abbott had no idea what shirtfront really meant. Putin laughed it off and Australia went down in Russian estimation. Because of our close defence ties with the US, Australia has often been drawn into issues that involve Russia.

Unemployment/Employment

Financial support for those unemployed has waned and many people are struggling. Rules on statistics have been changed and there is a steady increase in the underemployed. With a stroke of a pen, someone working one hour per week is considered employed. Newstart is an allowance given to the unemployed to support them when seeking new jobs. Those on these benefits must be actively seeking employment, even if there is none or they lose the benefits. They become easy targets for politicians and the media and named as dole bludgers. For many people particularly in rural regions there aren't jobs available and this causes an exodus to the city as it is difficult to survive on the allowance given. Australian manufacturing has all but shut down completely. There is a large amount of automation in many work places and that means that fewer people are needed. With a large pool of people to choose from, employers are able to suppress wages too. Traditional jobs gone, little change in education to expand opportunities, low wage growth and a very low unemployment benefit, young people cannot get into the job market and housing market. This just further stagnates the economy.

Unions

There has been a dramatic decline in union membership in Australia to the extent that the Labor Party, the traditional voice of the unions in parliament are losing their base and are being forced to look elsewhere. Many unions have become political and dominated by trying to achieve political ideological gains rather than act in the best interest of their members. This has led to the disenfranchisement of members and the loss of membership. However, the biggest change has been due to the Coalition government's push to undermine unions and change labour laws.

World trade

Countries and groups of nations have put in trade tariffs and barriers to protect their own producers. However, because there is a supply and demand backbone to all their economies, and multinational companies, governments have been trying to reach individual agreements between countries. Some of these are symbolic and trade can see the dumping of cheap or excess products which greatly affect an individual nation. Cheap labour in some countries undercuts others. Scarcity of one commodity can affect the capacity of another. There is no level playing field as countries try to woo individual companies with lucrative tax deals. China has entered the market and is now a powerful player and the once dominant US is finding it difficult to lose its stranglehold on world markets.

Return to Contents page